The Stations of the Cross in Colonial Mexico:

The *Via crucis en mexicano* by Fray Augustín de Vetancurt, and The Spread of a Devotion

The Stations of the Cross in Colonial Mexico: The *Via crucis en mexicano* by Fray Augustín de Vetancurt, and The Spread of a Devotion

John F. Schwaller

University of Oklahoma Press
Norman, Oklahoma
and
The Academy of American Franciscan History
San Diego, California
2021

Library of Congress Cataloging-in-Publication Data

Names: Schwaller, John Frederick, author. | 12 Vetancurt, Augustín de, 1620–1700. Via crucis. Engl | 12 Vetancurt, Augustín de, 1620–1700. Via crucis. Nahua
Title: The stations of the cross in colonial Mexico : the Via crucis en mexicano by Fray Augustín de Vetancurt / John F. Schwaller
Other titles: 3 Via crucis en mexicano by Fray Augustín de Vetan
Description: 1 Norman, Oklahoma : University of Oklahoma Press ; San Diego, California : The Academy of American Franciscan History, 2 | Includes bibliographical references and in | Summary: "The book studies the spread of the devotion of the Stations of the Cross in colonial Mexico, focusing on a Nahuatl version from 1580 translated by Fr. Agustin de Vetancurt. It looks at Native culture to see why the devotion was embraced so strongly after the Spanish invasion. The book places the devotion in the context of the Catholic Reformation and of the Baroque, the two trends that exalted this type of religious expression. Finally, it includes an analysis of the Nahuatl translation and of the illustrations of the work" — Provided by publisher
Identifiers: LCCN 2021043852 | ISBN 9780806176536 (cloth)
Subjects:
Classification: LCC BX1428.3 .S39 2022 | DDC 282/.72—dc23/eng/20211227
LC record available at https://lccn.loc.gov/2021043852

Table of Contents

List of Illustrations

Figures

Preface

As I repeat several times in this book, there are very few Catholic churches in which one does not find a set of plaques or paintings on the walls denoting the fourteen Stations of the Cross. The devotion is ubiquitous. It has spread to the Anglican Communion (the Church of England and the Episcopal Church in the United States, to name but two) and to many Lutheran churches. But surprisingly little has ever been written about the history of the devotion, and certainly nothing about its role in Latin America, except for one, which is a wonderful analysis of artwork associated with the devotion. This book seeks to correct that lack of study through the analysis of a delightful handbook cast in Nahuatl by Fr. Augustin de Vetancurt, a Franciscan who was born and lived in Mexico in the seventeenth century.

This book has its origins in two very disparate events. Back in the mid-1970s when my wife and I were living in Mexico City, on the occasional Sunday we would go to the open-air antiques market at Lagunilla. After several visits, I decided that I wanted an old book bound in vellum. As a poor graduate student I had a limited budget, but eventually we found a little paperback-size book for the equivalent of about $5, and I bought it. I really never paid much attention to the contents, since it was some sort of devotional manual. I really was just interested in the vellum binding. It remained on my shelf, more decorative than useful.

Fast-forward twenty years, and I had become the director of the Academy of American Franciscan History (AAFH). The academy had just moved from the Washington, DC, area, and I was hired as the first lay director. One of my challenges was to organize the rather large library of books and manuscripts that had been moved to California. This effort took me and two library assistants almost two years. Among the various papers in the collection, I happened upon a short illustrated manuscript written in Nahuatl. Since I knew Nahuatl, I quickly discerned that it was a devotion of the Stations of the Cross from the pen of Fr. Agustin de Vetancurt. At that point I enlisted the assistance of Barry Sell, one of the foremost Nahuatl scholars who also lived in California. Barry had worked extensively with colonial Nahuatl imprints and knew the work of Vetancurt. He and I labored on the manuscript for several months, making a clean translation. I discovered just how rare the piece was. While, according to Vetancurt himself, the text had been published, no copies of the printed editions still existed. Unfortunately, at that point my full-time employment with the Franciscans ended, and I went on to an academic administrative position in Montana.

In my spare time, I would pick up my photocopy of the manuscript and work with it, presenting a few conference papers here and there. At some point, I was thumbing through my own little vellum-bound book from Lagunilla and was shocked to see that the final twenty pages or so consisted of a set of prayers and meditations on the Stations of the Cross. As I worked more on the text, I noted that it had an uncanny resemblance to the Vetancurt piece that Sell and I had translated. But there were some significant differences. I assumed that these had been editorial decisions by Vetancurt and that this particular devotional book had been his model. In 2016, the AAFH presented me with the Antonine Tibesar Prize, and I used the occasion to outline my research on the Vetancurt Stations of the Cross. That Tibesar lecture was published in the journal *The Americas*. In the lecture and article, I presented my theory regarding my little devotional book from Lagunilla being the model for Vetancurt.

During the summer of 2018, I was honored to serve as a Maury A. Bromsen Memorial Fellow at the John Carter Brown Library (JCB). There, my goal was to further investigate the Vetancurt book on the Stations of the Cross. I had three main goals: First, determine whether there were existing illustrations in printed works from the period that might have been used in the Vetancurt book. Second, survey all the small devotional works from the period; fortunately the JCB has one of the most complete collections of extant imprints. Last, look more deeply into Ventacurt himself and his literary production, not to mention his use of Nahuatl; the JCB also holds the largest number of manuscripts attributed to Vetancurt. A serendipitous discovery was the documentation of Vetancurt's profession into the Franciscan Order. My profound thanks go to the trustees, director, and staff of the JCB for making this research possible and for all the assistance that they provided me during my residency.

In the collection at the JCB, there were many different types of spiritual guides and handbooks, including the few devotions that are now common as well as many dedicated to the ones that have become quite rare. At the same time, there were scores of editions intended to be used when following the most popular devotions, such as the Stations of the Cross and the Rosary. One of the most popular imprints was another version of the Stations of the Cross that differed from the one that I had acquired so many years ago in Mexico. Upon closer examination, I discovered that it lined up quite closely with the text in the Vetancurt work. I concluded that it was the Spanish precursor from which the friar had worked in developing his Nahuatl version.

As with all scholarly endeavors, although my name appears as the author of this book, there are scores of folks who have knowingly and unknowingly contributed to making this work possible. My deepest thanks must go to Dr. Jeffrey Burns, the director of the Academy of American Franciscan History, and to the academy itself. They own the Ventacurt manuscript and have been generous in allowing me to work with it for all these years. They have generously provided some of the funding for this publication. Being associated with the academy and the Franciscan Order has been one of the great joys of my academic career.

Barry Sell deserves a great deal of credit for his phenomenal work on Nahuatl language imprints. He has helped so many scholars with his transcriptions and translations of the many documents that have been uncovered in the last few decades. He is a tremendously talented scholar who has made so many impressive contributions. He and I worked closely with one another during during the initial translation of this work. His help was absolutely critical. In addition, Louise Burkhart, my colleague here at the University at Albany, has been a marvelous resource. She and I have spent much time discussing Passion plays and the Stations of the Cross because the two devotions cover much of the same biblical material. Her assistance with many of the more difficult Nahuatl terms has been essential. We offer a weekly Nahuatl seminar to students and members of the community, and we meet to work on texts that members bring. I have to thank all the people who have joined us over the last six years who have helped me immensely improve my command of Nahuatl and aided me in working through the odd words that pop up from time to time. I am very pleased to be a member of this community of scholars. I joke that we operate like a one-room schoolhouse where the more advanced students help the beginners and we all pitch in together to help one another. Beyond that, the fellowship of the Northeastern Group of Nahuatl Scholars has also been critical in my work on this topic. Sometime around 2008 we began to meet regularly, first in Albany, then in New Haven, and most recently back in Albany. Scholars from around the world spend three days together, totally immersed in Nahuatl and studies of the Nahua from precontact times up into the contemporary period. I have presented pieces of my work to the group and have always been aided greatly by their insights and suggestions. I am so very proud to have been and to continue to be a member of this group of *tlamachtianime*.

Everything that I write about Nahuatl can be traced back to R. Joe Campbell. He taught me Nahuatl while I was a graduate student at Indiana University. Without him, I would be at a loss for Nahuatl words. He has been a friend, mentor, and adviser these many years. I cannot claim that much of this book is truly original, since I have depended so thoroughly on the wisdom of others. One of the wisest is Frances Karttunen. Over the last decade and a half, we have spent many happy hours with her and the late Alfred Crosby at her home in Nantucket. Although she, too, studied with Joe Campbell, we all became friends while my wife and I lived in Mexico as I did my dissertation research. During the winter of 1974–75, Karttunen and James Lockhart did all the hard work to write *Nahuatl in the Middle Years*. That book completely revolutionized our understanding of language change and gave rise to the

New Philology as it exists in Nahuatl studies. Their work formed the basis of Lockhart's magisterial study *The Nahuas After the Conquest*. To both Joe and Fran go my deepest thanks. All the errors in the Nahuatl that others may find in these pages are entirely my own doing, and none of these great scholars may be implicated for my shortcomings.

Upon my arrival in Albany in 2013, I was very warmly greeted by my colleagues. I have benefited greatly from being a member of the faculty here. My primary assignment has been in History, but I have many great colleagues in a score of other departments. The History Department did not know what to make of a former college president who had asked to join their ranks as a simple professor. They have accorded me every bit of generosity and fellowship that one can hope to receive. I hope that my small contributions have helped the department during my tenure there. I have also been honored to be invited to serve on the board of the university's Institute for Mesoamerican Studies. Over many decades, this body has been dedicated to promoting the very best scholarship about Mesoamerica and to producing some of the world's leading scholars. Beyond the institute, the members of the Department of Anthropology have been exceedingly generous in their welcome to me, a total outsider. The members have proven to be excellent colleagues and good friends.

The final touches to this work were applied during the spring and summer of the Covid-19 pandemic. It made me think of the *huey cocoliztli* and *matlazahuatl* that overwhelmed the Nahua after the arrival of the Spanish. Along with so many others, my wife and I retreated to the confines of our home. Then, when we could, we departed from New York to spend the summer at our family cabin in northwestern Minnesota. The view from our home, on a rise overlooking our little lake, was powerful food for our souls. The great joy was that our children and grandchildren also escaped their confinements to come join us, after dutiful quarantines, for the better part of the summer. Our children and their spouses are all academics. Needless to say, this community of scholars nurtured me and provided the kind of candid criticism that can really improve one's scholarship. We are an odd assortment of scholars. One holds an MFA in Choreography and Dance, another is finishing up a PhD in Contemporary Art History focusing on Argentina in the 1970s, another earned a PhD in American Studies and focuses on religion and society in the United States, and the last also has a PhD in Colonial Latin American History and studies race. You can only imagine what our dinnertime conversation sounds like. But the joy of our lives are the grandchildren, with whom we spent the entire summer. To this beloved company I offer my love. I hope that this little work does not trigger too much controversy when next we meet.

Albany, NY
January 2021

Chapter One
Introduction

In a small village in central Mexico, sometime around 1700, the local priest gathered his flock for a prayer service on the afternoon of Good Friday. The congregation assembled in the narthex of the church while the priest fumbled with his vestments. Two acolytes carried candles, and the members of the parish lined up, jockeying with one another in the order of precedence, with the village leadership going to the front. The priest found the thing that he sought, a well-worn little book. Unlike the large liturgical book that he used on Sundays and feast days, this book was tiny. It easily fit in his hand, and on more than one occasion he had forgotten it, buried in the depths of his cassock pocket. The priest was comfortable speaking Nahuatl, the language of his parish, but for some of the occasional smaller devotions he still relied on printed guides. In this instance, the little book was helping him. It had been written by a spiritual brother of his: Fr. Augustín de Vetancurt.[1]

When all was ready, the group set off, leaving the church through the north door, which was on the left as they faced the altar. To many, it seemed odd to leave by that door, since it was supposedly a special entrance to the church, not an exit: ornately decorated on the outside, it welcomed all who entered so they could learn the mysteries of the faith. To the sound of flutes, a trumpet, and a drum, the procession began with participants singing the "Veni Sancte Spiritus" (Come, Holy Spirit). They slowly left the church and went to the first of the *posas*, small prayer cells placed around the patio of the churchyard. With this, the congregation began their celebration of the Stations of the Cross, the remembrance of Jesus's lonely, sorrowful, and terrifying walk to his crucifixion and death. They made three circuits of the patio, stopping for prayers and meditations at the *posas*, finally returning to the church, then entering the symbolic tomb where Jesus lay. In their church, the congregants were proud that they had a crystal coffin displaying the lifelike image of the broken and beaten Lord, the Santo Entierro (Holy Burial). In silence the faithful pondered Jesus's death, then quietly filtered back to their homes

1. As will be discussed in later chapters, throughout this work I will refer to the friar using the orthography of his name that he used himself and that appears in his printed books: Augustín de Vetancurt.

for two days of prayer and meditation, knowing they would see one another on Sunday in a happier celebration remembering Jesus's resurrection on Easter morning.

This book is a multifaceted study of the little prayer book and devotional guide that got lost in the priest's cassock, a truly unique document: the *Via crucis en mexicano* of Fr. Augustín de Vetancurt, a Nahuatl version of the Stations of the Cross. Vetancurt's book is unique for several reasons. It was published in Mexico in the last decades of the seventeenth century, a time when the papacy was only beginning to give formal recognition to the devotion in the Roman Catholic Church. The appearance of Vetancurt's *Via crucis* in 1680 fits well into the chronology of the devotion's development within the Franciscan Order and Roman Catholic Church. The publication of the book in Nahuatl came at just the right time: the devotion was just beginning to gain adherents. This also explains the popularity of the publication, which went through at least two printings in less than twenty years, linked as it was to the pope's formal recognition of the devotion and then the granting of indulgences to those who prayed it in its entirety. What we have come to learn is that Vetancurt, a Franciscan friar of Spanish origin born in Mexico—a Creole—translated the devotion into Nahuatl. The book that he used as his guide was written by a Spanish Franciscan friar living in the Spanish port city of Cadiz. But the devotion itself was based on a nearly-three-hundred-year-long development of this type of meditation and prayer. This present study will focus on the creation of the devotion in Europe as well as its adoption by the Franciscans, export to the New World, and eventual success among Natives and Spanish alike.

No printed copies of the Vetancurt book remain, only a manuscript copied from a printed edition, now held by the Academy of American Franciscan History (AAFH). In it, we can see the devotion's importance to the Natives of Mexico. The extant copy uses a local variant of Nahuatl, probably the language of the seventeenth-century population it served. It mirrors standard Spanish-language devotions of the same era but is not an exact translation. It is also indicative of a wave of popular devotions that were sweeping Mexico and the rest of the Roman Catholic world at the time. These were important elements of the Catholic Reformation period—the late seventeenth and early eighteenth centuries. In art and architecture, the period was also marked by the emergence of a new style of elaborate decoration that would be called the baroque.

This study of the text uses several terms to describe religious practices. Anyone familiar with specialists in the rituals and ceremonies of the Catholic Church will understand that there is a very precise vocabulary for nearly everything. In general, the word "liturgy," derived from the Greek *leitourgia*, meaning "a public duty or work done for the public," refers to "all the rites, ceremonies, prayers and sacraments of the Church." The public celebration of the Mass (also called the Eucharist or Holy Communion) is the central liturgy of the Church. One of the seven sacraments of the Church, it is performed for the good of the public (i.e., for the salvation of people through belief in Jesus Christ). A sacrament is an act that brings grace (divine blessings) to the individual who participates in it. Many children have to memorize the definition of "sacrament" when they go through religious instruction: "Sacraments are outward signs of inward grace."[2] The general category of "liturgy" also includes formal prayer services in which the Eucharist is not performed, such as the prayers and readings associated with the canonical hours. These are sets of prayers that are said or recited at specific times during the day, such as Matins, Vespers, and Compline.[3] Also included in the category of "liturgy" is a litany, a type of prayer in which there is a dialogue between the leader and the congregation, like a call and response. The most famous of these is the long Litany of the Saints, which is used on special holidays such as All Saints' Day.

Private devotions are separate from the liturgy. Strictly speaking, though it can involve a church service, the Stations of the Cross is categorized as a private devotion, not unlike the Rosary. These devotions are encouraged and can help the faithful in their relationship with God but can be practiced privately, without the intervention of clergy, though group (corporate) celebrations of these "private" devotions are common. Many churches host a public ceremony of the Rosary in which many can join together to pray. Similarly, especially during Lent and Holy Week, churches have organized celebrations of the Stations of the Cross, particularly on Good Friday, the Friday before Easter Sunday.

This book will also examine church architecture and decoration. In the evangelization of New Spain, the missionaries oversaw the construction of hundreds of early churches as well as the convents that adjoined them. Although in English we tend to use the term "monastery" in reference to a residence for male members of religious orders and "convent" for females, the difference between the two is not gender-based but depends, rather, on the rules of the groups to which the missionaries belong, frequently what are called religious orders. Catholic priests can be divided into two large categories. The majority are diocesan, or secular, priests, meaning they have taken the vows of the priesthood and are recognized by local bishops but live out

2. "Sacraments," *Catholic Encyclopedia*, New Advent, https://www.newadvent.org/cathen/13295a.htm. Episcopalians and Lutherans in the United States prefer the somewhat longer version: "Outward and visible sign of an inward and spiritual grace."

3. For example, our word "noon" comes from the canonical hour *nonce* (*nona hora* in Latin), which was the ninth hour after sunrise, a little later than 12 PM. Similarly, the *siesta* of the Hispanic world comes from *sext* (*sexta hora* in Latin), the sixth hour after sunrise.

in the world and serve as parish priests. On the other hand, some priests are members of religious orders, specialized groups frequently founded by individual saints who organized the lives of their followers around special sets of rules (*regulae* in Latin, thus members of those groups or orders are called "regular clergy"). Importantly, not all members of religious orders are priests—many are not—but all do take vows to follow the specific rules of the order to which they belong. Mendicants—that is, religious (i.e., members of religious orders) who live in poverty, are supported by alms, and follow special rules—live in convents. The term "mendicant" comes from the Latin *mendicare* (to beg). Franciscans, for instance, are mendicants who live in religious houses but work out in the world according to the calling or vocation of their order. On the other hand, some members of religious orders live in communities separate from the rest of the world, rarely leaving their residences, such as Benedictine monks, who live in monasteries. In New Spain, there were no monks. All of the early missionaries were members of the three Mendicant Orders and thus were friars.

The churches of sixteenth-century Mexico had several unique features, including the open chapel, the *posas*, and the atrium. In order to provide religious services to the large Native populations the missionaries encountered in early Mexico before churches could be built to accommodate the crowds, the friars designated a large open area as a sacred space, which was then surrounded by an ornamental wall. This large walled space was known as an atrium. An open chapel was essentially just the sanctuary of a chapel that had walls on three sides with the fourth side open to the atrium. It might be located beside a church or placed on the second floor of an adjoining convent. Such a chapel would allow for many people to celebrate services, many more than might possibly fit in the relatively small churches the friars were able to build. *Posas*, as will be discussed later, were small chapel-like structures, generally built in the corners of the atrium, linked by a pathway. This arrangement allowed for processions to go from one *posa* to another, using the atrium like a large outdoor church.

The conversion of Natives to Christianity was a core element in the Spanish colonial enterprise in the Americas. Even in the midst of military operations, priests and friars began attempting to convert the Natives to Christianity. Once Spanish rule was established, scores of missionaries from a variety of religious orders and members of the diocesan or secular clergy arrived to more fully Christianize the Natives. In Mexico, then called New Spain, the earliest missionaries came from the Franciscan Order. At first only a few friars arrived, but they were followed by a full contingent of twelve in 1524. Within the next decade, expeditions of Dominicans and Augustinians had also arrived to work on the Natives' conversion. Later in the sixteenth century, priests from the Mercedarian Order arrived, followed by members of the newly founded Jesuit Order.

Religious orders are self-regulating bodies. Friars elect their own leaders, frequently called a superior, prior, or abbot, and the various convents of a region or geographical area are organized into a larger unit called a province. Fr. Augustín de Vetancurt was a member of the first province of New Spain, the Holy Gospel Province of the Franciscans.

Christianity and the Stations of the Cross

The devotion of the Stations of the Cross has its roots in the story of what happened to Jesus Christ immediately leading up to his death, as celebrated in the Christian Church. Throughout the year, Christians celebrate events from Jesus's life. For many Christians these events begin with his birth, celebrated on Christmas, December 25. This is followed by his circumcision and naming on January 1; the visit of the Three Kings, or Wise Men, who were foretold of his birth, on January 6; and his presentation in the Temple, an ancient Jewish custom, on February 2. Shortly following these Church holidays, Christians prepare for Easter, the celebration of his death and resurrection. During the period called Lent, spanning the forty days before Easter, the faithful imitate Christ's fasting and prayer in the desert when he was discerning his ministry.[4] Lent culminates in Holy Week, the week between Palm Sunday and Easter, the rituals and celebrations of which serve to recall the end of Jesus's life and ministry. On Palm Sunday, Jesus is believed to have entered Jerusalem, where he was praised by the populace as the Messiah or Savior. On Thursday of Holy Week, since he was a practicing Jew, he celebrated the Passover feast, which recalls the last meal of the Jews in Egypt before Moses led them to their promised land.[5] Later that night, as Jesus was praying with his followers in the Garden of Gethsemane, he was arrested by officers of the Jewish Temple and began the twelve- to fifteen-hour period known as the Passion.

Christians base their understanding of the events of the Passion on the accounts in the biblical books of Matthew, Mark, and Luke, with a few incidental details from the book of John. These four books, accounts of Jesus's life collectively known as the Gospels, date from about a generation after Jesus's death to upwards of a century after. The books of Matthew, Mark, and Luke are called the Synoptic Gospels, from two Greek words meaning something like "joined view," because they narrate essentially the same events, with

4. Lent begins on Ash Wednesday and ends on Easter, the dates of which vary from year to year according to a lunar cycle. This is actually a period of forty-six days. But it also encompasses six Sundays, which in Christian teaching are always days of celebration and do not count toward the total.

5. It is worth noting, in this celebration, known to Christians as Holy (or Maundy) Thursday, Christians replicate a feast that the Jews instituted to replicate their salvation from slavery in Egypt.

small differences among them. John's Gospel is quite different from the other three, and it generally falls outside this study, since it does not contain details of the path Jesus took in his final hours other than the final crucifixion. Thus, only the Synoptic Gospels—Matthew, Mark, and Luke—discuss the final day of Jesus's life in any detail.

The events of the Passion, as narrated in the Synoptic Gospels, follow Jesus as he is taken from one court of law to another. Piecing together the various accounts to try to create a single narrative, it is generally believed that for the crime of having violated various Jewish laws regarding Sabbath practices and ritual purity, Jesus was taken first to appear before the Jewish ruling authorities in the Sanhedrin, which was the local tribunal of Jewish scholars and leaders. This group controlled the activities in the Temple, which was considered the holiest place in Judaism. Then Jesus was taken to the Roman courts for additional charges. Jewish law forbade capital punishment, but Roman law recognized execution as appropriate for various offenses, including treason and *lèse majesté* (usurping the role and powers of a king). According to the Gospels, Jesus's opponents felt that charges of treason provided them with a means of eliminating him since he had described himself as a king. The Gospels describe Jesus appearing before Pontius Pilate, the local Roman governor, at the Praetorian palace. Some traditions indicate that Pilate first sent Jesus to Herod Antipas, the Jewish king of the region, attempting to find an easy way out of the predicament. Some accounts, based on traditions outside the Bible, have Jesus being shuttled among three courts, that of the Jewish Temple authorities (including Caiaphas and Ananias), that of the Jewish monarch (Herod), and the Roman court of Pilate. Each court claimed to have some jurisdiction. The Gospels, however, make no mention of Herod or the other Jewish officials by name during the Passion.[6] Rather, the Gospels indicate that the case ended with Pilate because he could order Jesus's execution, something beyond the other courts' authority. The Gospels paint Pilate as unwilling to condemn Jesus to death; he attempted to free Jesus as part of a ritual pardon to celebrate the Jewish holiday of Passover. All four Gospels record that the crowd, rejected Jesus's release, calling instead for the freeing of Barabbas, the leader of a revolutionary insurrection who also had been condemned to death. In the end, Pilate found Jesus guilty of treason and condemned him to death by crucifixion. Following his condemnation by Pilate, Jesus was stripped, flogged, and then mocked. The mocking is presented variously as Jesus simply being beaten, wearing a crown of thorns, or being dressed in royal robes. The column to which he was tied during the flogging became one of the symbols of the Passion. The moment when Jesus was

6. These officials are firmly part of the Passion story. The rock opera *Jesus Christ Superstar* includes these non-Biblical figures.

revealed, beaten and wearing the royal robes, is called the *ecce homo* (behold the man). According to the Gospels, Jesus was then forced to carry the cross on which he would be executed from the Praetorian palace to the site of the crucifixion, Golgotha or Calvary (Golgotha and Calvary both mean "Place of the Skull," one in Aramaic, the other in Latin). The route from the palace to the crucifixion is called the *via dolorosa* (way of sorrow) or the *via crucis* (way of the cross); other traditions call it *amargura* (bitterness). The devotion of the Stations of the Cross allows the faithful to follow Jesus in prayer and meditation from his condemnation to his crucifixion and burial.

The devotion has the objective of assisting participants in imagining themselves walking alongside Jesus during his Passion. It is an imaginary spiritual pilgrimage to Jerusalem to share in Christ's suffering. Using prayers and meditations, the practice helps to insert the faithful into the events and incidents of Jesus's last hours, his crucifixion, and his eventual interment, with expectations for his resurrection. In order to accomplish this more fully, most modern Catholic, Anglican, and even Lutheran churches will have decorations on their interior walls symbolically representing the stops along the way. Although the devotion is one of the most popular in many churches in modern times, it is a relatively new practice, as will be discussed at length in chapter 2. With roots in early pilgrims' experiences in the Holy Land, the devotion in its current well-established format emerged in only the seventeenth century. By the late sixteenth or early seventeenth century, at least in Spain and Italy, the number of stations had stabilized at fourteen in a specific order, as they are now commonly found.[7]

1. Christ Is Condemned to Death
2. The Cross Is Laid upon Him
3. His First Fall
4. He Meets His Blessed Mother
5. Simon of Cyrene Is Made to Bear the Cross
6. Christ's Face Is Wiped by Veronica
7. His Second Fall
8. He Meets the Women of Jerusalem
9. His Third Fall
10. He Is Stripped of His Garments
11. He Is Laid on the Cross and His Crucifixion
12. The Crucifixion and His Death on the Cross
13. His Body Is Taken Down from the Cross (Deposition and Pietà)
14. He Is Laid in the Tomb (Interment)

7. Storme, *The Way of the Cross*, 142.

Of these events, only about eight come directly from Scripture. Jesus's three falls, his meeting with Mary, and Veronica's wiping of his face are absent from the biblical accounts in the Synoptic Gospels, and only Luke mentions his meeting the women of Jerusalem.[8] Consequently, while just over half of the events come from Scripture, some of the more emotional moments, such as falling, meeting his mother, and encountering Veronica, are pious legends, stories that may or may not be true but nonetheless serve to explore aspects of faith and belief.

The first station corresponds to an event that all the Gospels mention, namely Pilate's condemnation of Christ to death. Although Passion narratives generally begin with Jesus's entrance into Jerusalem (celebrated on Palm Sunday) and focus on the week before Easter, the Stations of the Cross are significantly tied to the events of Jesus's final hours. Thus, the sequence of events that led inexorably to the crucifixion began with the sentencing by Pilate. Immediately after the condemnation, all the Gospels agree, Jesus was beaten, tortured, made to wear a crown of thorns, dressed in royal robes, and mocked. Yet these events are not included in the Stations. They become important themes in the meditations and prayers, but they are not the specific focus of the first station.

The next moment common to all the Gospels, which is marked by the second station, was when Jesus was forced to carry his own cross as an additional punishment. The Gospels also agree that at some point along the route, the guards made a man known as Simon of Cyrene carry the cross for part of the route, although this does not appear until the fifth station.

The Gospels do not mention the events of the third and fourth stations. Over the years people must have imagined that Jesus fell on one or more occasions on the route of his Passion. As will be considered elsewhere, some traditions hold that there were as many as seven falls. In the established version of the Stations of the Cross, the general meditations for the first fall consider the weight of the cross and Christ's fatigue. Logic for the fall is based on the subsequent participation of Simon of Cyrene; it answers the question of why Simon was forced to carry the cross. Clearly, Jesus must have been unable to continue carrying it for the whole route. However, the story narrated through the Stations of the Cross implies that after Simon assisted him, Jesus took up the cross on his own yet again, because stations seven and nine relate his second and third falls.

---

8. Matthew and Mark mention only that Simon of Cyrene took up the cross for part of the journey (Matthew 27:32; Mark 15:21). Luke mentions Simon of Cyrene and also that Jesus met the women of Jerusalem (Luke 23:26–31). John does not mention Simon at all. All the accounts either have or imply Jesus's condemnation, the receiving of the cross, his being stripped, the crucifixion, the deposition, and the interment.

In Christian numerology both three and seven are important numbers. Three corresponds with the three members of the Christian Trinity, that is, the three aspects of the divinity: God the Father, God the Son, and God the Holy Spirit. Seven is commonly associated with both virtues and vices, and Mary is believed to have suffered seven times, which are called the seven sorrows.[9]

Just as the Gospels are silent regarding the number of falls, they also do not mention an encounter with Mary, although that is the focus of the fourth station. In fact, none of the Synoptic Gospels mention Mary at any time during the Passion, although John does include a dialogue between Jesus and his mother while he is on the cross. Thus, her presence on the route of the Passion seems to be a later addition. The encounter is included as one of the seven sorrows of Mary and so has an important place in the larger theological discussion of the Passion.

The fifth station, namely the role of Simon of Cyrene, as mentioned above, does come from the Synoptic Gospels. All three of those accounts include that Simon was forced to carry the cross either for or with Jesus. The Gospel of John does not include this episode and implies that Jesus carried the cross by himself through the whole route. Mark (15:21) tosses in a detail not mentioned elsewhere that Simon had two sons, Alexander and Rufus.

The next two stations also lack biblical references and are thus considered pious legends. The seventh station, the second fall, offers an opportunity for the sixth station, Veronica's wiping of Jesus's face, to occur. This meeting with Veronica is one of the unique encounters of the Stations of the Cross: a woman named Veronica wiped the sweat and blood from Jesus's face, and the cloth was then imprinted with his visage. This led to a double play on words popular in the Middle Ages: The name Berenice was not uncommon in Biblical times. In Greek it means "bearer of victory." Latin traditions have the name as Veronica, which has a similarity to the phrase *vero icon*, or "true image."

Jesus's meeting with the women of Jerusalem, the theme of the eighth station, comes directly from the Gospel of Luke (23:28–31), the only Gospel to mention the encounter. In the story, a group of women from Jerusalem followed Jesus along the route, beating their breasts and weeping. Jesus

---

9. The Church teaches that there are seven virtues (faith, hope, charity, prudence, temperance, fortitude, and justice) and seven deadly sins (pride, greed, lust, envy, gluttony, wrath, and sloth). Seven events in Mary's life were accorded the status of sorrows. Five of them occur during the Passion, including her meeting Jesus on the route to the crucifixion, the crucifixion itself, the moment when Jesus's side was pierced by the guards, his body's removal from the cross, and the burial.

became angry and told them that rather than grieve for him, they should grieve for themselves. Various passages throughout the Gospels include eschatological pronouncements—warnings of the end of times—and this is one of those inclusions, warning the women that fearful things were about to happen, so fearful that they themselves would wish to die rather than have to suffer through them.

The route to the crucifixion reaches its conclusion with the ninth station: the third fall. Although not documented, it denotes that Jesus was simply too fatigued to continue. Immediately following that last fall, Jesus was prepared for crucifixion. In the tenth station, the guards stripped him of his clothes, which were then divided up among the guards. Theologically this was an important step in the process and necessary because of previous prophetic statements about the Messiah, a millennial figure who would come to save Israel at the end times. All four of the Gospels agree on this point and look to an earlier biblical passage, Psalm 22:18. In it, the suffering psalmist laments that he has been stripped and his enemies have cast lots for his clothing. In Psalm 22 more generally the narrator looks to God for salvation while being assailed on all sides. The opening phrase of this psalm is "My God, my God, why have you forsaken me?" (Psalm 22:1) According to Mark and Matthew, these were also Jesus's last words.

The final stations, eleven through fourteen, recount events taken directly from the Bible. After he was stripped, Jesus was laid on the cross and crucified—nails were driven through his hands and feet. Station eleven marks the act of nailing Jesus to the cross. Station twelve corresponds to his death on the cross. The thirteenth station focuses on the removal of his body from the cross, and his burial is the focus of the fourteenth station.

The Bible provides many of the references and images included in the celebration of the Stations of the Cross, but not all, as has been seen. While in the celebration of Christmas, for example, Christians adopted earlier customs and traditions from the Mediterranean world, since the Stations of the Cross owes its origins not to practices of the early Church but to later centuries, very little of the pre-Christian devotional complex was incorporated. What the practitioners added generally came from other, later sources.

Each of the scenes from the Stations had been common in Christian art from the Middle Ages and before. The crucifixion of Jesus figures as one of the most important events in Christian thought, and it leads directly to the miracle of Jesus coming back to life three days later, his resurrection. Thus, over the course of three days—from noon on Friday until dawn on Sunday—Christians remember the Passion and suffering of Jesus, followed by his resurrection. The resurrection set the Christian movement apart from other Jewish sects of the time. Christians believe that Jesus was brought back to life and interacted with his followers for several weeks before being bodily transported into heaven in the ascension. Because of the emphasis on the resurrection, the events leading up to that critical moment were important as the religion developed over the centuries. This helps to explain the centrality of the Passion in many Christian devotions.

This book will focus on both the specific text of the Stations of the Cross as translated by Fr. Augustín de Vetancurt and on many broader issues that arise out of that work. The second chapter considers the general features of the devotion of the Stations of the Cross. The devotion has its origins in the Middle East, specifically in Jerusalem, where faithful Christians would make pilgrimages in order to walk the path that Jesus took to his crucifixion. The rise of Islam made that pilgrimage more difficult. By the late Middle Ages, some pilgrims, upon their return to Europe, built replicas of the holy places and invited others to pray there and revere them as if they were actually in Jerusalem. These actions, along with changes in the manner and style of spirituality, gave rise to the devotion known as the Stations of the Cross. Chapter 2 also considers the processions and other public rituals of the Mexica (Aztecs) that may have been familiar to Native peoples as the missionaries began their efforts. It looks at the important role that processions and celebrations of Holy Week played in the life of the colony into the late seventeenth century.

The life and times of Vetancurt provide the theme for the third chapter. Remarkably little is known about his life. The chapter traces the broad strokes, from Vetancurt's birth in the village of Ayotzingo in the Central Basin of Mexico to his entrance into the Franciscan Order in Puebla to his service as the priest in charge of the large Native parish of San Josef de los Naturales. But Vetancurt was just one of several intellectuals who were active in Mexico City at the time. The chapter also considers his relationship to other intellectuals of the period, specifically don Carlos de Sigüenza y Góngora and the poet Sor Juana Inés de la Cruz.

The fourth chapter considers the actual Nahuatl text as translated by Vetancurt. Devotionals of this type were extremely popular in the seventeenth and eighteenth centuries. One, however, stands out and the model upon which Vetancurt based his translation. With that knowledge, we can look at the Nahuatl words that Vetancurt used to describe events and places and get a better understanding of what the impact of the devotion might have been on the Natives who used it.

One of the unique elements of Vetancurt's manuscript is its illustrations. The work includes several small drawings that illustrate about half the stations. Chapter 5 analyzes the artistic expression of the colonial period as seen through works on the Stations of the Cross in particular and the elements of the Passion of Jesus more generally. Sculptures, paintings, and engravings were all used to represent scenes from Holy Week. This chapter then places the manuscript's drawings into that larger artistic context.

The appendices to the book contain the transcription of the translated text in English along with the original Nahuatl. This effort began back in the 1990s in collaboration with Barry Sell. He then graciously handed the work off to me, and I have continued to revise the transcription and translation over the ensuing decades.[10]

---

10. For those who are interested, a copy of the original Spanish text that Vetancurt used as his guide and a translation of that text into English is available on the book's site on oupress.com or go to https://www.oupress.com/9780806176536/the-stations-of-the-cross-in-colonial-mexico/.

Chapter Two
The European Origins of the Stations of the Cross

The devotion of the Stations of the Cross is ubiquitous in the Catholic Church. Nearly all churches have plaques or paintings on the walls denoting the Stations. Many other Christian denominations also provide for their members to pursue the devotion, particularly within the Anglican Communion (known as the Episcopal Church in the United States) and the Lutheran Church. The faithful practice the devotion specifically on Good Friday, but in some parishes, it is celebrated every Friday of the year. Additionally, some churches in the United State have constructed the Stations of the Cross in gardens and wooded areas, allowing the faithful to engage in the devotion while walking outdoors.

Although the devotion is widespread, most people who practice it are unaware of its history and would be surprised to learn that it does not come from remembrances developed immediately following Jesus's death. Rather, it is a practice that developed only in the last five or six centuries. While this might seem to be a long time, many rituals of the Church date back well over a thousand years, many some two thousand. The central ritual and liturgy—the Eucharist (the Last Supper or Holy Communion)—dates to the time of Christ, was mentioned explicitly in letters that became part of the Bible's New Testament, and appears in records from the first centuries of the Church. But not only did the Stations of the Cross originate fairly recently, it also has not been well studied. Indeed, only a handful of serious studies have explored the history of the devotion in Europe, and none have considered its exportation to the Americas.

The Origins of the Devotion

Most scholars date the rise of the Stations of the Cross to the Middle Ages. The modern devotion developed from a confluence of three rather disparate historical streams. First, the Holy Land offered a strong attraction to many Christians because it was the location of Jesus's life and death. By visiting the places where Jesus lived and died, faithful people could see the very scenery that had greeted him. The costs and difficulties of such a journey were so high that only a very few pilgrims could ever make the trip. The rise of Islam in the seventh century and Muslims' subsequent capture of Jerusalem were also critical elements deterring the practice. With Muslims installed in Jerusalem, European Christian pilgrims had an even more difficult time visiting the important Biblical sites. The few travelers to the Holy Land frequently wrote accounts that described holy places. Building on those accounts, a set of sites slowly developed that were included in most itineraries. Devotions then emerged that were associated with each of the sites in the holy city. In particular, these practices focused on the places associated with the final hours of Jesus's life. But, importantly, there was no fixed order in which the pilgrims would visit these sites, nor were they described in books in any particular order.[1]

The rise of a movement referred to as the *devotio moderna* in the fourteenth century provides the second stream influencing the development of the Stations of the Cross. This movement advocated for a return to the early practices of the Church. Included among these were the pursuit of humility and obedience and the living of a simple and unencumbered life. The movement had its roots in earlier devotional practices that emphasized the blending of interior and exterior forms of spirituality. In the early Church, silent prayer was an accepted form of devotion, but it was not until the Middle Ages that silent prayer took hold as a widespread practice with the rise of monastic orders whose members took vows of silence.[2] With tacit Church approval, the faithful would practice silent prayer and meditation in daily devotions. Beginning with various changes as early as the thirteenth century, but developing more fully in the fourteenth, a new set of religious practices evolved. While silent prayer and meditation continued to be important spiritual components, this passive, interior form of prayer gave way to a more physical style in which movement of the body assisted in creating the spiritual experience. The faithful would stand, kneel, sit, and walk about as dictated by specific prayers or meditations. This physical involvement allowed devotees, no matter where they actually found themselves, to imagine that they were at the holy sites and create a mental itinerary, which may or may not have corresponded to any physical reality. The *devotio moderna* developed manners of prayer that linked specific prayers and meditations that would focus on specific themes, often associated with and patterned to occupy the practitioner day by day, week by week, or even month by month in some instances.[3]

---

1. This discussion is a synthesis of arguments made by Thurston, *The Stations of the Cross*; Zedelgem, "Aperçu historique"; Storme, *The Way of the Cross*; Lenzi, *The Stations of the Cross*; and Kirkland-Ives, "Alternate Routes."
2. Van der Horst, "Silent Prayer in Antiquity," 20–21.
3. Battle, *Blessed Are the Peacemakers*, 68.

The third historical stream sprang from efforts in late medieval Europe to build imagined sacred landscapes. Throughout Western Europe in the late Middle Ages, various devotional sites were constructed in an attempt to recreate those holy places. Frequently at the edge of a town or village, a devotional cross would be erected marking the town's limits. On the Iberian Peninsula, in particular, these came to be known as *humilladeros.* These sites provided travelers with places to offer prayers at the beginnings and the ends of their journeys. In a parallel but distinct manner, both in the Low Countries and on the Iberian Peninsula, some convents, monasteries, and wealthy patrons would build replicas of holy places from the Levant. These functioned as late medieval tourist attractions, allowing the faithful opportunities to see what those holy places might look like without having to undertake the arduous and dangerous journey.

The Franciscan friars came to play an important role in the development and spread of the Stations of the Cross, although they were not the only religious order involved. Although the Franciscan Order was not even founded until the thirteenth century, from the time of its founding, it became involved in several of the threads that came together to create the devotion of the Stations of the Cross. In particular, the friars eventually became the official Roman Catholic presence in Jerusalem. Their practices, including their early adoption of apostolic poverty, renunciation of the world, and imitation of Christ, were important components in what came to be the *devotio moderna.*

The Stations of the Cross as a devotion came to exist in three separate modalities. The words of the prayers and meditations lie at the heart of the devotion. These were recorded in books so that they could be invoked at any time. But from the very beginning, alongside the words were images. Sometimes there were plaques, paintings, sculptures, bas-reliefs, or even chapels created not just to evoke a visual response in the faithful but also to transport them mentally to the Holy Land and into the steps of Jesus's Passion. While none of the handbooks examined for this project from colonial Mexico were illustrated, modern handbooks certainly do have images of the Stations to allow practitioners to participate in the event on a visual level. At the same time when the words and images were being developed and attention was focused on physical objects, there was an equally important performative aspect. The faithful could pray the Stations of the Cross privately, either sitting or kneeling, but from the earliest days of the devotion one particular aspect was important: walking from one spot to another, be it inside a church, in a courtyard, or along a series of chapels or monuments to replicate or evoke the holy places. At each station, the faithful would stand, kneel, touch the ground, and be involved in other physical activities to further transport them into the emotional state of the experience. Thus, in reality, the devotion of the Stations of the Cross exists as two texts and one performative element.

One text was written—the prayers and meditations—and the other text encompassed the images, of whatever type, that accompanied the words. These were then enhanced by the performance. To complicate matters further, the devotion of the Stations of the Cross did not necessarily need to be performed, that is, accompanied by movement. People could, and many did, merely walk all by themselves or sit quietly in a space designated for the Stations, praying silently with the use of a book of prayers and meditations, although most handbooks do include suggestions for actions such as kneeling or standing. The historic evidence for physical responses to the devotion is extremely difficult to come by; there are very few traces, only the directions listed in manuals. Thus, scholarly attention usually ends up focused on the records of processions, the physical evidence of decorations, and the publishing history of handbooks destined for the devotion.

In spite of the widespread practice of the Stations of the Cross, within the Catholic Church in particular and several Protestant churches in general, there are really only a few serious modern studies of the devotion's history and development.[4] The Jesuit scholar Herbert Thurston wrote the earliest of these, published in London in 1906.[5] Thurston had an eclectic and wide-ranging interest in spiritual matters and mysticism. He published several very popular books on topics such as theosophy, spiritualism, ghosts, and poltergeists. In his work on the Stations of the Cross, he presents a solid history of the devotion's development and also considers the more immediate practical aspects of how one prays the stations.[6]

The next scholar to tackle the history of the Stations was Amédée de Zedelgem, a member of the Capuchin Order (the Order of Friars Minor Capuchin), one of the religious orders within the Franciscan family.[7] The Capuchins emerged as distinct from the main Franciscan Order in the early sixteenth century when some friars sought to return to what they perceived

4. In addition to the devotions described below, Sandro Sticca wrote a short article on the development of the devotion that appeared in 1993, Sticca, "The Via Crucis." Another author, Antonius A Sant'Elia A Pianisi, a Capuchin friar, also known as Antonino da Sant'Elia a Pianisi, wrote a more extensive study in Latin in 1950, Antonius A Sant'Elia A Pianisi, *De pio Viae Crucis*. For reasons of access, neither of these studies has made a lasting impact on the field.

5. Thurston, *The Stations of the Cross.*

6. A loving biography was printed at his death: Martindale, "Father Herbert Thurston."

7. Zedelgem, "Aperçu historique." The Capuchin order of Franciscans takes its name from the pointed hood that was part of their habit. *Cappuccio* translates as "little hood" from Italian. There is a species of monkey known as capuchin because their coloration, white face and brown or dark body, reminded early naturalists of the brown cassock worn by the friars. Similarly, the drink *cappuccino* received its name from that same coloration, white on top, brown below.

as a purer interpretation of the rules laid down for the order by Saint Francis, which dated from the early thirteenth century. Zedelgem, who was Belgian and had an impressive command of several languages, constructed a detailed and well-documented study of all the possible precursors to the Stations of the Cross and a wide-ranging essay on local differences. He took particular care to consider both textual and artistic renderings. Zedelgem closely read and critiqued Thurston's work and expanded significantly beyond it. As a native son of Belgium, he concluded that the devotion came from the Flemish region of his country, then was transplanted to Spain, Italy, and the rest of the world by the Franciscans.[8]

Albert Storme, a Franciscan friar, published his historical sketch of the development of the Stations of the Cross in 1984.[9] Storme was a member of the faculty of the Studium Biblicum Franciscanum, a house of study of the Franciscan Order located in Jerusalem. It was part of the Custody of the Holy Land, where the Franciscan Order had special regional authority. Founded in 1924, the Studium is affiliated academically with the Pontifical University Antonianum in Rome. Quite literally, Storme's institution was located on the Via Dolorosa (Way of Sorrow), the supposed path Jesus walked to his crucifixion in Jerusalem. He used his location and knowledge of Franciscan traditions to develop his historical sketch. Like Thurston, and to a degree Zedelgem, Storme also saw the devotion of the Stations as having evolved out of pilgrimages to the Holy Land. The roots of his work can be seen in some short books that he wrote about the holy places of Palestine such as Bethany and Gethsemane.

A fourth author to tackle the topic of the Stations of the Cross is Sarah Lenzi.[10] Her work draws on Thurston, Zedelgem, and Storme, but does not slavishly follow them. She critically analyzes their assumptions and provides a rather different interpretation of the facts. The task of pursuing the research is daunting because the essential texts are written in a wide variety of languages ranging over at least four centuries. Lenzi was trained in divinity at Harvard and completed her doctorate in religious studies at the University of Pennsylvania. An ordained Unitarian minister, she brings great nuance into the study of the Stations. While her book has an important section on the history of the devotion, her principal focus is that the devotion did not spring up from the Holy Land, or even from one particular place or another, but that it manifested a wide range of spiritual practices that were popular in the late medieval and early modern periods.

The discussion that follows draws heavily on these authors in an attempt to summarize their broad-ranging arguments and to better understand how

---

8. Zedelgem, "Aperçu historique," 142.
9. Storme, *The Way of the Cross.*
10. Lenzi, *The Stations of the Cross.*

the Stations of the Cross came to be celebrated in early modern Spain and then was exported to New Spain. Thurston, Zedelgem, and Storme all looked to the history of Christian possession of the Holy Land to discover the roots of the Stations of the Cross. But scholars differ on the question of whether there is any direct connection between pilgrimages to the Holy Land and the development of the devotion of the Stations of the Cross. Certainly, the fact that the sites depicted in Stations of the Cross are all located in Jerusalem points to the importance of a basic understanding of that city's relationship to Europe—the probable origin of the devotion.

Fascination with the Holy Land

After the rise of Islam in the seventh century, Muslims took possession of most of the Middle East, leaving enclaves of Christians, Jews, and other religious minorities in the area. The Christian church also split into two rough geographical parts, with important theological differences between them. Much of the Middle East and Eastern Europe embraced what would come to be known as Orthodox Christianity. Churches in the West continued to look to Rome and the pope for leadership and thus were part of what is known as the Roman Catholic Church. Eventually Christian rulers gained control of Jerusalem in 1099, only to lose it again shortly. By the thirteenth century, some Catholic religious orders had gained the right to inhabit and guard some of the holy places. Local Muslim rulers had first given Orthodox priests permission to practice their religion in the Church of the Holy Sepulchre (the traditional burial place of Christ) in the late twelfth century. By the time Saint Francis began his ministry in the early thirteenth century, the city had undergone various political changes. Importantly, Francis desired to preach the Gospel to the Muslims in Jerusalem. After several failed attempts, some think he may have reached the Holy City in 1219–20. Thereafter Franciscans established themselves in several places in the Holy Land, but in 1291 the friars were expelled and took up exile on the island of Cyprus. Pope John XXII granted the Dominicans authority to establish houses in Syria, keeping a fair distance from any previously developed Franciscan convents. Then, in 1322, the King of Aragón requested that the sultan in Damascus allow some Catholic friars or monks to take control of the Church of the Holy Sepulchre. The members of Catholic religious orders would serve alongside the Orthodox priests already there. It looked like these Catholic religious would be Dominicans, but at the last minute their mission ended. Instead, Franciscan friars arrived by 1327, seemingly acting on permission gained by Aragón.[11]

---

11. Zedelgem, "Aperçu historique," 62–64; Lenzi, *The Stations of the Cross*, 19–20.

Within a few years, the Franciscans had also acquired the site where Christ was supposed to have celebrated the Last Supper, known as the Cenacle House. This building had previously been under the control of Augustinians, but had been abandoned before the Franciscans began their work. Franciscan presence in the Holy Land was confirmed in 1342 when Pope Clement VI gave authority for the creation of the Franciscan Custody of the Holy Land under a special minister provincial in the order.[12] As a result, these Franciscans became known as the Guardians of Mount Zion in Jerusalem. By the mid-fourteenth century, the Franciscans had begun to perform rites at two other important sites in the Holy Land, including the Church of the Nativity in Bethlehem and the Tomb of the Virgin Mary in the Kidron Valley, over which they had been granted control by local ecclesiastical authorities, political authorities in both the Middle East and Europe, and the papacy.[13] This gave the Franciscans a unique and important place among religious orders of the Catholic Church, having been entrusted with so many of the places that were specifically mentioned in the Bible and infused with such sanctity.[14] The Franciscans, as late as the latter part of the fifteenth century, extolled the spiritual benefits of visiting the holy places. Francesco Suriano, a Franciscan, wrote a *Treatise on the Holy Land*, ostensibly to an Italian nun, noting, "Those things which touched Christ only for a while were strongly imbued with His virtue and grace. . . . Because of that the [Holy Land's] trees, woods, vegetables, grass, bread, water, stones, and everything else there is holy, and filled with virtue."[15]

Although many visitors to the Holy Land from as early as the fourth century described various processions in the city commemorating Holy Week, none of them outlined a path that clearly corresponds to Jesus's route. In fact, most of the extant guides are simply that: guides to the sites of Jerusalem. Pilgrims were concerned with having visited all the religious sites and gaining the specific indulgences associated with each place.[16] The term "station" does

12. In the Franciscan world a custody is usually a new region that is created under an existing province, frequently as a missionary field. For example, the Franciscan presence in New Spain began as the Custody of the Holy Gospel under the Spanish province in Extremadura. The Holy Gospel eventually became its own province. Thus, a custody functions as a small provincial unit with a larger province.

13. "The Custody," Custodia Terrae Sanctae, https://www.custodia.org/en/custody-and-its-history. According to Catholic teachings, the Tomb of the Virgin would be empty since she was assumed bodily into heaven.

14. Lenzi, *The Stations of the Cross*, 20–26.

15. Quoted in Bacci, "Materiality and Liminality," 129.

16. An indulgence was a spiritual gift that relieved the recipient from spending a specified period in purgatory, a place where the souls of the faithful were purged of their sins before entering heaven. Visiting specified holy places, saying certain prayers, and providing sources of income to the church would all grant indulgences to the faithful.

not appear in travelers' accounts until the middle of the fifteenth century.[17] Again, the sites mentioned frequently did not have to do with Christ's route but rather were sites felt to be important to the Christian story, not necessarily the Passion. When the term *via crucis* (way of the cross) appeared, often as not it referred to a specific street that carried that name.[18] Only in the mid- to late sixteenth century did the devotion finally coalesce around the fourteen stations that are recognized today.

A few travelers' accounts trace the final steps of Jesus in his Passion. One of the most influential of these is *Aetheriae peregrinatio ad loca sancta*. The account dates to the fourth century and was circulated in manuscript form, gaining more fame in the Roman Catholic Church in the eleventh century. It describes a procession among the various holy places.[19] Though the many accounts do not describe anything matching what came to be known as the Stations of the Cross, these descriptions do demonstrate a continued interest in visiting and reading about visits to the holy places associated with Jesus's Passion. The guidebooks are not unlike modern guides, listing the important sites to see in a city and region deeply invested in religious history. Tourists to the Holy Land were taken on a wide variety of visits but without any specific itinerary. Frequently the first place was the Church of the Holy Sepulchre, and then the tour would move backward chronologically to Pilate's praetorium and even to the Garden of Gethsemane.[20]

Devotio Moderna

Saint Francis advocated a radical practice of *imitatio cristi* (imitation of Christ): he gave up his possessions, acted like an itinerant preacher, gathered a group of followers, and came to bear the stigmata.[21] In the fourteenth century, in the tradition of Francis, other authors called upon their readers to likewise imitate Christ. The most important of these was Thomas à Kempis, a late fourteenth- and early fifteenth-century author who wrote a book on the theme of the imitation of Christ. Unlike the Franciscans, who emphasized acting in a manner like Christ, Kempis calls upon his readers to focus on their own inte-

---

17. Lenzi, *The Stations of the Cross*, 97–98.

18. Thurston, *The Stations of the Cross*, 45–61; Zedelgem, "Aperçu historique," 96–104; Lenzi, *The Stations of the Cross*, 27–36, 96–98. The street also carried alternate names in many of the guides, including Amargura (Bitterness) or Via dolorosa (Way of Sorrow).

19. Sticca, "The Via Crucis," 105–6. See also, Thurston, *The Stations of the Cross*, 57–61; Zedelgem, "Aperçu historique," 46–53.

20. Thurston, *The Stations of the Cross*, 22–23; Zedelgem, "Aperçu historique," 60–64.

21. The best brief introduction to Francis and the Franciscan Order is Short, *The Franciscans*. The stigmata consists of the wounds of Christ. According to legend, God marked Francis with wounds on his hands, feet, and side that imitated those of Christ.

rior spiritual lives—to withdraw from the world and contemplate divine things. Building on this theme, various other authors wrote devotional books that call upon readers to consider various scenes of the Passion and to put themselves into Jesus's suffering as part of this focus on one's own spiritual life.

Many spiritual leaders and authors considered Jesus's Passion through a variety of works with many different themes and focuses. Several popular devotions emerged as Christians embraced the many elements of the Passion.[22] The variety among them is somewhat confusing. Several devotions focus on Jesus's falls throughout the Passion narrative, not the specific falls along the route to Calvary. Two forms within this genre became fairly widespread: the Three Falls, which are included in the Stations of the Cross, and the Seven Falls, covering events beyond the route of the Passion. Of course, seven was a popular theological number, which may have contributed to the emergence of that form of the devotion. As these devotions made their way into print, frequently the devotional handbooks also contained engravings and woodcuts to allow faithful practitioners to more fully enter into the experience.[23] In a genre that may have influenced the Stations of the Cross, a devotion known as the Nine Steps, or Nine Movements, also had a wide popularity in the fourteenth and fifteenth centuries. It is a crucial element in the development of the Stations because it incorporates movement into the devotion itself and focuses on moving from one place to another. In this, it differs significantly from the Falls and the Stations themselves in that they have specific moments as their focus: the instance when Jesus took up his cross or when he met the women of Jerusalem. In the devotion of the Nine Steps, the movements are less tied to a specific moment or place.[24]

Another very popular devotion was the Seven Sorrows of Mary. Unlike the other stational devotions that focus on events around Jesus's Passion, this devotion runs the gamut of Mary's life and experiences, beginning with the circumcision of Jesus as an infant and culminating in his crucifixion. Nonetheless, as with the other devotions, the Sorrows of Mary also became associated with a set of sculptural pieces that evoke the emotions of the specific moments commemorated in the devotion. Parallel to the development of the Seven Sorrows was a devotion dedicated to commemorating the Seven Joys of Mary. A form of this devotion using the Rosary is known as the Franciscan Crown. In that variant, the Rosary contains seven groups of ten beads for which the practitioner remembers each of the joys and says a set of prayers, such as the Lord's

22. Thurston, *The Stations of the Cross*, 62–75; Zedelgem, "Aperçu historique," 72–76. Zedelgem devotes many pages to exploring all the various different types of assemblages such as the seven falls, the seven sorrows, the seven paths, and more: 72–96. "Devotions," *Catholic Encyclopedia*, New Advent, http://www.newadvent.org/cathen/12275b.htm.

23. Kirkland-Ives, "Alternate Routes," 258–59.

24. Kirkland-Ives, "Alternate Routes," 261–62.

Prayer and the Hail Mary.[25] As with so many other devotions, there are also alternate devotions focusing on numbers other than the holy number seven. One variant, for example, is the Five Joys of Mary. The most famous of the sculptural displays for the Seven Sorrows dates from the late fifteenth century in Antwerp. A papal indulgence, issued in 1620, was granted to those who performed the devotion.[26] One might well consider that the Seven Sorrows of Mary also played an important role in the creation of the devotion of the Rosary. The Seven Sorrows was also popular in early colonial New Spain, and one of the bas-reliefs commemorating it adorned a *posa* in the atrium of the Franciscan church in Calpan, Puebla.

One genre of devotions that played directly into some versions of the Stations of the Cross focused on the Wounds of Christ and the Effusions of Christ's Blood. The Five Wounds of Christ, a popular devotion in the fourteenth century, focuses on the wounds to Jesus's hands, feet, and side incurred during the Passion. The visual representation of the wounds became the seal of the Franciscan Province of the Holy Gospel in Mexico. In contrast to the Five Wounds, the Effusions devotions consider all the blood that Jesus shed in his Passion, from his scourging to the imposition of the crown of thorns to cuts incurred along the road to Calvary to his final crucifixion. As with the other devotions studied here, several variants were based on different numbers of effusions from seven to fifteen and beyond.[27] This focus on the amount of blood shed by Jesus during his Passion also became a feature of several books of meditation for the Stations of the Cross in that the penitent should reflect on Jesus's suffering through his blood loss.

Many of these devotions, along with the Stations of the Cross, are considered "stational devotions" by Mitzi Kirkland-Ives. She and other scholars have written about this broad array of devotions. While often viewed as a spiritual species that became extinct, these practices had a brief popularity but were eventually overwhelmed by the Stations of the Cross, and study of them helps to better contextualize the spiritual environment within which the Stations of the Cross took its form. Kirkland-Ives has characterized each of these practices as "but one expression of many wider somatic and kinetic responses to Christ's Passion."[28] Indeed, in various churches, convents, and monasteries, representational objects such as paintings, plaques, and sculptures were placed to assist practitioners in their practice of these devotions, something that would also occur with the Stations of the Cross.

---

25. "Franciscan Crown," *Catholic Encyclopedia*, New Advent, http://www.newadvent.org/cathen/04540a.htm.

26. Kirkland-Ives, "Alternate Routes," 264–65.

27. Kirkland-Ives, "Alternate Routes," 265–66.

28. Kirkland-Ives, "Alternate Routes," 251.

FIGURE 2.1. Five Wounds of Christ, Molina, *Confessionario breve*, John Carter Brown Library.

From earliest times, pilgrims to Jerusalem would visit the sites associated with Christ and his suffering on Good Friday. Denied access to the actual sites of Christ's Passion because of political and religious upheaval, the faithful were admonished to prayerfully contemplate Christ's suffering and imagine Jerusalem and the events of Holy Week as an internal devotion. Nonetheless, by the early thirteenth century, Saint Francis and others began to encourage the faithful to engage in a more physical recollection of Christ's life and Passion. For instance, Francis encouraged churches, and even households, to create replicas of Jesus's birth. These would allow the faithful to imagine what it was like on the night Christ was born. Nativity scenes soon became popular throughout Europe as Christians attempted to insert themselves into the experience of Christ's life. Iconography and legends of the saint describe Francis as being focused on Christ's Passion and suffering to such a great extent that he received the stigmata: his own flesh bore the wounds of Christ, on his hands, feet, and side. Even though Francis has come to be seen in the light of the movement called *imitatio christi*, his own spirituality was not so much an imitation of Christ as it was a call to his spiritual brothers and sisters to "follow" Christ and the example he set. Unlike Kempis, theirs was both an internal and an external imitation of Christ. Not only did they imagine Christ within themselves, they acted in the world in a manner they felt was consistent with Jesus. Franciscans and others saw Saint Francis both acting like Jesus and contemplating Jesus in his heart: a true imitation of Jesus.[29] The new physical devotion also held that if Christians could imagine walking along the route that Christ took, aided by physically creating a place in their own home or religious establishment, they would participate more fully in Christ's Passion. In keeping with this approach, some members of the Franciscan family (priests, friars, nuns, and tertiaries) wrote handbooks to guide individuals in their devotions.[30]

Throughout Europe many different devotions of the Passion continued to develop, and many were published while others circulated in manuscript form. They varied greatly in the number of stops or stations and in the exact location of the stations. Sometimes the stations were to be visited in the order that Christ passed through the events: from the Last Supper (Cenacle House), to the Garden of Gethsemane, to Pilate's house, and then toward Calvary, crucifixion, deposition, and interment. But others took the pilgrim backward, from the tomb to the Cenacle House. As will be seen, some of these variations made their way across the Atlantic and appeared in books published in seventeenth- and eighteenth-century New Spain.

While Thurston and Zedelgem continued to look to the Holy Land for the roots of the Stations of the Cross, the key pieces that began to outline the devotion were not travelers' accounts but rather devotional pieces written in northern Europe. In the early sixteenth century, around 1530, Jan Pascha wrote a spiritual handbook titled *The Spiritual Pilgrimage of Hierusalem*. Rescued from oblivion, it was published in 1563 and then, within about a century, was translated into French and English. Pascha, a Carmelite from Louvain, included fifteen stations in his account, which correspond generally to what would become the canonical fourteen, with some stations lumping together and some unique features that do not appear in the modern set. For instance, Pascha included all seven of the falls but combined them with some other events.[31] Nonetheless, it is close enough to clearly mark the beginning of the process whereby the canonical Stations emerged. Following Pascha, Christiaan van Adrichem, known as Adrichomius, published a devotional booklet in Cologne in 1584 that included twelve stops. The falls were consolidated to

29. Lenzi, *The Stations of the Cross*, 122–27.

30. Thurston, *The Stations of the* Cross, 45–61; Zedelgem, "Aperçu historique," 64–68; Lenzi, *The Stations of the Cross*, 10–16. Kirkland-Ives, "Alternate Routes," 254–56. Tertiaries are members of the Third Order of Saint Francis, generally lay people who take as many vows as they feel called to take and who otherwise follow the Franciscan Rule to the best of their ability. See below where this is more fully explained.

31. Thurston, *The Stations of the Cross*, 76–95; Zedelgem, "Aperçu historique," 99–102; Lenzi, *The Stations of the Cross*, 42–43, 154–57.

become three, and the remaining ones were added into other events. The result was a series of stations that fit exactly into the now-traditional fourteen, excepting the deposition and the burial.[32]

When the devotion of the Stations of the Cross did finally emerge in its final form, with fourteen stations and prayers and meditations for each, it was not like a traveler's account of a visit to the Holy Land but rather an attempt to create an environment for a deeper union with Christ. As Lenzi writes: "The Stations of the Cross ritual uses scriptural sources and adds apocryphal materials to create a new practice that works to imitate Christ's life as the ultimate prototype."[33] One of the common features of the devotion is the inclusion of the number of steps between each station, and sometimes there is a description of the physical location of each station. These distances are pure fiction, and many of the local descriptions are as well, but they serve to help create a full reality into which the participant can become immersed. Similarly, they provide milestones to aid memory. The sites and distances become vehicles whereby the faithful can remember the sequence, prayers, and meditations.[34] In modern times this technique is known as a method of loci, or a memory palace: by constructing an imaginary building or landscape, a person can then associate specific things with each space, allowing for later recall. The desired action of the Stations of the Cross is not merely an imaginary trip to Jerusalem but rather an imaginary walk with Jesus in his final Passion.[35]

Imagined Sacred Landscape

By virtue of their presence in Jerusalem and the Holy Land, Franciscans encouraged others to come visit them. As early as 1342, the pope endorsed a set of indulgences in recognition of their guardianship of the Holy City that would be granted to those who visited these special places.. Well before this, as early as the sixth century, some churches in Europe had constructed chapels to represent locations along the route of Christ's Passion in Jerusalem.

In the Middle Ages, pilgrims routinely carried off bits and pieces of the holy places as spiritual souvenirs from their journeys. These, as well as true relics of the Holy Land, were distributed throughout Europe on various trade routes. Given this practice, then, it was only a matter of time before full-scale replicas of the holy places were built outside the Middle East as evocative mementos. Some of these marked places where the saints had trod, such as

---

32. Storme, *The Way of the* Cross, 125; Zedelgem, "Aperçu historique," 102–4; Lenzi, *The Stations of the Cross*, 43–44, 157–58.

33. Lenzi, *The Stations of the Cross*, 130.

34. Lenzi, *The Stations of the Cross*, 129–30.

35. Lenzi, *The Stations of the Cross*, 132–33.

where Paul landed at Crete and Malta. The number of true relics associated with Jesus were limited, but they became the focal points of many churches throughout the West. These artifacts include pieces of the true cross, parts of the crown of thorns, parts of the column where Christ was beaten, and even drops of his precious blood. But for many communities, residents looked to the local landscape to provide an analogy to Jerusalem. Thus, any nearby hill could be termed the local Golgotha or Calvary. In some instances, the local landscape was transformed to match the Holy Land more closely.[36] As chapels and churches were built to enhance the local landscape, they could be further elevated spiritually though the placement of sacred relics, not just Christological relics but mementos of other saints, including Catherine, George, and Barbara among many others. In some instances, assemblages of structures were used to create symbolic Jerusalems. On the island of Rhodes in the early sixteenth century the Hospitallers built a copy of the holy sepulchre and then assigned symbolic value to a series of stops along a route to visit the imitation tomb. This might have then been copied in other places in Europe. Accounts tell of a Way of the Cross in Fribourg in 1516 based on the Rhodes model.[37] Sometimes these structures were imbued with mysterious and divine power, much like the House of the Virgin at Loreto, which was reported to have flown there from Nazareth.[38]

Elsewhere in Europe, when the faithful could not make the trip to Jerusalem to reenact Christ's Passion, some thought to replicate the experience at home. Indeed, some successful pilgrims to the Holy Land, upon returning home, built models and replicas of the holy places as souvenirs of their travels. While Thurston and Storme see these as precursors to structures used for the Stations of the Cross, Lenzi notes that these structures did not truly imitate the originals but rather took specific elements from them and then used those details more thematically; for instance, a local hill might be a stand-in for Calvary. These structures were evocative, not imitative. It was more that the structures evoked the places' original function. The structure thus linked past and present into a conflated time.[39] By 1520 the pope granted a set of indulgences to the faithful who visited a set of Stations in the cemetery of the Franciscan friary in Antwerp, which had been built in imitation of the Holy Land.

In medieval Spain, many cities had constructed *humilladeros*, small chapel-like structures, usually with a canopy or roof (*baldaquin*) covering a large stone cross. These *humilladeros* frequently marked the limits of cities or territories

36. Bacci, "Materiality and Liminality," 137.
37. Bacci, "Materiality and Liminality," 143.
38. Vélez, *The Miraculous Flying House of Loreto*, 3–5.
39. Lenzi, *The Stations of the Cross*, 115–21.

and thus were placed on roads leading into and out of cities. Incorporating these structures into routes celebrating Jesus's Passion could be relatively simple, using a *humilladero* as a stand-in for Calvary. In the fifteenth century, the eastern Spanish kingdom of Aragón worked to reestablish its claims in the Holy Land by building a hospice there for travelers from Western Europe. Spanish members of religious orders then took their experiences in the Holy Land back to the Iberian Peninsula and began creating their own virtual replicas of holy sites, often circuits meant for visitation.[40] One popular form, for example, was a chapel or church built as a replica of the Church of the Holy Sepulchre, complete with a crystal coffin bearing a lifelike statue of the tortured body of Christ, a theme that would be exported to Latin America.[41] One nobleman, upon his return from a pilgrimage to the Holy Land in 1519–20, redesigned his Seville palace to resemble Pilate's praetorian palace. In later centuries it even came to be known as the Casa de Pilatos (Pilate's House).[42]

In Spain there is evidence of the sixteenth-century construction of several Ways of the Cross that had fourteen stations, although some scholars date them to the early seventeenth century.[43] Importantly, around that time Spain had close ties to the Catholic Low Countries, since they were all part of the same Hapsburg domain. Particularly in the sixteenth century, there was significant communication between the two regions, so devotions and other trends that had begun in the Low Countries could easily spread to Spain. Works such as that of Adrichomius were translated into Spanish relatively quickly and found an audience on the Iberian Peninsula.[44] Other publications in that period were certainly part of the larger literature emulating the Passion, while not necessarily articulating the canonical form of the Stations of the Cross.[45] By the late sixteenth century in Spain, two elements of the Stations of the Cross had emerged: devotional literature that took the canonical form and structures that could be used as focal points for the devotion. One of the earliest known devotionals in Spanish containing the prayers and meditations for the fourteen stations is reported to have been published in 1625.[46]

While the Franciscans were not the sole originators of the Stations of the Cross, in Spain the devotion became associated with the order, and in partic-

40. Gil Atrio, "Cuestionario histórico," 68–72. Like Thurston, Zedelgem, and Storme, Gil-Atrio attempts to see actual experiences in the Holy Land as the basis for the development of the Stations.

41. Gil Atrio, "Cuestionario histórico," 72–77; Lara, *Christian Texts*, 217–24.

42. Wunder, "Classical, Christian, and Muslim Remains," 197–99.

43. Storme, *The Way of the Cross*, 146; Gil Atrio, "Cuestionario histórico," 77– 81, passim; Sticca, "The Via Crucis, 115.

44. Gil Atrio, "Cuestionario histórico," 77–79.

45. Storme, *The Way of the Cross*, 131.

46. Gil Atrio, "Cuestionario histórico," 88–90.

ular with Third Order Franciscans.[47] In various kingdoms of Spain, Third Order Franciscans had either built or taken control of structures associated with the celebration of the events of Holy Week.[48] Later, the devotion gained wide popularity and renown due to the efforts of an Italian Franciscan, Saint Leonard of Port Maurice (1676–1751), who is credited with building more than 570 Stations of the Cross throughout the Italian peninsula.[49]

By the seventeenth century the Stations had become more common in the West, and the number of stations within the devotion was regularized at fourteen.[50] Eventually, in 1686, Pope Innocent XI granted the Franciscan Order the right to place stations in their churches. Moreover, Franciscans and those affiliated with the order could gain indulgences by visiting these stations. The indulgences granted to participants were the same as those granted for pilgrimages to the Holy Land, reflecting how difficult it was for most people to visit Jerusalem. This privilege for Franciscans was confirmed in 1694, and in 1726 it was extended to all the faithful, though the Franciscans were the clear promotors of these indulgences.[51] Nonetheless, people from other orders wrote some of the early devotional books dedicated to the practice. Similarly, as the devotion became popular, Stations of the Cross were placed in churches associated with different orders, as were similar stations for the Seven Falls and Seven Sorrows.[52] But the Franciscans remained widely associated with the Stations of the Cross and its indulgences. Just as in the Holy Land, the Franciscans were not the first order to focus on the holy places, but by the mid-fourteenth century they had developed a monopoly on many of the important ones.

---

47. Within each family of religious orders there are three subgroups. The First Order is the male order, the Second Order is the female order, and the order for the laity is called the Third Order. Members of the Third Orders are generally not required to take vows of celibacy and thus may be married. Some of the other vows of the order may be modified for the laity as well, such as poverty. They are not required to live in a community nor to wear the distinctive habit of the order at all times. Individual members may, however, follow the rules of the order as completely as they are able.

48. Gil Atrio, "Cuestionario histórico," 82–84.

49. "St. Leonard of Port Maurice," *Catholic Encyclopedia*, New Advent, http://www.newadvent.org/cathen/09178c.htm.

50. Thurston, *The Stations of the* Cross, 159–74. The devotion of the Stations of the Cross never developed as completely in the Orthodox churches as it did in the Roman Catholic Church.

51. Storme, *The Way of the Cross*, 148; Robin, *Las capillas*, 23–24. "Stations of the Cross," *Catholic Encyclopedia*, New Advent, http://www.newadvent.org/cathen/15569a.htm.

52. The Stations of the Cross were strongly embraced in New Spain, as will be seen. But this did not mean the disappearance of other Passion devotions. In the early eighteenth century, a booklet titled *Desagravios de Jesus nuestro bien; y tiernas meditaciones, para meditar y contemplar lo que padeció en la noche del jueves en el asqueroso e indecente aposentillo* was published by Nicolás Espindola. It contains meditations and acts of contrition for what it characterizes as the Seven Mysteries of Christ's Passion.

In 1731, Pope Clement XII extended the privilege of indulgences for the Stations of the Cross to all churches so long as they were created with Franciscan assistance and licensed by the local bishop. Clement's brief also established the official number of stations at fourteen, since some variation continued until that time and beyond.[53]

The Stations of the Cross evolved from a variety of several similar devotions, all based around the notion of stations and movement from one station to another while engaged in prayer and meditation. Another devotion that developed a little bit later but was largely contemporaneous with the Stations was the Rosary. The Rosary uses beads as a mnemonic device, not dissimilar to the use of the stations. The Stations of the Cross has some Marian components and evolved from other devotions focused on Mary, such as the Seven Sorrows of Mary. But the Rosary, as it became popular in the fifteenth and sixteenth centuries, focused more completely on the life of Mary as the mother of God. Yet just as the Stations of the Cross includes two stations that focus particularly on Mary (station 4, He Meets His Blessed Mother, and 13, His Body Is Taken Down from the Cross), the Rosary also features a series of five Mysteries (prayers and meditations) that focus on Jesus's Passion. These "sorrowful events comprise: (1) the Agony in the Garden, (2) the Scourging, (3) the Crowning with Thorns, (4) the Carrying of the Cross, and (5) the Crucifixion."[54]

Like the Stations of the Cross, the Rosary also includes the interplay of visual experiences with prayers and meditations. This combination seeks "to open new modes of perception rather than to arouse discursive thought or propose novel ideas."[55] The practice thus heightens the emotional and transcendent character of the devotion. The Rosary, like the Stations of the Cross, evolved from prayers and mediations of the fourteenth-century *devotio moderna*, which focused on the juxtaposition of Jesus's humanity with his divine nature by focusing on the elements of his Passion. These were reinterpreted in the sixteenth century as a result of the canons and decrees of the Council of Trent and of the influences of the *Spiritual Exercises* of Saint Ignatius Loyola, the founder of the Jesuit Order, to create two powerful tools used by Catholics as part of new traditions that emerged after the Protestant Refor-

53. "Way of the Cross," *Catholic Encyclopedia*, New Advent, https://www.newadvent.org/cathen/15569a.htm. See also Storme, *The Way of the Cross*, 146–48; Zedelgem, "Aperçu historique," 129–30. The individual associated with the pope's final approval and for fierce advocacy for the devotion was the Franciscan friar, Saint Leonard of Port Maurice (1676–1751), who reportedly established some six hundred sets in early eighteenth-century Italy. "St. Leonard of Port Maurice," *Catholic Encyclopedia*, New Advent, http://www.newadvent.org/cathen/09178c.htm.

54. Winston-Allen, *Stories of the Rose*, 3

55. Mitchell, *The Mystery of the Rosary*, 78.

mation.[56] These two devotions were thus associated with two different religious orders: the Stations of the Cross with the Franciscans and the Rosary with the Dominicans.[57]

While both the Rosary and the Stations of the Cross could be pursued by individuals sitting alone in contemplation, the devotion of the Stations lent itself to a more public celebration. Many churches would organize processions, especially on Good Friday, in order to celebrate the Stations of the Cross. These might be within a church, a convent, or a monastery, but also occurred frequently in the streets and roads of towns, moving from chapel to chapel. Thus, the Stations, in particular, have an important performative aspect as the participant walks, considering the moments of Christ's Passion. This aspect became particularly important as Christianity moved from Western Europe into the rest of the world and into central Mexico in particular.

Processions in Pre-Hispanic Mexico

Religious processions played an important role in several months of the Mexica (Aztec) solar year, the *xiuhpohualli*.[58] The solar calendar contained eighteen months of twenty days each, plus five unnamed days, the *nemontemi*. During the months of Toxcatl and Panquetzaliztli there were processions that made a specific series of stops at important places on the island of Tenochtitlán-Tlatelolco, the ancient site of Mexico City, as well as in other parts of the Central Basin, where the city is located. In addition to these two important processions, many of the monthly festivals included processions within the sacred precinct of Tenochtitlán in which young people paraded from one place to another and priests conducted processions from temple to temple. During several months, lines of priests, sacrificial victims, and the general populace might process from one place to another for a specific ceremony or ritual, frequently dancing as they went along. For example, in the month of Tepeilhuitl, five women representing mountains were carried by other women and paraded in a procession. The route was not stipulated, merely that they all must arrive at the Templo Mayor, the main temple in the center of Mexico-Tenochtitlán, and then were sacrificed to the god of rain, Tlaloc.[59] This brief study, however,

56. Mitchell, *The Mystery of the Rosary*, 19.

57. Winston-Allen, *Stories of the Rosary*, 76–79.

58. While many books and authors refer to the residents of central Mexico in pre-Hispanic times as the Aztecs, that is not a name that they commonly used for themselves. In general, they used the name Mexica. In this essay, I will follow that convention. When discussing all the Native groups who also spoke the Aztec language, Nahuatl, I will refer to the larger group as the Nahua.

59. Sahagún, *Florentine Codex*, 2:133. The *Florentine Codex* was a twelve-volume compilation of Mexica history and traditions collected by a Spanish friar, Bernardino de Sahagún, written in Nahuatl and Spanish.

will look specifically at processions that involved several stops along a predetermined route and where unique rituals were enacted at each stop.

The feast of Toxcatl, the fifth month of the solar year, was dedicated to the god Tezcatlipoca (Smoking Mirror). The central ceremony of the feast was the celebration of a god impersonator, a *teixiptla*, a man who, for a year, lived as the physical embodiment of the god Titlacahuan (We, His Men), an aspect or avatar of Tezcatlipoca.[60] He was given wives and the best food, drink, and clothing. Fr. Bernardino de Sahagún, a Franciscan missionary who worked with Native informants to collect information about the ancient customs, listed in book 2 of the *Florentine Codex* all the possible physical defects to be avoided in the imitator the priests chose. An important consideration was that in every respect people treated the impersonator as if he truly were the god. In Nahua theology, he was considered a local embodiment of the deity.[61]

An important ritual in Toxcatl was a four-day procession of the god impersonator to a series of ritual sites starting five days before the end of the month. On the first day of the journey the god impersonator and his entourage traveled to a place called Tecanman. They sang and danced in their procession and at the places where they stopped to spend the night. On the second day, he went to the place where the temple to Titlahuacan was located, the very temple dedicated to the god. There the impersonator stayed in the home of the official in charge of the temple. The third day of travel included a boat trip to Tepetzinco in the middle of Lake Tetzcoco.[62] The fourth day involved a trip to Tepepulco (Sahagún notes that it was located near Tepetzinco, but in reality it was not very close, nearly fifty kilometers away). From Tepepulco, the god impersonator and his entourage returned by boat to Acaquilpan, where the *teixiptla* eventually met his death by sacrifice at the temple called the Tlalcochcalco.[63] This site has been described as being near Chalco Atenco, to the southeast of Tenochtitlán.[64] Toxcatl did not end with the death of the impersonator. It was, however, a very important ritual wherein a religious procession marked a landscape with performances of smaller rituals along the way.

During the month of Huey Tecuilhuitl the goddess of corn, Xilonen, was revered. Just as in Toxcatl, when a man served as a god impersonator (*teix-*

60. Olivier, *Mockeries and Metamorphoses*, 44. Bassett, *The Fate of Earthly Things*, 132–35.

61. Sahagún, *Florentine Codex*, 2:66–68.

62. There is still a hill named Tepetzingo in what was Lake Texcoco, to the west of Chiconcuac and to the east of Ecatepec. In preconquest times this hill would have been a small island in the lake. There is another Tepetzingo in the modern-day state of Hidalgo, not too far from Tepepulco, but it would not have been in Lake Tetzcoco

63. Sahagún, *Florentine Codex*, 2:70–71.

64. Carrasco, "The Sacrifice of Tezcatlipoca," in *To Change Place*, 36.

iptla), a woman was chosen to become the deity. Unlike the description for Toxcatl in which Sahagún spent several paragraphs describing the criteria for selecting the impersonator, in Huey Tecuilhuitl he merely wrote that a woman was chosen. He did describe her adornment in a bit of detail: The impersonator was dressed in all the raiment associated with the deity. She wore two colors of face paint—yellow around her lips and red on her forehead—and a four-cornered paper hat with quetzal feathers dangling like corn tassels. She had a necklace made of many strands of turquoise beads and a golden pectoral. Her skirt and blouse were adorned in a lily pattern. She wore the carmine-colored sandals of the nobility. To finish the effect, she carried a red shield and rattle sticks. The ritual leading up to her sacrificial death consisted of a procession to four distinct places: Tetamazolco, Necoquixecan, Atenchicalan, and Xolloco. In each place, she participated in a ritual bathing ceremony known as *xalaquia* (entering sand as water). These four stops were symbolic of the four eras through which creation had passed prior to the present, according to Mexica thought. On the next day, with much ceremony and following several other preliminary rituals, the impersonator was taken to the temple of Cinteotl, the young corn god, and sacrificed there through decapitation.[65]

These were but two of four major celebrations of the Mexica year. During these four months emissaries from foreign regions were required to pay their tribute to the Mexica overlords. While staying in Tenochtitlán, the foreigners were given an opportunity to see some of the most impressive ceremonies of the Mexica ritual cycle.

Panquetzaliztli was dedicated to the national god of the Mexica, Huitzilopochtli (Hummingbird on the Left). The rituals and ceremonies continued throughout the twenty days of the month and culminated in a running procession. The most famous procession associated with the festival of Panquetzaliztli was known as Ipaina Huitzilopochtli (the Swiftness of Huitzilopochtli). It featured a priest who ran while carrying an image of the god made of amaranth-dough (*tzoalli*) along a circuit in the Central Basin of Mexico. The priest ran from the Templo Mayor to the divine ball court within the sacred precinct. There, two people were sacrificed. The runner then proceeded to Tlatelolco, the twin city of Tenochtitlán located just to the north. From there he ran along the causeway toward Tlacopan, stopping in Tlaxotlan and Popotlan. From Tlacopan the running procession passed just to the east of the outcropping of Chapultepec to arrive at Izquitlan, where sacrifices were made. The runner continued south to Coyohuacan and Huitzilopochco, where more sacrifices occurred. He then ran up the causeway to Acachinanco and eventually back to the Templo Mayor. The route of travel was symbolic

65. Sahagún, *Florentine Codex*, 2:103–5; Dibble, "The Xalaquia Ceremony"; Durán, *Book of the Gods*, 439–40

of the original migration of the Mexica, which had taken them from their mythic homeland of Aztlan to Tenochtitlán. Moreover, the events that occurred at the Templo Mayor after the return of the priest and deity figurine recapitulated the elements of the birth of Huitzilopochtli. Thus, in the month of Panquetzaliztli the running procession with fixed stops was used to recall the Mexica migration and the birth and apotheosis of Huitzilopochtli as a solar deity, since the ceremony roughly corresponded to the winter solstice. Also, importantly, the direction of the running procession was counterclockwise. The overall movement traced the perceived direction of the movement of the sun in Nahua thought, which was from east to west, then to the south, and around to the east again.[66] Just as in the Toxcatl procession, the Panquetzaliztli ceremony defined the physical space with a series of rituals at fixed and predetermined places, all to reenact the Mexica migration. Both were symbolic re-creations of mythic-historical events central to the Mexica religion.

The Stations in Early Colonial New Spain

Authors have long assumed that the early missionaries used processions and other very public displays of piety as key features of their evangelization.[67] As mentioned earlier, the architecture of the early missionary churches included the features of an enclosed patio, known as an atrium (*atrio*), and small chapels placed around its perimeter, usually in the corners, called *posas* because of their resemblance to covered wells. The assembly of structures provided the early missionaries with a place to conduct most of the essential business of evangelization until such a time when a church and other permanent structures could be erected.[68]

The procession seems to have been both a missionary technique and a ritual understood and embraced by the Natives. Writing about the very earliest years of the colony, the friar known as Motolinia, Fr. Toribio de Benavente, noted that by about 1528, seven years after the conquest, the Natives of Texcoco organized a religious procession to beseech God to relieve their suffering caused by flooding that year.[69] The friar also described the processions of the Natives during the commemoration of Holy Thursday and Friday. These were penitential acts in which the Natives used so-called disciplines (ropes embedded with pieces of metal) to scourge themselves. Otherwise the processions seem to have resembled the processions found in many Spanish cities during

66. Schwaller, *The Fifteenth Month*, 80–104.
67. McAndrew, *The Open-Air Churches*, 216–17; Kirkland-Ives, "Alternate Routes," 266.
68. Valadés, *Rhetorica cristiana*, folios 210–14.
69. Motolinia, *Memoriales*, 119.

Holy Week: penitents walking defined routes, carrying lighted candles, crosses, and scourges. While in procession, the penitents would recite a set of prayers and sing songs appropriate to the day.[70] The devotion they recited in all likelihood contained elements that would later be associated with the Stations of the Cross.

It must be noted that the processions of the Mexica and the processions used by the missionaries were two very different things. It is more than possible that the missionaries used processions as a means of attracting the Natives to the new faith, knowing that such rituals had been present prior to the conquest. Nonetheless, conflating the two different traditions into a single experience in New Spain must be approached with great caution. In all likelihood, the use of processions by the missionaries figured as part of what James Lockhart describes as "Double Mistaken Identity."[71] Under this principle, the missionaries noticed that the Nahuas used religious processions and then assumed that they functioned in a manner not unlike processions in Christianity. For their part, the Natives observed the processions of the Spanish and assumed that they functioned in a manner not unlike precontact Mesoamerican processions. Neither assumption was correct, but both observers were confident in their assumptions and acted accordingly. Louise M. Burkhart also explores this same epistemological realm, noting that some aspects of Christianity "passed easily across the cultural barrier" but were "transformed in the process of their translation."[72] Consequently, Natives might have participated in Christian processions because of the similarity with the precontact practice without fully embracing or even understanding the deep cultural differences.

Diego de Valadés, one of the early missionaries, published an extensive work in Latin about the evangelization, and his sketch of the ideal atrium is reproduced in many places. In the description of what he explains as appropriate practices, Valadés also includes processions. He notes that initially the processions were solely for displaying the Blessed Sacrament, such as on Corpus Christi, and were confined to the atrium, but eventually they began to spill out into the adjoining streets and would also occur on different feast days. Nonetheless, he criticizes the practice of going outside the atrium because it gave way to "immoderate costs."[73] Slightly later in the work, Valadés lists the major feast days during which processions might be made. These include Maundy Thursday (Thursday of Holy Week), Easter Sunday, Corpus Christi (the Feast of the Blessed Sacrament), and the Feast of Saint Francis.[74]

70. Motolinia, *Memoriales*, 93–94.
71. Lockhart, *Nahuas after the Conquest*, 445–56.
72. Burkhart, *The Slippery Earth*, 185–88.
73. Valadés, *Rhetorica cristiana*, folio 210, "immodici sumptus."
74. Valadés, *Rhetorica cristiana*, folio 227.

Another Franciscan missionary, Motolinia, describes the events of Easter 1536 in some detail. He notes that the Blessed Sacrament was displayed on Good Friday and Holy Saturday, and the Natives would come forward and give offerings in front of the consecrated host. These included a wide variety of blankets in many different styles and a wide variety of fabrics, from rabbit fur to cotton. Candles and some crosses were left as well. The crosses also reflected a wide variety of composition, from simple wood to gilt and even semiprecious stones such as jade and turquoise. Natives would present their gifts while kneeling down, spreading out the blanket or carefully placing the candle or cross. Frequently, some people brought copal incense to burn and made offerings of food. All these items were collected by Native officials and later used in the hospital or sold for its support. On Easter morning the Natives would then process, singing joyful songs and dancing along the way. Thereafter the friars would conduct the Easter Mass.[75]

In these passages focusing on the early Franciscans' missionary activities, it is clear that processions with established liturgies were a common part of the indoctrination process. The numbers of Natives who participated in these events is staggering—frequently several thousand. But at the same time, Motolinia is well known for his exaggerations. He claims to have baptized a huge number of Natives, estimating between four and nine million in the first fifteen years of the evangelization, which is an astounding number.[76] The number can be discounted by an order of ten and still indicate a considerable level of engagement. Quite simply, no one can believe the huge numbers presented by Motolinia. Nonetheless, they do provide an indication of the importance the friars placed on these activities.

While Motolinia comments that the Natives participated in processions in the opening years of Spanish rule, he also notes that the practice continued well into the mid-sixteenth century, when he was writing. In describing the activities in the parishes, the friar explains that on procession days, the streets would be filled. The faithful would sing or pray the Te Deum Laudamos (Thee, O God, We Praise), various hymns to the Virgin and to the Holy Spirit (Veni Sancte Spiritus, Come Holy Spirit), and prayers such as the Our Father and the Hail Mary and would recite the Ten Commandments, all in the Native languages.[77] Thus, it seems that the performance of processions with liturgies and songs became essential parts of the missionary effort even beyond the immediate conquest period.

Processions on certain holy days clearly played an important role in the spiritual life of early colonial New Spain. The Spanish colonists had brought

---

75. Motolinia, *Memoriales*, 94–96.
76. Motolinia, *Memoriales*, 120–22.
77. Motolinia, *Memoriales*, 156.

this medieval Spanish tradition with them.[78] Others occurred with special intentions to relieve droughts or stop floods and pestilence and at other times while seeking divine intervention. Relics of saints and important religious images were similarly paraded in the streets for a variety of purposes. Indeed, processions were so important and integral to the full religious experience that one of the very first books published in Mexico was a short treatise by Dionisio Richel, a Carthusian monk, on the manner in which to hold processions.[79]

Writing in the 1590s, the Franciscan missionary Fr. Gerónimo de Mendieta describes the participation of the Natives in religious processions through the liturgical year. Starting in November, there were processions to parade the Blessed Sacrament through the neighborhood near the church compound. Flowered arches would be placed in the street in such quantities that they would block out the sun. The friar counted more than a thousand arches in one route. He also describes processions within the atrium surrounding the church. The group would pass from the church door to one of the *posas*, where they would stop and dance to songs sung by choirs with musicians.[80]

Some of these celebrations involved props and other physical reminders of the event being celebrated. As noted, the Franciscans were early supporters of Nativity crèches as a spiritual aid allowing the faithful to better envision the event, to imagine themselves as participants in the scene. Mendieta notes that this was also a feature of a Christmas procession in early colonial Mexico. A large Nativity scene was erected in one of the church doorways that was so clever, he notes, that even Spaniards came by to take a peek.[81]

Mendieta describes a scene from the celebration of Corpus Christi, which he indicates corresponded to a principal ceremony before the conquest. Since it is a moveable feast, depending on when Easter falls in the calendar, it can be celebrated as early as May 21 or as late as June 24.[82] The association referred to by the friar might well be to Toxcatl, described above, one of the Mexicas' important late-spring festivals. Mendieta writes that the procession featured a priest in finest vestments surrounded by acolytes carrying a monstrance in which was placed the consecrated host: the Body of Christ, the focus of the celebration. The congregation knelt in the atrium during the

78. Truitt, *Sustaining the Divine*, 162–63, provides a table showing all of the regularly scheduled processions in Mexico City in this period.

79. Richel, *Este es un cōp dio breue.*

80. Mendieta, *Historia eclesiastica Indiana*, 3:84 (book 4, chap. 19).

81. Mendieta, *Historia eclesiastica Indiana*, 3:85 (book 4, chap. 19).

82. Easter is the critical moveable feast around which other celebrations take their date in any given year. In the Roman Catholic Church, Easter is celebrated on the first Sunday after the first full moon on or after the spring equinox. Thus, Easter can fall between March 22 and April 25. Ash Wednesday is calculated by counting backward from Easter, while Pentecost and Corpus Christi are calculated by counting forward from Easter.

procession, singing psalms along with the Gloria Patri (Glory to the Father) and Magnificat (My Soul Magnifies the Lord). At about two or three in the morning the procession ended with church bells ringing in the host's return to the church. At that point, the Natives would quickly prepare the atrium and then begin their traditional dances, but to the songs of the new religion. When the church bell rang for Prime (about 6 or 7 AM) the dancing would end, and the congregation would prepare itself for Mass.[83] This description shows how the two religious cultures had begun to blend by the end of the sixteenth century. Beyond that, it shows the process of grafting Christian practices onto Native traditions using of processions, singing, and dancing.

In ceremonies that seem much closer to the solemnity of the Stations of the Cross, Mendieta remembers Holy Week celebrations beginning with Palm Sunday and lasting until Easter. Recalling his experience in Tlaxcala, the friar notes that the leading Native nobles would spread out their cloaks so that the priest and acolytes might walk on them. As in many communities, the palms and branches that they waved during this ceremony were put away and guarded. The following year these would be burned to provide the ashes for the Ash Wednesday ceremony. During Holy Week, Mendieta writes, from Maundy Thursday until Holy Saturday (Easter eve) the Natives engaged in penitential processions similar to those celebrated in Mexico City.[84]

The arrangement of the *posas* in the atrium allowed for processions to occur either as a supplement to regular church services or as an extension of them. The way that the *posas* were erected, in at least some of these churchyards, anticipated a counterclockwise movement. In atria where the *posas* remain and in several where we have only drawings of their organization, the intended movement was counterclockwise to the north, west, south, and then east, which was the same orientation as at least one of the most important preconquest rituals, that of the Swiftness of Huitzilopochtli in Panquetzaliztli.[85]

While Mendieta provides great detail for many of the ceremonies and processions, he makes only oblique references to the Stations of the Cross and the rituals of Good Friday. The friar notes that celebrations did occur, with penance on Friday and rejoicing on Easter Sunday, but he defers any details to the next chapter, where he writes of practices in the chapel of San José, a sanctuary specifically for the Natives, where Vetancurt spent much of his career. But in the next chapter Mendieta glosses over any details, merely noting that 7,700 penitents associated with the confraternity of Our Lady of Solitude processed through the streets. Even in these celebrations there were

83. Mendieta, *Historia eclesiastica Indiana*, 3:84–85 (book 4, chap. 19). Prime is the first of the canonical hours of the day in the church.

84. Mendieta, *Historia eclesiastica Indiana*, 3:86–87 (book 4, chap. 19).

85. Wake, *Framing the Sacred*, 118–19; Schwaller, *The Fifteenth Month*.

some vestiges of the old pre-Hispanic social order. Mendieta notes that the Natives were organized by neighborhood according to the precedent established in pre-Hispanic times. The friar comments that the celebrations of Holy Week were so remarkable that the viceroy don Martín Enríquez (who served 1568–80) declared that he had never seen anything like it in his life.[86]

Certainly, themes of the Stations of the Cross such as scenes from the Passion of Christ were common throughout early colonial Mexico. Some of the more famous of these will be analyzed in a later chapter. In constructing their convent churches, the friars consciously used scenes from the Passion both in the architecture and in the decoration. In the center of the atrium they frequently placed a highly decorated cross, normally on top of a mound or pedestal. In a small way, this was used to represent Golgotha or Calvary, the hill where Jesus was crucified. Additionally, the crosses were frequently decorated in bas-relief showing items that were used during the crucifixion. These items, called the symbols of the Passion, include things such as the nails, the hammer, a pair of tongs that held the nails, a spear, a sponge, the crown of thorns, and a ladder among others. Taken as a whole, the atrium cross, then, became a Golgotha in miniature.[87] The base of the cross, the representation of the hill of Calvary, also resembled the small platform altars known as *momoztli* that dotted pre-Hispanic Nahua cities. Indeed, some of the Nahua platforms might have been reused and recycled for the new Christian purpose.[88]

Many of the convent churches that dot central Mexico have highly decorated north doors. In church architecture the main door is called the "west" door, regardless of the actual orientation of the church. Traditionally churches aligned from east (altar) to west (main door). On the north side, to the left while facing the altar, doors had ornate exterior decorations surrounding them. In the Franciscan church of Huejotzingo, this door came to be known as the *porciúncula*, referring to the shrine to the Virgin Mary that Saint Francis refurbished outside Assisi.[89] These decorated entrances served two purposes. There was an Old Testament tradition associating the north with pagans; thus, the north door became linked to individuals who sought to enter the church for the first time and to become Christians. Later, these doors also became associated with the gates of Jerusalem, and the convent churches became the New Jerusalem.[90]

---

86. Mendieta, *Historia eclesiastica Indiana*, 3:90–91 (book 4, chap. 20).

87. McAndrew, *Open-Air Churches*, 247–54.

88. Lara, *City, Temple, Stage*, 170–71.

89. *Porciúncula* means "a little portion" because the Assisi chapel was first built on a plot of land apportioned to the Benedictines. Francis found the chapel in a state of disrepair and refurbished it. The little place was then granted to him for his use. It is considered the founding place of the Franciscan order. See also McAndrew, *Open-Air Churches*, 155.

90. Lara, *City, Temple, Stage*, 32–33, 139; Kubler, *Mexican Architecture*, 250–51; McAndrew, *Open-Air Churches*, 155, 344.

FIGURE 2.2. Los cuatro postes, Humilladero in Ávila, Spain, photographed by the author.

If the interiors of the church and atrium could be considered the New Jerusalem, then the space outside the walls represented the surrounding countryside. The place of Christ's crucifixion was outside the walls, on Golgotha/Calvary. Thus, many friars established representations of Calvary, called *calvarios* or *humilladeros* outside their atria. These were very similar to those found in Spain. The placement of these objects, chapels, and crosses created a spiritual landscape in which the faithful could follow the *via sacra* from the church to the site of the crucifixion. Along the way, as the devotion of the Stations of the Cross began to spread in the New World, stops could be developed to correspond to the stations as one passed from the church and atrium to the *calvario*.[91]

The interiors of the churches and convents were decorated with other things that also evoked Christ's Passion. Many of the wall paintings included images of the crucifixion or the ecce homo, when Pilate presented Christ after his sentencing, both of which are elements in the Stations of the Cross. Other murals depicted religious processions or various scenes from the Bible. By the early seventeenth century, many churches also had statues of saints, Jesus, and the Virgin Mary. In some instances, these statues represented events of the Passion, such as Christ after he was beaten at the column or even the holy interment, where the battered and bruised body of Christ lay in a crystal

91. Lara, *City, Temple, Stage*, 108–9.

coffin. As was the case in Spain, on special holidays, and in particular during Holy Week, these images would be placed on large wooden frames, like large tables, and carried through the streets. Some scholars have seen the veneration of these images as a carryover of the Nahua tradition of *teixiptla*, local embodiments of the divine. For the Nahua, the *teixiptla* could be a statue of wood, stone, or dough or even a person dressed in the garb of a deity. These objects actually took on the power and characteristics of the deity represented.[92]

By the end of the sixteenth century, processions continued to be an essential part of religious expression in Mexico. Don Antonio de San Antón Muñón Chimalpahin Quauhtlehuanitzin, known to scholars as Chimalpahin, wrote of the extraordinary number of processions, both civil and religious, that occurred regularly in Mexico City. As was noted earlier, there were parades and processions to welcome newly appointed viceroys. These lavish displays of the Spanish colonial state's wealth and power were exceeded only by the celebrations of the coronation of a new monarch in Spain and the requisite taking of an oath of allegiance to that new monarch, the *jura del rey*. The oathtaking ceremony eventually became so expensive that legislation was issued to curb the outlay.[93] But in addition, the city also hosted processions and parades for important religious holidays such as Corpus Christi or Holy Week. Holy Week and Corpus Christi marked two important moments in the Church calendar. Holy Week is the week between Palm Sunday and Easter, in late March or April. Then, two months later, Corpus Christi is celebrated in late May or June.[94] In addition to these two important religious feasts, in times of drought or famine, religious processions might also be organized to implore God and the saints for assistance.

Chimalpahin chronicled the events that marked life in Mexico City from 1577 until shortly before his death in 1615. The pages of his account, written in Nahuatl, are replete with descriptions of a wide variety of processions. The first procession that he describes occurred in 1585 when the Third Provincial Council met in Mexico, assembling together all the bishops of the region in order to bring local canon law in line with the Council of Trent. His account ends with a brief note that on Wednesday, October 14, 1615, there were prayers and processions to implore God to save the realm from the depredations of pirates, who were then sailing along the Pacific Coast of the kingdom.[95]

---

92. Molly Bassett calls the *teixiptla* "the localized embodiment" of the divine figure. Bassett, *The Fate of Earthly Things*, 132–35; Lara, *Christian Texts*, 217–19; Taylor, *Theater of a Thousand Wonders*, 517–18.

93. Curcio-Nagy, *The Great Festivals*, 33.

94. As noted above, Easter is a moveable feast. Corpus Christi and Pentecost are two feasts that depend on Easter's timing and thus move in the calendar as well. For Mexican processions, see Curcio-Nagy, *The Great Festivals*, 27–32.

95. Chimalpahin, *Annals of His Time*, 26–27, 306–7.

The celebrations of Holy Week in general, and Good Friday in particular, attracted a great deal of attention and popular outpourings of emotion and religious devotion. The first Good Friday procession mentioned by Chimalpahin occurred in 1598, although we know from other sources that they had been a regular feature of life in the city for decades. Chimalpahin probably mentions this particular celebration because the prestige of sponsorship of the procession was hotly contested among the four Native neighborhoods of the city. In that particular year, the residents of the San Pablo district had sought a specific license from the viceroy to organize the event. Nonetheless, the residents of the San Sebastian district succeeded in leading the parade, a sure sign of favor.[96]

Chimalpahin devoted many pages to Holy Week in 1613. His narrative begins with the ceremonies on Monday, April 1. He describes many of the religious processions that wound through the city in the week, from the confraternity of the Souls in Purgatory, who processed on Monday, carrying a float of Saint Francis and the instruments of the Passion, to the several processions at the end of the week. On Good Friday ceremonies began shortly after midnight with the residents of Santa Cruz Contzinco processing in darkness, arriving back in their homes at 4 AM. They were competing with the residents of San Pablo Tlachcuititlan, the head town of their district, over the right to process with el entierro (the interment of Christ). The residents of San Pablo emerged in their parade at 5 AM. After them, at dawn, the residents of Santiago Tlatelolco, a confraternity called the Nazarenos, processed to the cathedral and then to the Church of San Francisco. In those early hours another Tlatelolco confraternity, one dedicated to Nuestra Señora del Tránsito (the Dormition of Our Lady), paraded, too, going to the cathedral then past San Francisco and back home. Next, a procession called the Mixtecos (ostensibly for Natives from Oaxaca) emerged from the Church of Santo Domingo, carrying an image of Our Lady of the Rosary.[97] In the afternoon, yet another group from Tlatelolco carried the image of the interment of Christ, El Entierro. Clearly, several parishes had images of the interment, and each claimed to have a right of precedence in the Good Friday processions, since the celebration of Good Friday ended with the burial.[98] One other important aspect of this competition was that each neighborhood church had a specific image of a saint, Jesus, or Mary in their church that would be mounted on a *paso* for processions. Clearly the baroque tradition of highly emotional sculpture pieces had reached Mexico by this time.

96. Chimalpahin, *Annals of His Time*, 62–63. To better understand the rivalries among the districts of the city, see Truitt, *Sustaining the Divine*, 15–34.

97. Truitt, *Sustaining the Divine*, 43.

98. Chimalpahin, *Annals of His Time*, 241–49. Truitt has a good analysis of these chapels, *Sustaining the Divine*, 34–45.

At roughly the same time, the chronicler of the Dominican Order, Fr. Agustín de Dávila Padilla, recorded processions during Holy Week, on Good Friday in particular. What is important about this account is that he refers to some of the stops along the route as "stations." The specific procession that he describes began at the Dominican church. From there the participants proceeded to the cathedral, three blocks south. The procession then went all the way to the edge of town, three blocks west, to where the main Franciscan church was located. From the Franciscan church, the Dominican procession then went to the convent of Nuestra Señora de la Concepción, three blocks to the north and a bit to the east. After that stop, the Dominicans returned to their home church, three blocks back to the east. Theirs was a clockwise procession.[99]

In New Spain there is some evidence that the devotion of the Stations of the Cross formed an important part of religious life in the colony by the late sixteenth and early seventeenth centuries, becoming widespread much earlier than it did in Europe. In 1612, the *actas de cabildo* (minutes of the municipal council) of Mexico City mention a procession, perhaps related to the Stations of the Cross that departed from the Franciscan convent on the edge of the center city and then passed out of the populated area to the west, along the road that went to Tacuba, to a *humilladero*. The procession and its route came to the attention of the city fathers because of flooding along the road. A few months later, the aldermen discussed a request to help improve the *humilladero*.[100] In 1616, the archbishop, don Juan Pérez de la Serna, reported a ritual similar to the Stations of the Cross processing from the Franciscan monastery along a road he called Amargura (Bitterness), of a distance and length similar to the route taken by Christ in his Passion.[101] In all likelihood, this is the same procession and route as the other, with the street named Amargura being the road to Tacuba, which is the modern-day Avenida Juárez. Thus, between 1611 and 1612, it seems that chapels were built along the road from San Francisco to the edge of town and the *humilladero*, as will be seen below. In 1616, the Franciscans received approval for an indulgence to be granted to individuals who prayed the whole devotion.[102] Taken as a whole, there is clear evidence that there was a formally established route for the Stations of the Cross in Mexico City. The procession began in the Church of Saint Francis, passed along the south side of the municipal park known as the Alameda, and then went west to the *humilladero* located on the western edge of the city.

---

99. Dávila Padilla, *Historia de la fundación*, 565–68.
100. Robin, *Las capillas del Vía crucis*, 42–43.
101. Robin, *Las capillas del Vía crucis*, 43–44.
102. Iguiniz, *Breve historia*, 89–90.

By the early seventeenth century, the devotion of the Stations of the Cross had become more firmly established as a unique ritual, one particularly associated with the Third Order Franciscans. The Third Order had been officially founded in Mexico in 1614 at a meeting of the provincial leadership. In colonial Mexico, the Third Order existed as a hybrid between a traditional religious sodality or confraternity and a religious order itself. Members seldom became friars or nuns. They were expected to comply with the spirit of the Franciscan Rule, but without taking the necessary vows of celibacy, poverty, and obedience. Nonetheless, many chose to dress in the habit of the order and follow the precepts of the order as best they could.[103] The account books of the Third Order Franciscans in Mexico City indicate that they annually spent varying amounts on the preparations for and execution of the Stations of the Cross. The expenditures occurred between January and May, peaking in March and April. As noted, since Easter is a moveable feast, it wanders through the calendar from late March to late April. Unfortunately, the records are incomplete, so it is difficult to determine when the practice began after the order's founding in 1614. Nonetheless, it is clear that the ceremony became an important ritual for the capital in the early to mid-seventeenth century.[104]

In her study of the chapels associated with the devotion of the Stations of the Cross, Alena Robin notes that the first structures date from 1612, about the same time as the foundation of the Third Order. As has been seen, this was at roughly the same time that similar structures were built in Puebla and Antigua, Guatemala.[105] As noted above, the collection of structures included the *humilladero* and a large covered cross, along with small chapels or devotional structures along the path leading to it westward from the convent of the Franciscans. In paintings of the city from the seventeenth century, these structures look like small monuments built in a row leading west. Thus, the *humilladero* and monuments would have been located to the south of the Alameda in Mexico City, stretching along what is now Avenida Juárez.[106]

Maps and paintings of Mexico from the seventeenth and eighteenth centuries clearly show the presence of these chapels lining the south side of the Alameda park, heading west toward the edge of the city. A map of the city from 1625 depicts the chapels as a series of connected buildings along the road in the first block west of the Franciscan church (see fig. 2.3). As Robin

103. Belanger, "Between the Cloister and the World," 157–59. In modern times, some Third Order Franciscans do take full vows in the order but do not take Holy Orders and thus are not priests or deacons.

104. Robin, *Las capillas del Vía crucis*, 49–50.

105. Robin, *Las capillas del Vía crucis*, 55.

106. Robin, *Las capillas del Vía crucis*, 46–55.

FIGURE 2.3. Map of Mexico City, 1628 (detail). Benson Latin American Collection, University of Texas.

notes, the early chapels had fallen into disrepair. Over the course of the seventeenth century they would be removed and new chapels erected farther west from the original location.

A seventeenth-century map decorating part of a painted screen, called a *biombo*, includes the chapels as part of the developed landscape of the city. While they are not the central feature of the map, they do appear. The map on the screen depicts central Mexico City in an elevated view, as if one were several hundred feet above west-central Mexico City, more or less where the modern Monument to the Revolution is located, looking to the east. Running from the lower-right corner and into the front-central part of the city is the aqueduct that brought fresh water to the city from the springs of Chapultepec. The aqueduct bends toward the east, and just along the last block of its run, one can see a green space, which is the Alameda, a public park whose construction began in 1592. Located along the south side of the park are three small buildings lining the street, which are chapels. Then, just beyond, toward the viewer, a series of four crosses leads to a grouping of another three. Right behind the three crosses is a baldachin that represents the *humilladero* located on the western edge of the old downtown part of the city. The depiction of the chapels shows that the seventeenth-century reconstruction in the city moved the chapels several blocks westward.

The chapels and crosses are all parts of a set of Stations of the Cross that were built in the city in the late sixteenth and early seventeenth centuries. Between 1684 and 1700, larger, freestanding chapels marking the Stations of the Cross replaced the earlier monuments and were placed farther west, away from the center of the city. These structures and the art associated with the Stations of the Cross will be studied more thoroughly in chapter 5.

Quite clearly, interest in and fervor for the celebration of the Stations of the Cross in Mexico began as a simple outgrowth of the missionary endeavor, but the devotion developed as the friars encouraged it and as the faithful embraced it as a visible affirmation of Christianity. This trend was not limited to Latin America but was part of the baroque style and the Catholic Reformation that were spreading across much of the Christian world at the time.[107]

As Robin notes, the chapels remained part of the Mexico City landscape for several generations. Looking at the historical record and the various paintings and maps of the city from the eighteenth century, the chapels persisted well into the nineteenth century and were only destroyed in 1861.[108] Nonetheless, throughout the seventeenth and eighteenth centuries, the chapels and crosses were permanent reminders of the devotion of the Stations of the Cross. Over the course of a century and a half, the structures were replaced several times with larger and more opulent buildings.

The most important of these was the chapel associated with Calvary, located on the western edge of the city, not far from where Paseo de la Reforma and Avenida Madero intersect in modern Mexico City. According to inventories, in the early eighteenth century Calvary Chapel had three altars. The principal altar, in the apse of the chapel, directly across from the entrance, featured an impressive painting of Jerusalem. It also had a figure of Christ crucified with a silver crown and silver rays, known as *potencias*, emanating from it.[109] The plaque reading INRI was silver, as were the nails holding it in place. Beside it was an image of Our Lady of Sorrows (Nuestra Señora de los Dolores) of approximately the same size with silver ornaments. The inventories also suggest that there was a wooden replica of Calvary, with two crosses on which the two thieves were also crucified. Thus, the assemblage was a

107. Llewellyn, "The Stations of the Cross and Popular Piety," 216–17.
108. Robin, *Las capillas del Vía crucis*, 223–28.
109. See chapter 5 for a fuller discussion of the *potencias*.

replica of Christ's crucifixion. On either side of the crossing were altars dedicated to the descent from the cross and to the holy burial.[110] Thus, the three final Stations of the Cross were depicted in Calvary Chapel, which was the last of the set to be destroyed.

At about the same time that the chapels associated with the Stations of the Cross were being built in Mexico City, the Third Order Franciscans of Puebla were developing their own. The Third Order was founded in that city in 1614, and over the next few years the order accumulated property and set about constructing small chapels associated with the Stations. Documents point to 1615 as the starting date for the project, and the Puebla set of chapels was completed by 1622 when the viceroy, Marquis of Serralvo, gave a formal title of possession to the Third Order. Additional grants were forthcoming in 1628 by local authorities, with spiritual supervision vested in the friars based on grants from the dean of the Puebla cathedral.[111]

The route for the processions was similar to the contemporaneous procession route in Mexico City. Beginning inside the Franciscan church, the procession stopped at two of the *posas* in the atrium. It then left the church property and proceeded through the streets of the city. Unlike in Mexico City, where the procession route immediately moved to the outskirts of the city, the procession in Puebla actually moved into the more developed urban area before exiting to the countryside. Five stops occurred at chapels along the city streets. The procession then went to the hillside known in those times as the Cerro de Belén (Hill of Bethlehem).[112] The chapels outside the church atrium were initially built of adobe, but with the passage of time they began to deteriorate, and eventually they were replaced with ones made of brick or stone.[113] Nonetheless, with the ravages of time, by the middle of the nineteenth century several, but not all, had been destroyed. Many others had been converted to purposes other than those for which they were originally intended and had taken on new names.[114]

There is a late seventeenth-century description of the chapels penned by the chronicler of the Franciscan Order, Fr. Augustín de Vetancurt. After pointing out that the construction began in 1615, thanks to a gift of land, he describes the chapels. Each of the chapels measured twelve varas long and

110. Robin, *Las capillas del Vía crucis*, 165–71.

111. Ruiz Martínez and Armenta Olvera, *Las capillas del vía crucis*, 11–12; Vetancurt, *Teatro mexicano*, 3:136–37.

112. The hill is better known today as the location of Forts Loreto and Guadalupe. In the nineteenth century it was at these forts that the Mexican forces defeated the invading French in the battle known as "El Cinco de Mayo."

113. Ruiz Martínez and Armenta Olvera, *Las capillas del vía crucis*, 13–17.

114. Ruiz Martínez and Armenta Olvera, *Las capillas del vía crucis*, 17–34. The authors provide a fairly detailed history of each of the chapels and their ultimate destruction.

six wide.[115] They all had barrel vaults and housed altars that enhanced the specific theme of each station. Each chapel had a sacristy where the vestments and utensils could be safely stored. The property also included a small interior patio with a garden and a small residence where a secular priest could live to guard it. A custom developed in which people would visit the chapel's stations each Friday of the year. But the ceremonies on Good Friday eclipsed all others. Women would pray the devotion in the morning, while men took to the path in the afternoon. The Third Order Franciscans attended a mass in the Franciscan church in the afternoon and then walked the stations in the early evening as a group. The last chapel, called Calvary, was built on the top of the hill and was larger than the others. In addition to the regular features, it had an underground chamber dedicated to the Holy Sepulchre (Santo Sepulchro).[116]

At the same time when devotees of the Stations of the Cross were constructing these chapels, the followers of the Rosary were also having a profound impact on liturgical architecture both in Mexico in particular and throughout Latin America. In the mid- to late seventeenth century, Rosary chapels were built as part of Dominican churches. Some of the most famous were located in provincial capitals in New Spain, particularly in Puebla and Oaxaca. The Rosary chapel in Puebla is still held as one of the culminating works of the Mexican baroque style. Every surface of the chapel is covered with carved plaster that has been painted or gilded. It is a riot of movement and completely astounding at first glance. It became an exemplar for the creativity and extravagance associated with Mexican baroque.[117]

Later Missionary Activities and the Stations of the Cross

In the early seventeenth century the Catholic Church began to shift the manner in which it addressed missionary activity. The first missions were simply groups of dedicated friars and priests who set out into the wilderness to convert Natives to Christianity. By the seventeenth century most core areas of Latin America had been Christianized. But many people, both Natives and Spaniards, had only a rudimentary grasp of the religion. Since the sixteenth century, various groups within the Church had been active in organizing internal missions, that is, efforts to deepen the faith of those already in the Church and also to convert Protestants back to Catholicism. In New Spain, for all

---

115. The vara was measured with slightly different lengths at different places at different times, but it was approximately equivalent to thirty-three inches, slightly less than a yard.

116. Vetancurt, *Teatro mexicano*, 3:136–37.

117. Mullen, *Architecture and Its Sculpture*, 130–33.

intents and purposes, there were no Protestants. Those Protestants who did reside there lived in fear of being discovered by the Inquisition, but their numbers were never large. Missionaries had ample opportunity to enrich and deepen the faith of those who were already nominally Catholic. The papacy recognized that these two goals, deepening the faith of Catholics and converting Protestants, were important challenges for the health of the Church, adding to the long-term goal of converting others to the faith who had never been presented with Christianity. In 1622, Pope Gregory XV created a new office charged with efforts to convert and strengthen the faith of Catholics. It was named the Congregation for the Propagation of the Faith, known by its Latin name, Propaganda Fide. The congregation is now known by a more modern name: the Congregation for the Evangelization of People. This movement to spread the Gospel among those who were already Christian, as well as to non-Christians, gained wide support in the Franciscan Order, such that within a few decades organized groups of friars were setting out on missions both in Europe and in the New World. In New Spain, their efforts began with the creation of missionary colleges that served both as educational institutions to train friars in missionary techniques and also as a home base for the missions. The first of these was erected in Querétaro: the Colegio de Santa Cruz, founded in 1683.[118]

A routine part of the missionary techniques used by the Franciscan missionaries from the colleges included the teaching and practice of the Stations of the Cross. One missionary, Fr. Melchor López de Jesús, became an avid proponent for the devotion, spreading the Stations of the Cross wherever he went, erecting crosses and *calvarios* to encourage the faithful to pursue the devotion. López de Jesús was a colleague and frequent companion of Fray Antonio Margil de Jesús, who shared López's dedication to the Stations of the Cross.[119] The activities of Margil and López correspond exactly to the period when the devotion was expanding in its importance in New Spain: the end of the seventeenth and beginning of the eighteenth centuries. The missionary friars generated interest in this devotion and others by pointing out that an important benefit to Catholics of the Catholic Reformation were the indulgences that the participants could gain to reduce their stay in purgatory.[120] The missionaries would remind the faithful that by pursuing the devotion, they earned the same indulgences as if they had made a pilgrimage to

---

118. McCarty, "Apostolic Colleges," 53–58; McCloskey, *The Formative Years*, 32–35.

119. Brading, *The First America*, 43, 377.

120. As will be seen later, the Catholic response to the Protestant Reformation has been called the Counter-Reformation. Nonetheless, recently scholars have preferred to use the term Catholic Reformation, since there were reform efforts internal to the Church prior to Luther and the rise of Protestantism.

Jerusalem. Even after the missionaries departed, the faithful were encouraged to continue to practice the Stations of the Cross, along with praying the Rosary and performing other pious acts. The missionaries would assist by refurbishing Stations where they existed, sometimes erecting crosses to denote a route where none had been present before.[121]

The chronicle of the colleges outlines in great detail many of the efforts undertaken by Margil and López in establishing the devotion of the Stations. López was born in the village of Almonacid in the province of Toledo, Spain, in 1639. The Franciscan author of the chronicle reflects that from an early age López found consolation in the devotion of the Stations: "In the Via Sacra he found his path, truth, and life, and along this road he directed his steps all his life."[122] López joined the Franciscan Recollects in Spain at age fifteen, in the province of Castile. He passed his novitiate and early training in the convent of Santa María del Castañar, some eighteen miles from Toledo. He took his vows as a Franciscan and was ordained a priest, which meant he was licensed to preach and confess. When the first missionaries of Propaganda Fide were organized in Spain, López joined the expedition, and in 1683 he set sail for Mexico. For the next sixteen years he traveled extensively in New Spain as a missionary in some of the most difficult regions, from the jungles of Central America to the coastal plains of Texas. In many of his missions he was a companion to Fr. Antonio Margil de Jesús.[123]

On one particular mission trip, in 1684, López accompanied three other friars from Querétaro to Campeche in order to found a Franciscan Recollect convent in the latter city. During their stay in Veracruz, the friars ministered to the residents of the town and even to the prisoners in the fort that guarded the city, the famous Fort of San Juan Ulúa. The friars admonished the prisoners to reject their sinful ways and to pledge to live new lives. In order to assist them in their conversion, López and his companions admonished them that they should pray the Rosary as a group every day and on Fridays all pray the Stations of the Cross. Obviously, in this context the devotion of the Stations consisted only of the meditations and prayers and not the movement from station to station. The missionaries also preached in the port itself, where they charged the two missionaries who would remain there to publicly celebrate the Stations of the Cross every Friday of the year.[124]

In 1694, López and a group of fellow missionaries traveled to Guatemala to create a missionary college there. Third Order Franciscans of Guatemala City,

---

121. Melvin, *Building Colonial Cities of God*, 138, 160–61.

122. Espinosa, *Crónica de los colegios*, 531.

123. Espinosa spends twenty-three chapters outlining the details of López's life. Espinosa, *Crónica de los colegios*, 529–639.

124. Espinosa, *Crónica de los colegios*, 472, 475.

now Antigua, had already built a *calvario* in the city, and this site was selected as the location of the new college. As had become the practice upon completing a mission in a given town or city, López and his companions charged the friars of the college to follow all the rules of the order and the colleges. And on all Sundays and feasts, as a community, they were to pray the Crown of Mary Queen of Angels and on every Friday the Stations of the Cross.[125]

The importance of the Stations of the Cross as a missionary tool for the colleges can be seen in a letter written by Margil de Jesús about the missionaries in Guatemala. He singled out Fr. Melchor López, in particular, detailing his activities in furtherance of their mission. The missionaries were working with groups of men and women gathered at the church. Margil noted that "Everyone was gathered, they drank their drinks of chocolate and then, kneeling, they prayed Matins. With the sign of the cross, they brought the men together. Then, very late, they walked the Stations of the Cross inside the church, and everything ended quite late."[126]

Obviously, the devotion was being spread to the faithful as an essential part of the deeper and more emotional brand of religion that the colleges of Propaganda Fide used as part of the effort to renew the faith among Christians and to implant the faith in those who had not yet become Christians.

Another member of López's group also became closely identified with the devotion of the Stations of the Cross. Fr. Francisco de Casañas from Barcelona also joined the first expedition of Propaganda Fide missionaries. As with López, Casañas came to embrace the devotion of the Stations of the Cross to such a degree that upon his death, they found in his cell crosses denoting the *via sacra*. Moreover, the other friars said that Fr. Francisco would pray the Stations nightly in the cloister of the convent, carrying a cross of his own in imitation of Christ.[127]

As has been seen, the close association of the devotion to the Franciscan Order and the Missionary Colleges' use of and dedication to the devotion only served to emphasize the two institutions' ties with the devotion. But at the same time, the order also secured papal bulls to provide spiritual benefits to anyone who followed the devotion and allowed stations to be erected in non-Franciscan churches. By virtue of these two threads, the practice of the Stations of the Cross was spread to many communities in New Spain in the waning years of the seventeenth century.

---

125. Espinosa, *Crónica de los colegios*, 792. The Crown of Mary devotion is also known as the Franciscan Rosary or Franciscan Crown. It differs from the traditional Rosary in that it focuses on the Seven Joys of Mary. "Franciscan Crown," *Catholic Encyclopedia*, New Advent, http://www.newadvent.org/cathen/04540a.htm.

126. Espinosa, *Crónica de los colegios*, 549.

127. Espinosa, *Crónica de los colegios*, 481–82

From this survey, we can see that the Stations of the Cross began in Europe but spread to the New World, where processions and public manifestations of piety were used by the missionary friars to establish the Christian faith in Mexico. When the devotion of the Stations of the Cross was exported to the New World, practices there followed their own unique path. Upon the devotion's arrival, it settled on fertile soil prepared by earlier rituals, celebrations, and activities. It also became a part of a series of processions, festivals, and other holidays that served both to create unity in the colony and to manifest difference. The festivals and processions called all members of society to share in their common faith and culture. Organized around political and religious events, they allowed all participants to become members of one body politic. Yet because of how the festivals and processions were organized, Natives and Creoles usually took supporting roles, while the leadership fell to Spanish elites.[128]

As noted earlier, the Stations of the Cross implies two distinct things. On the one hand there is the devotion: the combination of prayers and meditations that focus the practitioner on the suffering of Christ as he moved from the palace of Pontius Pilate to his ultimate death by crucifixion and burial. But as we have just seen, the Stations of the Cross can also refer to a set of paintings, plaques, bas-reliefs, or chapels indicating specific places for the devotion and serving as aides to the practitioner to participate more fully in the emotional power of the remembrance of Christ's Passion.

The devotion for the Stations of the Cross has historically been flexible. Several guides and handbooks were published in the seventeenth century offering prayers and mediations for use at the different stations. Eventually the standard of fourteen stations became widespread, but even today there are many different texts for the devotion. At the same time, in Mexico in the late seventeenth and early eighteenth centuries publishers began printing many other titles that used the concept of the station as an organizing trope for a serial religious devotion.

The Stations of the Cross has its spiritual roots in Jerusalem, where pilgrims sought to commemorate Jesus's final hours. But the devotion did not begin to take a concrete and recognizable form until many centuries later. Between the eighth and thirteenth centuries, the rise of Islam made travel to the Holy Land difficult. Various pilgrims still made the trek, and religious orders took control of the holy sites. Yet precisely because travel was so difficult and not all the faithful could visit Jerusalem, a few churches, convents, and monasteries in Western Europe developed replicas or commemorations of the holy places on their grounds. These would allow the faithful to imagine

128. Merrim, *The Spectacular City*, 156.

that they were in the Holy Land, visiting the holy places, and perhaps even accompanying Jesus in his Passion. With the passage of time, prayers and meditations developed to accompany these visits to the replicas. There was great variation in both the replicas and in the meditations. Some venerated the Falls of Jesus, some the Sorrows of Mary, and some just the Last Supper, imprisonment, and trial before Pilate. But by the sixteenth century, both the form and numbers of stations had been settled, but this was not confirmed by the papacy for many decades. The devotion of the Stations of the Cross also began to gain widespread popularity in the late sixteenth century. It was then transported across the Atlantic to Mexico, where it found an eager audience.

Religious processions were an important part of both Mexica religion and Spanish Christianity. The two religious traditions seem to have recognized this in each other. The missionaries used processions as an important tool in the evangelization of the Natives, and they enthusiastically embraced them. The devotion became so popular that small chapels or prayer stations were built in several major cities, using the Franciscan monastery as a starting point and then moving to the edge of town, to a replica of Calvary, frequently at a *humilladero.*

Chapter Three
Religious and Literary Culture in Mexico in the Middle Colonial Period

"[Some say] there are many printed books that do nothing, holding that the expense of money in printing them is useless, being thus: there is no book, no matter how bad, that does not have much from which we can learn."[1]

The devotion of the Stations of the Cross found a very receptive audience in early colonial New Spain. It tapped into a religiosity that had developed in Europe and then was exported to the New World. The small Spanish population of the colony saw their ancient embrace of Christianity as a clear point of distinction between themselves and the millions of Natives who surrounded them. In the thinking of the Spanish, the Natives were, after all, neophytes to the faith. Additionally, European residents of the colony were all deeply invested in their Catholic identity. The kings of Spain had emerged as leading the Catholic opposition to the Protestant Reformation. Devotions such as the Stations of the Cross provided a visible contrast to the early Protestants who tended to eschew public demonstrations of piety in favor of a quiet, private set of devotional practices.

The Stations of the Cross, as it developed in the sixteenth and early seventeenth centuries, relied on the formulaic recitation of prayers in remembrance of the specific suffering of Jesus recognized at each station. As time passed, these prayers and meditations began to become standardized, just as the number and theme of the stations themselves did. This standardization

1. Vetancurt, *Teatro Mexicano*, 4:379: "ay muchos libros impresos que no sirven teniendo el dispendio del dinero en las impressiones por inutil, siendo assi que no ay libro por malo que sea, no tenga mucho que aprender." This may be a secular paraphrase of 2 Timothy 3:16–17, "All scripture is inspired by God and is useful for teaching, for reproof, for correction, and for training in righteousness." Vetancurt must have been fond of this epigram, because it also appears in the preface to his *Arte de la Lengua Mexicana*, Biblioteca Virtual Miguel de Cervantes, http://www.cervantesvirtual.com/obra-visor/arte-de-lengua-mexicana—0/html/00965b84-82b2-11df-acc7-002185ce6064_12.htm.

was facilitated by the printing press, which could provide scores of identical prayer books to accompany the devotion. The earliest of these appeared in Europe, but by the mid-seventeenth century, presses in the New World had begun to publish their own handbooks for the devotion.

Print Culture in Mid-colonial Mexico

A measure of how popular the Stations of the Cross was in colonial Mexico can be found in the print culture of colonial New Spain. A printing press was established in Mexico City in 1536, some fifteen years after the conquest. Both the civil and ecclesiastical authorities were actively involved in print culture, helping to guide its direction in areas where they perceived a need. The output of the first press reflected the issues that the colonial authorities felt were important and that the printer felt could make money. At the same time, print production was closely regulated. Ecclesiastical works needed permission from the local bishop before they could be printed. Works on secular topics were also subject to scrutiny as their themes dictated. Because of the sixteenth-century Mexican presses' importance to the Church authorities of the missionary effort among the Natives, a significant portion of all their output focused on themes essential to evangelization. Thus, several score books were printed in the sixteenth and early seventeenth centuries that would be used for that purpose. Prominent among these were grammars and dictionaries of Native languages written for Spanish priests to use in their missionary activity. There were also confessional guides and other handbooks to assist the priests in the indoctrination of the Natives. Manuals that outlined the administration of the sacraments in Native languages also appeared, as did many collections of sermons written in those languages.

With the passage of time, fewer and fewer confessional guides, grammars, and other books used for evangelization came from the Mexican presses. The production of works in Native languages in general began to diminish after 1600 and sharply declined in the late seventeenth century. Yet Mexican presses were very busy turning out devotional material for an eager Spanish-language readership. Sermons, novenas (a set of prayers to be said over a nine-day period), descriptions of public events, and handbooks for private piety soon began to overwhelm the reading public. There were a few chronicles recording the religious orders' histories since their inception in the New World. Other important works attempted to capture the natural history of the region. In the publications one can see the beginnings of an important literary culture that, while not completely divorced from the Catholic Church, did manifest more secular interests in poetry and history.

In his survey of piety in the mid-colonial period, Brian Larkin sees several different types of penitential devotion. One of these was mortification, which consists of Christians wounding or inflicting pain on themselves as a form of penance. The practice of self-inflicted pain was a carryover from earlier forms of performative piety in Europe. It was well enough established in New Spain to have been mentioned by the bishops as they assembled in the Third Provincial Council in 1585. Flagellants—individuals who whipped themselves—were known to parade through major cities mortifying themselves. The practice also occurred in private with cilices, whips, and other instruments. A second type of penitential devotion consisted of simple gestures of performative piety, such as making the sign of the cross with the hand (touching the head, the stomach, and each shoulder) or making small crosses with the thumb on the forehead, mouth, and heart when listening to the reading of the Gospel. Numeric symbolism played an important role, focusing on thirty-three for the number of years that Jesus lived on earth along with three for the Trinity and seven for the number of mortal sins and cardinal virtues among others. Temporal symbolism also appeared, involving the celebration of the saints' days and the liturgical calendar. Additionally, there were works recognizing each week as a remembrance of Christ's Passion, from his entrance into Jerusalem to his crucifixion and resurrection. Thus, in many popular devotions, all or some of these features might be involved.[2]

New emotional and public displays of religion that emerged were part of the Catholicism that developed following the Council of Trent (1545–63). The council was called to review and potentially modify Church teachings and practices in reaction to the threat posed by the rise of Protestantism in Europe. The Catholic response embodied in the council's decrees has been variously characterized as the Counter-Reformation or, more recently, the Catholic Reformation. The council sought to clarify the essential elements of Catholic faith and practice. As various Protestant groups stripped churches of ornamentation, pared down services to focus more exclusively on Biblical readings and sermons, and streamlined ceremonies, the Catholic Church tended to embrace the emotional content that was part of the elaborate ceremonies, what modern observers call the "smells and bells": vestments, incense, and music.[3] Emotionally charged devotions such as the Stations of the Cross, wherein the faithful fervently sought to capture the suffering of Christ in the Passion, became hallmarks of the Catholic Reformation. Not only did the devotion itself—and the ceremonies it engendered—enhance

2. Larkin, *The Very Nature of God*, 56–61.

3. Within the Catholic and Anglican churches, in particular, ornate ceremonies are often disparagingly called "smells and bells," by those who prefer a less ornate and complex ritual. The "smells" refers to the use of incense throughout the mass for the sanctification of the altar, the priest, and the congregation. "Bells" are a reference to the use of small bells or chimes that are rung during the blessing of the wine and wafers during the Eucharist, or Last Supper, the core section of the mass.

this emotionally charged Catholicism, the use of ornate plaques, paintings, and even chapels also conformed to Catholic Reformation sensibilities, serving as stimulants to piety.[4]

In New Spain, from the late seventeenth century through the eighteenth century, at least twenty-eight different books featured stational religious devotions. Many of these were principally for use during Holy Week but could be adapted for many other occasions. Quite a few were so popular that they went through multiple printings. For example, one popular title, *Practica para andar las estaciones de la Semana Santa*, was published four times in Mexico City between 1720 and 1826. In fact, there seem to have been two books circulating with the same title, since the 1754 edition is very different from the 1758 edition. This illustrates some of the variations that one finds in these devotional books.

The version from 1754, which consists of a devotion of only seven stations, follows Jesus through the Passion and ends with the crucifixion. Nonetheless, it is a very different devotion, including several stops that are not part of the traditional fourteen and skipping over nearly all the traditional stations. This version of the *Practica para andar* begins at the Last Supper; proceeds to the Garden of Gethsemane; proceeds to Ananias's house, Caiaphas's house, Pilate's palace, and Herod's palace; goes back to Pilate's palace; then turns to the walk to Calvary. A curious feature of this version is the suggestion that each station should be performed in a different church, thus spreading participation in the devotion among several locales.[5]

The version in the putative 1758 edition has only four stations. Rather than focus on specific places, this devotional considers both specific sites and the movement from one place to another during Christ's Passion: walking from Pilate's palace to Herod's, remaining at Herod's palace, standing before the priests and scribes, and then going back to Herod's palace again. The meditations focus mostly on the events in the middle of the sequence, between visits to Herod and Pilate. Moreover, these are events that occur fairly early in the whole Passion narrative. Rather specifically, these events do not contain any of the stations included in the papally recognized devotion of the Stations of the Cross. In the copy of this edition held at the John Carter Brown Library, someone has taken a pen and edited the work. Various words have been blacked out: specifically, words suggesting madness, such as *loco* and *locura*. At one station in particular, when Pilate sentences Jesus, this version reads: "Dio sentencia contra su juicio" (He gave sentence [being] out of his judgment). In another passage the original author has Herod imply that Jesus must be mad. That, too, is crossed out. Words meaning "simple-minded" or

4. Larkin, *The Very Nature of God*. 92–92.
5. *Practica para andar* (1754).

"addled" are also blacked out.[6] For some reason, the secondary editor had strong feelings that there should be no suggestion of madness in either Jesus or Pilate. There is a good theological reason for that stance, since it would imply that the process was somehow tainted. On the one hand, Jesus, as one aspect of the divinity, cannot be mad. On the other, Pilate must act out of his own free will, and his judgement cannot be tainted by madness.

Nicolás de Espíndola, a priest from Mexico who was extremely active in eighteenth-century Mexico, wrote several different stational devotions. The earliest of his four or five titles appeared in 1709, *Desagravios de Jesus nuestro bien*.[7] It was specifically developed for use on Maundy Thursday and Good Friday. Espíndola organized his book around seven stations associated with the seven mysteries of Christ's Passion. The series begins with Jesus's arrest in the Garden of Gethsemane; continues through his imprisonment, appearance before Caiaphas, and humiliation; followed by the appearance of his mother as the Mother of Sorrows (Madre Dolorosa); his imprisonment again; and finally his crucifixion.[8] This particular devotion was fairly popular and went through some thirteen printings over the course of the eighteenth century.

Espíndola published another devotion for Holy Week in 1725: *Exercicios de los desagravios de Christo*. This work is very different from all the others and much less organized around stations. It contains three prayers and a meditation on Christ's Passion to be used on Palm Sunday as well as Monday and Tuesday of Holy Week.[9] This devotional handbook is not as stational as the others since it merely builds on themes associated with each of the three days at the beginning of Holy Week. Yet another stational devotion from the pen of Espíndola is simply titled *Via dolorosa*. In that manual, he organized his stations in a completely different manner, one that harks back to some of the earlier formats used in Europe. This work was printed in 1721 and 1761, and possibly more times. Rather than move in what became the traditional direction, from Pilate's palace to the crucifixion and entombment, the direction of movement in this guide is reversed. Espíndola starts with the entombment and goes backward to the Garden of Gethsemane and the Last Supper. There are only nine stations in the work, plus opening and closing prayers to the Virgin Mary. The stations include the holy sepulchre, the Mount of Calvary, the third fall, the second fall, Mary meets her son, the first fall, the Holy City of Jerusalem, the patio of Pilate's palace, and the Last Supper. This order must

6. *Practica para andar* (1758).

7. The full title is *Desagravios de Jesus, nuestro bien, y tiernas memorias, para meditar, y contemplar lo que padeció en la noche del jueves en el asqueroso è indecente aposentillo*, "The Redress of Jesus our Good, and Tender Memories, to Meditate and Contemplate on what He Suffered on Thursday Night in the Disgusting and Indecent Little Room."

8. Espíndola, *Desagravios* (ca. 1707–14).

9. Espíndola, *Exercicios* (1725).

have disturbed at least one reader, for in the copy in the John Carter Brown Library, the ordinal numbers describing the three falls are blacked out, possibly because it proceeds from third to second to first.[10]

Espíndola was a particularly active author in the early and mid-eighteenth century. Records indicate that he composed a total of twelve books, all dealing with spiritual exercises of one type or another, such as those described above. He was a secular priest in the Diocese of Mexico and a graduate of the University of Mexico. He seems to have eventually received the licentiate degree, since several title pages refer to him in that manner. But because his earlier works were continually reprinted, there are later imprints that continue to refer to him as a *bachiller*. He also clearly maintained close ties to several female convents in the city since many of his works were written at the prompting of nuns or for the benefit of female religious.[11]

In the seventeenth century, there were efforts to remove references to specific numbers from the Passion-based meditations. In the 1745 edition of María de la Antigua's *Cadena de oro* held at the John Carter Brown Library, there is a section on the sufferings of Christ where many numbers have been blacked out. In a different copy of the 1752 edition, the pages containing offending numbers have been removed completely, cut out of the binding. These sections included descriptions of the numbers of times Jesus was kicked, hit, and beaten. The figures that were later blacked out include the number of drops of blood spilled (730,500) and the number of tears shed for sinners (700,200). There was a fixation among the faithful in this period on counting the punishments meted out on Jesus. These were included in sections with titles such as "The Compilation of the Suffering of Our Redeemer."[12] This fascination with the many wounds of Christ and the blood that he shed harks back to one of the earlier devotions, the Effusions of Christ. Clearly, by the mid-eighteenth century, there had begun to develop an opposition to this fixation on drops of blood along with the hits, kicks, drops of spit, and other affronts suffered by Christ. This is seen in the unknown redactor's effort to try to remove references to the numbers of punishments.

Sor María de la Antigua (1566–1617) was one of the more prolific authors of the period. It is not clear if the nun was actually the author or whether the devotions were merely inspired by her. Devotions published under her name were quite popular in eighteenth-century Mexico, and several different versions of Stations of the Cross are attributed to her, particularly

10. Espíndola, *Via dolorosa* (1761), John Carter Brown Library (hereafter JCB) BA761 E77v.

11. León, *Bibliografía Mexicana*, Secc. 1, Part 4a, 279–85.

12. Antigua, *Cadena de oro* (1745), "Recopilacion de los Dolores de Nro. Redentor," JCB BA745 A629c.

the *Cadena de oro*.[13] Sor María de la Antigua was an important proponent of the celebration of the Stations of the Cross. She was born in Cazalla de la Sierra, in the province of Seville, Spain. When she became a member of the Order of Saint Clare (Poor Clares, the female Franciscan Second Order), she took the name "de la Antigua" in recognition of the Dominican convent of Nuestra Señora de la Antigua in Utera, some sixty miles away, where supposedly her parents had worked as servants. She eventually founded a convent in Marchena, a few miles east of Seville, in a former palace of the Dukes of Arcos.[14] She was revered for her piety and her devotion to meditation on the Passion of Jesus.

As noted, a significant number of spiritual handbooks followed devotions other than the Stations of the Cross. One of the popular books was a European devotion devoted to the Five Wounds of Christ, which competed with the Stations in the early development of stational devotions. The theme of the Five Wounds was particularly important in Mexico among Franciscans. Although the province of the Franciscan Order that encompassed all of central New Spain was called the Holy Gospel Province (Santo Evangelio), the crest that the order used was one depicting the five wounds of Christ: the nails wounds on his hands and feet and the spear wound in his side [see fig. 2.1]. The five wounds were particularly meaningful to the Franciscans because Saint Francis had a divine vision while on a retreat in the hills of central Italy, at a place called Mount Alverno. There he saw the vision of a seraph hovering in the sky. At that moment, Francis was inflicted with the wounds of Christ, called the stigmata, as seen earlier. Among the many different stational devotions that appeared in eighteenth-century Mexico is an anonymous pamphlet titled *Salutacion a las Sacratissimas cinco Llagas de Christo* (Greeting to the Most Sacred Five Wounds of Christ), which appeared in 1777. In this devotion the faithful person is to perform the Act of Contrition,[15] and then have a meditation and prayer for each of the five wounds: left foot, right foot, left hand, right hand, and side.[16]

---

13. The full title is: *Cadena de oro evangelica red, arrojada a la diestra de los electos, y escogidos,: que muestra el mas cierto, seguro, y breve camino para la salvacion eterna[.] Las estaciones de la dolorosa passion, y muerte de Nuestro amantissimo redemptor Jesus.* It was published several times in colonial Mexico including, 1729, 1741, 1745, ca. 1752, 1755, 1764, 1766, 1772, 1773, 1775, 1776, 1782, 1791, and 1795. Moreover, in 1775 editions came out in Puebla and Guatemala.

14. "Franciscanas Clarisas," Clarisas de Marchena, https://clarisas.es/content/14-franciscanas-clarisas; Robin, "Via crucis," 142–43. The ducal title refers to Arcos de la Frontera in the modern province of Cadiz, south of Seville.

15. An Act of Contrition is a common prayer that may take many different forms. The basic outline of the prayer is to acknowledge that a person has sinned, to be truly sorry for the sins, and to offer a sincere desire to not sin again.

16. *Salutacion a las Sacratissimas* (1777), JCB BA773 A385c.

The fluid nature of stational devotions in the late seventeenth century and into the eighteenth century in New Spain was marked by the publication of different imprints that had different numbers of stations and slightly different organizational schemes. Of the stational devotions that focus specifically on Christ's Passion, there appear to have been two general formats: one with at least twenty stations to be followed over the entirety of Holy Week and a short version of just fourteen stations. The fourteen-station version, however, differs significantly from what would become the canonical form approved by the pope early in the eighteenth century. An anonymous priest of the congregation of San Felipe Neri followed one of the traditions that includes the visits to Pilate, Herod, and Caiaphas that were not part of what would become the accepted version. The stations include the Garden of Gethsemane, Ananias's house, Caiaphas's house, Pilate's palace, Herod's palace, Pilate's palace, the imposition of the crown of thorns, the presentation of Jesus to the mob (the ecce homo), the death sentence, the imposition of the cross, the crucifixion, the last seven words, the descent from the cross and pietà, and the interment.[17]

Some versions of stations focusing on Christ's Passion follow a longer format with well over twenty stations. In these, the stations are distributed among the days of Holy Week and are not intended to be prayed over the course of an hour or even an afternoon. In this longer scheme, for example, on Maundy Thursday the devotee is to pray three stations. These correspond to Jesus being crowned with thorns, Pilate offering Barabbas, and Pilate condemning Jesus to death. There is another suggested format within the larger work that allows the faithful to pray the stations over a three-week period. As can be seen, the formats for these devotions are flexible enough to allow the practitioner to take the prayers and meditations as a basic template that can then be used in any number of different ways. They can be prayed consecutively in a morning or afternoon; they can be distributed over a number of days or weeks; they can be prayed on specific Church holidays, such as Maundy Thursday or Good Friday; or they can be used routinely throughout the church year.

In 1760, Fr. Joaquin de Osuna published another very complex set of devotions that resembles the Stations of the Cross. It was published various times in mid-eighteenth-century Mexico. Osuna was a Discalced Franciscan from the Mexican province of San Diego, located in and around Mexico City.[18]

---

17. *Via dolorosa o estaciones de la sagrada passion* (1722), bound with other versions of the same or similar work, JCB BA706 D498t.

18. Discalced Franciscans were members of a particularly strict branch of the order. They were known as Alcantarines after their founder San Pedro de Alcantara, a Spanish mystic of the sixteenth century. He embraced a very austere form of the Franciscan Rule that included going around barefoot, which then gave rise to the epithet of "discalced" meaning "barefoot." All branches of the Franciscan family were united under one hierarchy in 1897.

Osuna marketed his devotion as being "in the style of the Via Crucis" (*al modo del Via Crucis*). This demonstrates the ascendency of the canonical form of the Stations of the Cross, since other variants were also being marketed "in the style of," demonstrating that the fourteen-station model had become an established norm. Osuna's devotional consists of twelve *jornadas* (implying a day's occupation or journey), which are meant to actually take two days to perform. Within each *jornada* there are fourteen stations. Within each of these are four sets of prayers called *hospicios* (hospices), which are meant to be followed on the Sundays of the devotion. As a result, the full devotion takes four weeks to complete.[19] The choice of the term *hospicio* is curious since it normally means "hospice" or "hospital," although it has an extended meaning of "resting place" or "asylum."

Although the pope had established that the Stations of the Cross would have fourteen stations in the bull of 1731, that decision did not end the practice of having different numbers or different arrangements of the stations. Presses continued to publish and republish devotionals that did not conform to the papal decision. Not even Franciscans completely complied with the canonical fourteen stations approved by the pope. One Franciscan to offer a different approach was Fr. Diego Romero, who was a member of the Holy Gospel Province of Mexico, which means that he was either born in Mexico or took his vows as a Franciscan there, having been born elsewhere. His work predates the papal approval, appearing in Puebla as early as 1683, but later editions were published in Mexico City in the eighteenth century. Romero's devotional is also a very complex system of readings, prayers, and meditations. Ostensibly it is supposed to last a week, and on every day of the week there are readings, preparations, meditations, thanksgiving, and prayer offerings. Each day is then given over to a specific theme: Sunday—Intolerable Life; Monday—Fearful Death; Tuesday—Formidable Judgment; Wednesday—Doubtful Salvation; Thursday—Irrevocable Sentence; Friday—Frightful Eternity; and Saturday—Without Doubt, My Soul Reposes. But beyond these prayers and meditations, Romero also takes the faithful person through the events of the Passion, including fourteen stations covering the end of Christ's life, but not the ones approved by the pope. Romero begins with the end of the Last Supper, then proceeds through Jesus's prayer in the Garden of Gethsemane; his arrest; his appearances before Ananias, Caiaphas, Pilate, Herod, and Pilate again; and then his suffering under the cross along the Street of Bitterness (Amargura) and his crucifixion on Calvary. But then the devotion turns back to events normally included earlier—Jesus tied to the column, the crown of thorns, the ecce homo—and then ending with the descent from the cross. It seems that in each of the daily meditations, the penitent is to consider

19. Osuna, *Peregrinacion Cristiana* (1760).

these fourteen stations along with the theme for the day.[20] It is a terribly complex set of devotions that evokes the ambience of Christ's suffering although it does not strictly follow the established chronology of events.

The printed devotional guides, including those for the Stations of the Cross, are generally quite small physically. There are two formats in which most appear. One is slightly larger, about 4 inches by 5½ inches (9½ cm by 14 cm). The other, smaller one is approximately 2 inches by 3 inches (5 cm by less than 8 cm). The very long and complex booklets can run to many pages, although most have about twenty-four. Because these little books are so small, it seems that contemporaries collected them and bound them into small anthologies. In the collections of the John Carter Brown Library, there are several small tomes that include four or more small devotional handbooks all bound together in a single volume. These create problems for catalogers, but for folks who were eager to participate in the devotions, they were a practical response to owning many very small, slim books. One little book having only twenty-some pages could get lost easily, but a collection of four or more would have more than a hundred pages and would be much less likely to get lost, though it would still fit easily in the pocket of a cassock or cloak.

The popularity of these guides to various devotions of Christ's Passion was impressive. One of the most widely embraced was the version published under the title *Manual de exercicios para los desagravios de Christo*, ostensibly by Francisco de Soria, a Franciscan friar. Although Soria appears as the author, the title page lists Fr. Diego de Oviedo, whose role is not explained and who dedicates the work to the Third Order of Saint Francis. One of the editions has the note that it was originally licensed for publication in Madrid in 1705 by the press of Antonio Gonzalez de Reyes.[21] Soria's little guide was reprinted in New Spain at least twenty-seven times between 1686 and 1793, just over a century. Scholars also know of editions that appeared in Mexico City (twenty), Puebla (six), and Guatemala (one). The prayers, meditations, and other devotions prescribed by Soria were intended to unite the penitent with the image of Jesus known as *Santo Cristo de los Desagravios* (Holy Christ of Redress).[22] This was a specific

20. Romero, *Meditaciones* (1683).

21. Soria, *Manual de exercicios* (Puebla, 1729), title page.

22. *Desagravios* is a difficult word to translate, some authors use "atonement" or "reparations." It means "to erase or repair an offense to one's honor or fame resulting in complete satisfaction." Taylor, "An 'Evolved' Devotional Book," 69, translates it as "atonement." But theologically, "atonement" refers to Christ having suffered to erase the sins of humanity. The term *desagravio* in this context is the action of humans providing redress for the abuses caused to Jesus. Others have suggested "reparation" or "redress," which are closer to the meaning. Berdette, "Reparations," 358. Some editions, such as the 1810 in Mexico, attribute authorship to Fr. Fernando Martagon, of the Propaganda Fide College. Biblioteca Nacional de México, Obras Antiguas, Raras, RSM 1810 M4MAR. That edition does not have the Stations of the Cross appended to it.

image of Christ that was found in the chapel of San Josef de los Naturales within the Franciscan convent complex in downtown Mexico City.[23] Soria's complex set of devotions was meant to help the penitent provide a ritual atonement for the death of Christ. His series of rituals includes self-mortification, prayer, and meditation as part of a stational or performative devotion. There are ritual actions, fasting, and other disciplines spread across a thirty-three-day period. More gruesome instructions include flagellating oneself 155 times each night and other mortifications.[24] For the modern reader, it is sometimes surprising that a book instructing such extreme mortification would have gone through well over twenty printings.

In several of the editions, the final twenty pages consists of a set of meditations and prayers for the celebration of the Stations of the Cross featuring the traditional fourteen stations. Upon closer analysis there are at least two different versions of the prayers and meditations for the Stations of the Cross appended to the Soria *Manual de exercicios.* The simpler version is attributed to Fr. Antonio de la Anunciación and carries the title of "Luz para saber andar la Via Sacra."[25] In yet other editions of the Soria *Manual*, a slightly different devotional of the Stations of the Cross appears for which no clear attribution is provided. Rather, the text explains, "Other authors, Holy Fathers, Supreme Pontiffs, can see the well-reasoned, in the Via Crucis published in Rome, in the year 1702, which was in our convent of Aracoeli, and in the very learned, cautious, and most devout writing about the Via Sacra or Via Crucis, also published in Rome by our very reverend Father Fray Miguel Angel Candia, in 1703."[26] The Aracoeli church is known as Saint Mary of the Altar of Heaven.[27]

---

23. The history of the image is not clear. It seems to have originally belonged to the family of the Counts of the Valley of Orizaba, who owned the palace, known as the House of Tiles, across the street from the Franciscans. An earthquake struck in 1731, during which the statue of Christ crucified seemed to come to life and blood began to flow from its side. The religious authorities had the image moved across the street into the Chapel of San Josef. In 1780 it was moved into the main convent church to the Chapel of Cristo de Burgos. Taylor, "An 'Evolved' Devotional Book," 75–76.

24. Burdette, "Reparations," 367–72.

25. Soria, *Manual de exercicios* (Mexico, 1778). Little is known of Anunciación. In all likelihood he was a Franciscan from Cadiz. A reader in theology, he also published a book in Cadiz in 1669 that argued in favor of receiving communion daily: *Tratado de la communion quotidiana* (Cadiz: Juan Lorenzo Machado, 1669).

26. "Otros muchos Authores, Santos Padres, Summos Pontifices, podrâ veer el curioso, en la Via Crucis impressa en Roma, el año de 1702, el cual se anda en nuestro Convento de Aracoeli, y en la doctissima, curiosa, y devotissima Escritura de la Via Sacra, o Via Crucis, impressa tambien en Roma por nuestro muy Reverendo Padre Fray Miguel Angel Candia, el año de 1703." The word *curioso* was used twice, and in this period would be a false cognate of "curious." It means, "cautious," "well reasoned," or "neat." Soria, *Manual de exercicios* (Puebla, 1729), 86.

27. Located on the Campidoglio, it is reached through a long staircase of 124 steps. In the late thirteenth century it was assigned to the Franciscans. It is one of the titular

These two guides to the devotion of the Stations of the Cross are very similar in that they have the traditional ordering: each station corresponds to the events that eventually became canonical, and each of the devotionals features the same fourteen stations in exactly the same order. While the meditations and prayers are similar, they are not copies of each other. Thus, there are two versions: one that we might call the Anunciación version and the other, which might be called the Candia version. But what is most confusing is that both appear as appendices or additions to the Soria *Manual de exercicios.*

The Anunciación version of the devotion of the Stations of the Cross is in some ways simpler. Each station has a meditation and a prayer that deal with the specific nature of the station. There is a set of prayers and actions that the practitioner is supposed to undertake following each station. The faithful person is to kiss the earth, then say an Act of Contrition asking for forgiveness, kiss the ground again, and say another short litany followed by an Amen. The meditation for the next station always begins with a statement about how many steps it lies from the previous one. As seen earlier, several of the stational devotions that appeared in Europe also concentrated on the location of each station with reference to the others. This attempt to make the practitioner walk a circuit seems to imply that it copies, as closely as possible, the actual steps taken by Jesus during his Passion. At the very end of the devotional, the Anunciación version has a meditation that focuses on the offenses and affronts that Jesus had to suffer during his Passion. At the end of each of these offenses, the faithful person is asked to say, "Blessed and Praised be for ever such [a] great Lord." The devotion then lists Jesus's agony in the Garden of Gethsemane, his imprisonment, the guards' hits and blows, Jesus's suffering, the officials' false testimony and calumnies, and so on. This is a list of afflictions that is quite similar to one seen in another devotional in which the exact number of blows, kicks, and the like were enumerated, such as in the *Cadena de Oro.* As noted before, the fixation with enumerating the offenses against Jesus is also seen in early stational devotions developed in Europe.

What we might call the Candia version of the devotional for the Stations of the Cross is slightly more complex than the Anunciación version. The whole devotional ritual begins with an introductory Act of Contrition followed by a quatrain of poetry. There is a brief prayer that serves as a beginning for the Stations. The ritual for each station consists of a meditation, a snippet of poetry of varying length, and a prayer for that specific station. Just as with the Anunciación version, a reference is made in the meditation to the number of steps from station to station, but the number of steps differs between the Candia and Anunciación versions. Candia's poetry varies in length from one

---

basilicas of the city, meaning that it is recognized as one of the historic parishes to which cardinals are assigned by the pope. It is the official church of the City Council of Rome.

station to another and touches on the themes of the station. The poetry is followed by instructions directing the penitent to meditate on the number of steps taken and then say the Lord's Prayer, the Ave Maria, and the Gloria Patri at each station. Directly after that set prayers, a closing prayer for that particular station focuses on the details and themes of the station. Then there is a formula for forgiveness, similar to the Anunciación version, and a closing prayer that is repeated after each station. At the very end, the Candia version also has the devotion of affronts that is seemingly identical to the devotion in the Anunciación version. While the meditations and prayers in the two versions are worded distinctly, the general themes covered in the stations are quite similar.

The Anunciación version has a much longer publication history, although both were incorporated into other books, so there were many more copies and editions than we can possibly document. An early edition was printed in Seville in 1670.[28] In New Spain, it appeared as a standalone booklet sixteen times between 1727 and 1853; the latter edition was a translation into Tarascan (Purépecha). All the editions came from presses in Mexico City except for the Purépecha version, which was published in the town of Taréjaro, Michoacán. The Candia version seems to have appeared only in some editions of the Soria *Manual de exercicios* and never as a standalone imprint.

A detailed look at these two distinct versions of the Stations of the Cross can be illustrative. Even though the pope established the number of stations at fourteen and also stipulated the focus of each of the stations, the specific prayers and meditations were not formally decreed. Thus, there were, and continue to be, variations among devotional guides in their prayers and meditations. In general, however, different versions are remarkably similar because they deal with similar themes for each station. The complexity of the Candia version is clear when one considers the meditation for the first station:

Candia
Praetorium, house of Pilate,
where our Redeemer was cruelly
whipped, crowned with thorns, and
condemned to death.[29]

Anunciación
This is the first station. It is the
Praetorium and house of Pilate,
where the Redeemer of the world was
rigorously whipped, by the hands of
six ferocious soldiers, with various
thorns, with knotted ropes, and in

28. "Luz para saber como se ha de hazer la deuoción de visitar las cruzes y estaciones de la Vía sacra, y las sin número de indulgencias que se ganan visitándola," Worldcat, http://www.worldcat.org/oclc/919863064.

29. "Primera Estación. Pretorio, casa de Pilatos, donde cruelmente fue azotado nuestro Redemptor coronado de espinas, y condenado a muerte." Candia, "Del santo exercicio," 87.

them [were] spikes, chains, and steel hooks that pulled out his flesh with each blow they landed.[30]

The Candia version then goes on with a complex and evocative meditation on this scene:

> Soul, consider in this first station, our most beloved Lord, tied to the column, his flesh in pieces, his body bathed in blood that flows onto the ground from the cruel blows that the furious minister and executioners brought down on his divine majesty as if he were their worst enemy; collect in your heart the blood that flows from his wounds; open the eyes of faith in this praetorium and tribunal and look at your Lord, crowned with the penetrating thorns, the defiled Son of God, mocked by men, he whom the angels adore. Consider him who is the true judge of the living and the dead, full of privations and placed as a convict in the presence of Pilate, and how this iniquitous judge condemns our most innocent Jesus to the ignominy of death on the cross, and the humility, patience, and love with which our Redeemer admitted that iniquitous sentence, for our health and remediation.[31]

Moreover, the Candia devotional guide also contains a few lines of poetry between the meditation and the closing prayer. Thus, by and large, while the two are quite similar, and appended to the same larger devotional book, the Anunciación is shorter and less complex.

This study has focused on known and extant copies of various forms of stational devotions from colonial Mexico. But in addition to books held in libraries, we know that there are imprints that are missing from libraries and archives. Scholars such as José Toribio Medina have attempted to list all imprints from colonial Latin America. From time to time, copies of these reputed books have eventually surfaced. One that is relevant to the development of the Stations of the Cross was supposedly printed in Mexico in 1680. The Franciscan scholar, Fr. Augustín de Vetancurt noted that among his other publications was "The *Via crucis* [Way of the Cross] in Nahuatl, published two times, both by Francisco Rodríguez Lupercio."[32] Nevertheless, none of the scholars who study the history of printing in colonial Mexico has been able to find a copy. The work was popular. According to Vetancurt, it was

---

30. "Esta es la primera Estacion, es el Pretorio, y Casa de Pilatos, donde fue rigorosamente azotado el Redentor del Mundo, por mano de seis ferozes Soldados, con varas espinosas, con cordeles nudosos, y en ellos abrojos, cadenas, y garfios de de hierro, y le arrancaban la carne con cada azote que le daban." Anunciación, "Luz para saber andar," 2.

31. Candia, "Del santo exercicio," 88.

32. "El Via Crucis en mexicano, dos veces impreso, todo por Francisco Rodríguez Lupercio."

published twice before 1700. Some of the guides to early printing have descriptions of the book—for example, that it consisted of eleven leaves, some twenty-two pages, and was approximately the size of many other devotional manuals already seen.

Within the manuscript collection of the Academy of American Franciscan History there is a piece titled "To Know How to Walk the Stations of the Cross and the Indulgences That One Gains Following It, translated by the Reverend Father Fr. Agu[stín] de Vetancurt."[33] The title page carries a date of 1680. Certainly the theme of the work and the date it carries correspond to what little we know about the via crucis mentioned by Vetancurt himself. Upon further examination, the manuscript dates from 1738 and was copied by Matheo de San Juan Chicahuastla. Based on this limited information, it is fair to conclude that the manuscript held by the Academy is in fact a manuscript copy of the published edition of the Vetancurt work.

The manuscript held by the Academy is octavo size (16 cm by 22 cm) and is twenty-eight leaves long. The paper is European and has some parts that are badly worm-eaten, which poses a greater challenge to the reading of the text. The handwriting is typical of seventeenth-century Nahuatl found in many different manuscripts. It is a far cry from the elegant hands of transcribers in the capital and, along with the inscription, leads one to believe that the author was not a professional scribe. The name and the handwriting also give the impression that the copyist was a Native and not a European. The most engaging features of the work are the numerous illustrations found throughout. There is no indication that the original printed copy might have been so illustrated. The manuscript copy consists of an introduction, the fourteen Stations of the Cross, some final material including the Act of Contrition in Nahuatl, and a listing of the indulgences to be gained through the celebration of the Stations of the Cross. The contents are all consistent with other devotions of the Stations of the Cross published in the era, as will be seen. The remaining chapters of this book will look at the author, Vetancurt, and the text and illustrations of the work.

Looking at the growth in popularity of devotions dedicated to the Stations of the Cross, the Nahuatl version by Vetancurt, ostensibly published in 1680, makes it one of the earlier versions. Even if we use the putative date of the copy, 1738, it is still early in the overall development of the practice of the devotion in Mexico. Among the Spanish-language imprints, the two that

33. "Para saber andar las estaciones de la via sacra y las yndulgencias que ganan Vitando [*sic*] la traducido en lengua mexicana por el R. P. Fr_ Augn de Vetacurt." *Vitando* means "avoiding," but that does not fit here. It might be a contraction of *visitando* which would mean more like "visiting" or "following." The original Spanish version, as will be seen in chapter 4, used the word *visitando*.

were just discussed, by Candia and Anunciación, stand out as possible sources for Vetancurt's translation. Because of the absence of poetry in the Nahuatl version, and a few other salient features, it seems likely that Vetancurt used the Anunciación version as the basis for his setting of the via crucis and not the Candia version. A closer analysis suggests that Vetancurt did not slavishly translate the Spanish into Nahuatl but sought to express the same concepts using the nuances of the Nahuatl language. The language and the illustrations will be discussed in later chapters.

Fr. Augustín de Vetancurt

Fr. Augustín de Vetancurt is one of the better-known Franciscans of colonial Mexico. His surname was spelled in various ways both during his life and afterward. In several documents, he appears as Betangort, and in his petition to enter the Franciscan Order it was written Betancort. Nonetheless, in the books he wrote that found their way into print, his name appears as Vetancurt. Even his given name has caused some problems. Many scholars have chosen to use the more common Agustín as the name would appear in modern Spanish. Nonetheless, in the books that he published in his lifetime, his name was usually rendered Augustín. As a result, in keeping with how he seems to have preferred it, his name in this book will be rendered as Augustín de Vetancurt.[34]

Fr. Augustín de Vetancurt's reputation as a scholar and author derives largely from his fame as a historian and chronicler, having written the monumental *Teatro mexicano* (1698), a four-volume description of the most important events of colonial New Spain. Nevertheless, in addition to his renown as a historian, he was also an accomplished scholar of Nahuatl and published several works in that language. In spite of his many accomplishments, very little is known about him. Some of his anonymity can be attributed to Franciscan modesty. Franciscans are characterized by being modest and self-effacing in an attempt to practice Christian humility in imitation of Christ. Once a friar joined the order, especially in the seventeenth and eighteenth centuries, he considered himself a member of a new family, the Franciscans, and he gave up his earthly ties of kinship. Many men took completely new names. The model for their religious name was to choose a first name from a Franciscan saint and a surname that indicated his hometown rather than a family surname. Vetancurt did not follow that tradition, however.

34. A sermon he wrote was published in 1674 listing his surname as "Ventacurt," but all other publications show his name as "Augustin de Vetancurt." Other variants of his surname in Latin America include "Bethancourt" and "Betancourt." The latter is common because there was a famous president of Venezuela who spelled his surname that way. The surname comes from the Canary Islands and represents one of the spellings of the surname of the Norman-French conqueror of the islands in the early fifteenth century.

The brief details of Fr. Augustín's life are relatively simple, as one finds them in most public sources. He was born in Mexico sometime around 1620, attended the University of Mexico, and received his baccalaureate degree. After attending the university, he entered the Franciscan Order in Puebla, where he eventually took his vows as a friar. In a rare twist of fate, because Vetancurt entered the order in Puebla and not in Mexico City, we actually have the documentation of his entrance into the order. These include the documents that he had to submit to the Franciscans preliminary to entering the novitiate. The Mexico City records have been dispersed and scattered, but the Puebla records, almost miraculously, remain intact and are housed at the John Carter Brown Library, in Providence, Rhode Island. Thanks to these we now have details about Fr. Augustín and his early life.

The novitiate papers list Fr. Augustín de Vetancurt's date of birth as being in about 1622, a few years later than commonly thought. Witnesses placed him as about seventeen or eighteen years old on entering the order in 1640. He did not come from Mexico City but from a village called Ayotzingo, in the Central Basin of Mexico in the Chalco region, at the southeastern tip of the great central lake. Shortly before his birth, the Augustinians had begun serving the town. While the Franciscans had dominated the Central Basin of Mexico in the early missionary effort, other orders had slowly carved out their own small regions of influence. By the early seventeenth century, the Chalco region was one where three major orders competed (Augustinians, Dominicans, and Franciscans). The village of Ayotzingo, linked politically with nearby Mixquic, remained largely intact following the Spanish invasion, unlike other towns and villages that were destroyed or broken up by the Spanish. While Mixquic was part of an encomienda eventually held by don Luis de Velasco the younger and his heirs, it is not clear if this also included Ayotzingo.[35]

Vetancurt's parents were Luis de Vetancurt and Mariana de Vetancurt, sometimes listed as Mariana de Vetancurt y Cabrera. Neither used the honorific don, so they must be considered commoners. Luis de Vetancurt was a native of the Canary Islands but had lived in New Spain for some thirty years, according to witnesses, meaning he had arrived in the colony as a child or young man. His wife, Mariana, had been born in Mexico to Spanish parents and thus was a Creole.[36] The fact that the two had the same surname suggests

---

35. An encomienda was a grant of tribute (taxes) from a village or set of villages that was paid to a colonist rather than to the crown. For a description of the area and its political and social history, see Gerhard, *Guide to the Historical Geography*, 102–6.

36. The surname Vetancurt, and its variants, was quite uncommon in late-sixteenth- and early-seventeenth-century Mexico. Indeed, during the first few decades of Spanish migration to the New World, no one of that surname was registered with the royal authorities. Boyd-Bowman, *Indice geobiográfico*. This could be because the name was mostly found in the Canaries, and residents of the islands would have sailed to the New World without

that they might have been relatives. This suggests that Mariana, too, was from a Canarian family. In the colonial period it was rather common for folks to marry individuals from the same home region in Spain. According to witnesses, neither was descended from Jews, Muslims, or heretics.

The witnesses also noted that even if Augustín were not to enter the Franciscans, the family had sufficient resources to support him. The record is silent on his parents' occupations, but given the rich soils in the Chalco region, one might assume that they were farmers. Another possibility, given the Canarian heritage, is that Luis de Vetancurt worked on the water, perhaps hauling cargo into Mexico City or possibly fishing in the lake. The witnesses to Augustín's request to join the Franciscans included Lic. Juan de Villanueva, a priest and professor at the University of Mexico.[37] This implies that Augustín had previously been a student there, as is suggested by several biographers. Another witness, Lorenzo de Celi, might have come from one of the oldest Spanish families in the colony. Bartolomé de Celi, one of the early settlers in the colony, had arrived around 1522 from Italy.[38] Lorenzo was possibly the son of Josef de Celi, a man who served as a solicitor for the Mexico City municipal council in the late sixteenth century.[39] And it is plausible that Josef might well have been the son of Bartolomé.

Augustín de Vetancurt remained in Puebla for several years. Once he passed through the novitiate, he began teaching other novices in the Franciscan house in the areas of humane letters and Nahuatl. In 1642, just two years after entering the order, he was appointed lector of arts within the province. This position gave him a modicum of power and prestige. He was responsible for reading all the works in those fields written by members of the order that had been submitted for publication. After his service in Puebla, Vetancurt was reassigned to the Central Basin of Mexico to serve as the priest of the Franciscan chapel and *doctrina* of San Josef de los Naturales in Mexico City.[40] He worked in San Josef for more than forty years in service to his order and the Natives of Mexico. In addition to his routine duties, on various occasions he served as a definitor of the Franciscan Province of the Holy Gospel. A definitor is a member of the governing council of the province who deals with administrative matters of the order. Vetancurt eventually became the official chron-

---

the documentation required to leave mainland Spain, and so their documents are simply not housed with the other migration records.

37. John Carter Brown Library, Cod. Sp. 10, Franciscans—Puebla, *Informaciones noviciorum*, vol. 3, folios 135–39.

38. Álvarez, *Diccionario*, vol. I, item 234, p. 126.

39. O'Gorman, *Guía de las actas*, item 5610, May 8, 1595, p. 815.

40. The founder of the chapel, Fr. Pedro de Gante, consistently called the chapel a *doctrina* rather than a parish. In general, in the period, Native parishes, especially in the countryside, were called *doctrinas*. Truitt, *Sustaining the Divine*, 15.

icler of the province, appointed by the *comisario general* of the Franciscans and confirmed by Pope Innocent XI.[41] In that position, he was able to draw upon the significant historical archives of the Franciscans and fully utilize materials that had been collected and organized by the likes of Mendieta and Torquemada. Vetancurt also served as a teacher of theology within the order, as one of the official preachers, and as a supervisor and official reader of works produced by friars in Nahuatl. He died in 1700.[42]

Several of his publications stand out as truly significant. The first of these was his *Arte de la lengua mexicana*, a Nahuatl grammar based on the principles laid down by the famous Latin grammarian Antonio de Nebrija. This book first appeared in 1673, published by Francisco Rodríguez Lupercio (Medina, Mexico, item 1103).[43] Vetancurt wrote a handbook for the administration of the sacraments, *Manual de administrar los Santos Sacramentos*, published in 1674 (Medina, Mexico, item 1118). This book draws upon two earlier handbooks published by Fr. Miguel de Zárate and Fr. Pedro de Contreras, both Franciscans. It would become one of the most popular works from Vetancurt's pen and was reprinted three times in his lifetime, including once in Seville. This was a significant contribution, 150 leaves long, yet because of the mundane nature and multiple printings, it is not normally accorded much renown.

Vetancurt was unquestionably the leading Nahuatl scholar of his era. His predecessors in the Franciscan Order had used Natives from the local community both as informants and as aides or assistants in their literary labors. The team assembled by Fr. Bernardino de Sahagún for his work on the *Florentine Codex* is well known. Fr. Juan Bautista similarly used a team of Natives to assist him in his work. In the case of Vetancurt, we simply lack specific information about such a practice. While Vetancurt was probably bilingual in Nahuatl from childhood, he also had cause to call on Native informants and assistants. There is evidence that one of Vetancurt's Native assistants, don Manuel de los Santos Salazar, went on to become a priest himself and continued his labors in the field of Nahuatl. Vetancurt served on the board of examiners when don Manuel sought entry into the priesthood. Later don Manuel

41. In the Franciscan Order, each convent was headed by a guardian, elected to a three-year term by the friars of that house. In turn, the guardians elected the leader of their province, called a provincial, also on a three-year basis. Three friars were also elected to serve as an advisory body to the provincial. This body was called the definitorium, and each member was a definitor. The *comisario general* was the Franciscan superior who served as the link between the order in the Spanish empire and the leadership in Rome.

42. Vetancurt, *Teatro Mexicano*, 4:378–79; Beristain de Souza, *Biblioteca Hispanoamericana septentrional*, 1:261–62; *Handbook of Middle American Indians*, 147–48. The comisario general was the head of the Franciscan Order in the Spanish-speaking world.

43. All references from Medina, *La imprenta en México*, vols. 2–3.

recalled fondly that Vetancurt had introduced him to the works of Fr. Juan de Torquemada and don Carlos de Sigüenza y Góngora.[44] Clearly, Vetancurt followed the lead of other important scholars of Nahuatl and used Native assistants in his work. Unfortunately, this is one area where we have little additional evidence, although it might well still be discovered. Consequently, throughout this book, when an attribution is made to Vetancurt, it correctly should be understood as being attributed to Vetancurt and his assistants.

As a historian, Vetancurt published several works of general interest and others of particular interest to Franciscans. One of these is his brief biography of Saint Anthony of Padua, one of the most revered Franciscan saints: *Epitome de la Vida, Muerte, y Milagros del Taumaturgo Español S. Antonio de Padua* from 1682 (Medina, Mexico, item 1263). It is curious that Vetancurt refers to Anthony as a Spaniard, for Anthony was one of the early Franciscans in Italy and became associated with Padua, but he was born in Portugal. In 1697, Vetancurt published a biography of the founder of the order, Saint Francis of Assisi, in his *Chronografia sagrada de la vida de Christo . . . y en el Serafico Padre S. Francisco, y su Apostolica Religion* (Medina, Mexico, item 1656).

The most famous of his works is the *Teatro mexicano*, which appeared in 1698. This was one of the largest books published in the period, a massive work consisting of four parts and a total of 1,815 pages plus introductory material. It was a major accomplishment. This book covers the history of the conquest and settlement of New Spain and some of the Iberian precursors as well as descriptions and histories of each of the dioceses of the region, the cities, and other important historical information. Several of the parts in *Teatro* appeared as independent books prior to the publication of the whole. His history of the Holy Gospel Province of Mexico, the *Chronica de la Provincia del Santo Evangelio de Mexico*, was published in 1697 (Medina, Mexico, item 1684), and became a section of the fourth part of *Teatro*.

The first volume of the *Teatro mexicano* covers what is now called natural history, looking first at the location, climate, flora, fauna, and geography of the region, followed by a section on the products and richness of the New World. The second volume deals with the pre-Hispanic civilization: the origins of the people, their government, and their gods and religion. The third volume discusses military events, focusing on the Spanish invasion of Mexico. The fourth volume is by far the most complex, including five major sections. The first section focuses on the foundation and development of the Franciscan Province of Santo Evangelio of Mexico. The second section describes all the friaries in the province along with their history and location. The third section illuminates the smaller, dependent units of the province called *custodias*. The fourth section focuses on the convents for female religious that were under

44. Townsend, *Annals of Native America*, 202–3, 206–7.

Franciscan control in the province. The last section covers all the expeditions and missionary activities of the province's friars and is enhanced by a description of all the holy images (paintings, sculptures, etc.) there. Vetancurt added a supplement to this volume—the *Menologia*—containing the biographies of the friars who were members of the Holy Gospel Province as they were known to Vetancurt. He also appended two final pieces to the fourth volume, almost as if he found it difficult to stop his work on the book. These include treatises that describe the greatness of the cities of Mexico and Puebla, the two major cities in the Santo Evangelio Province.

An equal part of Vetancurt's reputation for scholarship comes from his study of Nahuatl. By the late seventeenth century, the number of works published in Nahuatl had declined significantly, with far fewer being published than had been a century earlier. In the *Teatro mexicano*, Vetancurt lists his own works that he published and others that remained in manuscript. Because he died shortly after the publication of the *Teatro mexicano*, we can assume that the list is fairly definitive. As a result of this, we know more about his publications than about those of many of his contemporaries. Among the manuscripts that were not published was a set of sermons cast in Nahuatl and at least one play in that language.[45]

Vetancurt and Seventeenth-Century Mexico

The period in which Vetancurt lived and worked has been characterized by Woodrow Borah as "New Spain's century of depression."[46] An earlier generation of scholars noted that the seventeenth century had not received the kind of scholarly attention as the sixteenth or eighteenth centuries did. The sixteenth century had seen the crucial events of the arrival of the Spanish and the imposition of Spanish rule over the Native people of New Spain. The eighteenth century would witness the dramatic events that led eventually to independence: reforms in all areas of government, new ways of thinking, and the impact of revolutions in the United States and France. Scholars depict Mexico in the seventeenth century as a somewhat stagnant place, socially, economically, and politically. Nothing much occurred, at least nothing to grab historians' attention, other than a few floods, threats of slave uprisings, famine, pestilence, and urban riots. Recently, the study of the seventeenth century has expanded far beyond Borah's characterization. It was indeed an exciting time. In the seventeenth century things did change—some things dramatically. For the focus of this study, religion and the arts came to figure even more profoundly in the colony.

---

45. Vetancurt, *Teatro Mexicano*,4:378–79

46. Borah, *New Spain's Century of Depression*.

During most of his career, Vetancurt served the chapel of San Josef de los Naturales in Mexico City.[47] His focus on it is clearly demonstrated in the *Teatro mexicano*, where he describes all of the Franciscan parishes and *doctrinas* in the province, but he spends extra time on San Josef. The chapel was established on the remains of what had been the emperor Moteuczoma's pleasure retreat before the Spanish Invasion. Under the Mexica, it had contained tanks for exotic fish and cages for birds from distant lands and was planted with all types of exotic trees. After the Spanish invasion, the Franciscans took over the property to establish a chapel for the Natives. They built their first church several blocks away, in front of what is today the Cathedral of Mexico. San Josef was located beside the large Franciscan convent that was built slightly later on the western edge of the central district, beside what is now the Latin American Tower in modern-day Mexico City. Its location allowed Natives from the district of San Juan Moyotlan, where the chapel was located, to use the chapel as their preferred place of worship.

The Franciscans, under the direction of the lay brother Fr. Pedro de Gante (Peter of Ghent), built the Chapel of San Josef as a set of parallel naves supported by pillars in such a way that if there was a large crowd everyone could still see the actions of the priest at the altar. In this respect, it seems to have been similar to the Royal Chapel at San Gabriel Cholula, which had nine parallel naves.[48] The sizes of the naves grew and changed over time as a result of damage from earthquakes and floods. While it might have had as many as seven naves, each ending in an altar, in time the structure stabilized to have five naves, each about thirty varas long and ten varas wide with four large doors.[49] It was so large that in 1558 Gante claimed the atrium could hold fifty thousand people and the chapel itself another ten thousand.[50] In the 1570s, friars similarly reported that it could accommodate the entire population of the city, both Spanish and Native. Francisco Cervantes de Salazar, writing in 1560, indicated that it had seven naves, such that the chapel and atrium together could fit some forty thousand people.[51] It was considered to be the

---

47. To better understand the complexity of the ecclesiastical jurisdictions of Mexico City at this time, see Truitt, *Sustaining the Divine*, 15–67. In keeping with Truitt, I use the more appropriate name of San Josef de los Naturales as it appeared in most colonial documents.

48. McAndrew, *Open-Air Churches*, 400–411.

49. The Spanish vara of this time was about thirty-three inches, thus slightly shorter than a yard and significantly less than a meter. The description of San Josef largely comes from Vetancurt, *Teatro mexicano*, except where otherwise noted. Vetancurt, *Teatro mexicano*, 3:109; McAndrew, *The Open-Air Churches*, 376–86.

50. A transcription of the original, in Torre Villar, *Fray Pedro de Gante*, 119. Maza, "Fray Pedro de Gante y la capilla abierta," 33, has the size at sixty thousand and ten thousand, respectively.

51. *Códice franciscano*, 6. Cervantes de Salazar, *México en 1554*, 185.

principal Native *doctrina* of the city, with other churches dependent on it.[52] Thus, although Vetancurt served the chapel of San Josef, he also worked alongside his brothers in the mother church of San Francisco. The chapel was so important that the friars seem to have chosen carefully who would serve there. The friar who administered the *doctrina* had to be fluent in the Nahuatl language as well as be able to administer the sacraments in that language, particularly confession.[53]

The impact of pestilence and repercussions of the Spanish invasion of 1519 can easily be seen in comparing population figures beginning in 1570. In that year, the friars estimated that the *doctrina* served the equivalent of 5,706 households. The other outlying parishes and *doctrinas* accounted for about another 1,500 Native households.[54] By the end of the seventeenth century, one source indicated that there were only about 240 Native households in the central district of Mexico City, much of the immediate area served by San Josef de los Naturales. Laborers headed one half of the households and artisans the other half.[55]

Because of the church's primacy over all other Native *doctrinas*, the Spanish kings granted certain cathedral-like privileges to San Josef, such as ringing its main bell for the curfew. The curfew for Natives seems to have been an hour earlier than for Spaniards, since it rang in San Josef at eight but at nine in the cathedral. San Josef was also considered to be the first *doctrina* in all the Indies, although others had certainly been founded in the Antilles before it. On a site that today abuts the tallest building in Latin America, in the sixteenth century and early seventeenth century, the chapel boasted the tallest cross in the city, manufactured from a massive cypress that was found in the forest of Chapultepec, on the western edge of the lake. The large tree was accorded supernatural status by many. The friars were concerned that such a large cross might fall and damage the chapel, and so it was replaced with a smaller version made from just the crosspiece of the original. Nonetheless, in 1571 a windstorm brought down that smaller one, smashing it to pieces, which were then saved as relics.[56] The interior of the chapel had twelve altars, several decorated with paintings. The baptismal font was carved from local alabaster, and the sacristy had a collection of silverware used in the celebration of the Mass.

---

52. Truitt, *Sustaining the Divine*, 5–7, 15.

53. Gibson, *Aztecs Under Spanish Rule*, 372; *Códice franciscano*, 6.

54. Paso y Troncoso, *Papeles de la Nueva España*, 3:26. Households have been routinely estimated as containing five to seven members, for a total population of twenty-five to forty thousand, well in line with earlier population figures.

55. Cope, *The Limits of Racial Domination*, 89–90.

56. Vetancurt, *Teatro Mexicano*, 3:111–12. See also, Cervantes de Salazar, *México en 1554*, 50.

The spiritual life of the chapel allows us to glimpse into the daily routines of the friars and the faithful. By the late seventeenth century, the chapel was home to eight religious sodalities, also called confraternities.[57] These groups were of tremendous importance in later evangelization because of the support they provided for their members. They were organized around the collective veneration of an image or symbol, such as the Blessed Sacrament, Our Lady of Solitude, the Franciscan Cord, the Holy Burial, and others. Some of these organizations encompassed specific occupational groups. For instance, the tailors embraced the confraternity of the Trinity. Under the auspices of the sodalities, Masses were sung regularly for the souls of their dead members and on the organizations' own annual feast days. In addition, when a member died, Mass was said for that person, and other members were expected to attend.[58]

A sculpture of the *Santíssimo Cristo de los Desagravios* (Most Holy Christ of the Reparations) was also housed in the chapel. It became the central image of a cult that had broad influences in the colony. As noted above, the most popular devotional handbook in the late seventeenth century and early eighteenth century was the booklet written by Francisco de Soria, titled *Manual de los exercicios para los desagravios de Christo ntro. redemptor* (Manual of Exercises for the Redress of Christ Our Redeemer). It was to this devotional manual that one of the more common devotional guides to the Stations of the Cross was appended. A cult that developed around the image of *Christ of the Redress* began in 1731 as a result of an earthquake during which the sculpture appeared to take on human characteristics, including the emission of sweat and blood. In recognition of the miracle, a new chapel was erected in San Josef de los Naturales.[59] Yet, even before that moment, the rituals associated with *Christ of the Redress* had already been written down in the publication history of the Soria *Manual* in the late seventeenth century. Soria had been called upon by sisters of the Third Order Franciscans in Tlaxcala to write the devotion, which originally was handwritten and passed from sister to sister.[60] What is crucial about the devotion outlined by Soria is that he proposed that through their penitential acts, individuals could atone for their own sins and make amends for, or redress, the suffering of Christ.[61] This concept of redress is distinct from the theological principle of atonement, which holds that the sacrifice made by Jesus on behalf of mankind reconciled humans to God. But in the context of the devotions presented by Soria, the specific type of redress is the expiation of sin in the individual penitent through recog-

57. Vetancurt states that there were nine but lists eight. Truitt, *Sustaining the Divine*, 235.

58. Vetancurt, *Teatro Mexicano*, 3:113–14. Gibson, *Aztecs Under Spanish Rule*, 127.

59. Taylor, "An 'Evolved' Devotional Book," 75–76.

60. "A los lectores," in Soria, *Manual de exercícios.*

61. Burdette, "Reparations for Christ Our Lord," 367.

nition of Christ's sacrifice for humankind by becoming one with that suffering. In other words, by suffering along with Christ, the faithful would repay him for his Passion and death. It shifts the emphasis from Christ's suffering in order to redeem humankind to the suffering of individuals as a form of reparations to Christ. Indeed, it is extremely evocative that the cult of the Most Holy Christ of Redress was based in Vetancurt's San Josef de los Naturales and that one of the common guides to the devotion of the Stations of the Cross would be appended to Soria's devotional guide for that cult.

Vetancurt refers to his devotional book for the Stations of the Cross in discussing the processions organized out of the chapel. He notes that on Fridays during Lent, the parishioners practiced the Stations on a path to "Calvary," with a sermon in Nahuatl afterward. As will be seen, Calvary was represented by a cross placed on the outskirts of the city. In addition, the members of the sodality built religious floats, called *pasos* in Spanish, which held statues that were tableaux of moments from the Passion. These *pasos* would be carried on the shoulders of penitents through the streets with musical accompaniment from trumpets, drums, and songs. Each day of Holy Week different groups would take different *pasos* into the streets. Vetancurt notes that on one Holy Saturday in the past the procession of the Holy Burial had included as many as three thousand participants, although that number had diminished by the late seventeenth century.[62]

As San Josef de los Naturales was established initially, in addition to the four Native neighborhoods of the city, the chapel had served twenty villages with an additional eleven hermitages.[63] These hermitages were smaller chapels provided for access to religious services throughout the city and were staffed by a friar who served as hermit. The spiritual jurisdiction of San Josef had extended outside the city as well. There had been five churches located up to a few miles away in the hinterland that also fell under its jurisdiction. In the outer districts of the Central Basin of Mexico, the chapel had also ministered to Natives in six more-distant villages, such as Nativitas, Iztacalco, and Chapultepec.[64] By the time Vetancurt served the chapel, its jurisdiction had shrunk, but much of its prestige remained.

In addition to providing spiritual resources to the local Natives, San Josef was also the site of one of the two important early schools. Fr. Pedro de Gante had founded a school for the Native boys of Tenochtitlán, which he directed for nearly a half century. A twin college for the sons of the Native elite had

62. Vetancurt, *Teatro Mexicano*, 3:114–15; Taylor, *Magistrates of the Sacred*, 301–3.

63. Truitt, *Sustaining the Divine*, 34–45.

64. Vetancurt, *Teatro Mexicano*, 3:116–17; Gibson, *Aztecs under Spanish Rule*, 372–77. Gibson disputes Vetancurt's claims, noting that while these hermitages, chapels, and villages were at one time associated with San Josef, it was a fluid relationship, and with time, more and more became free-standing entities, parishes or doctrinas.

been erected in Tlatelolco in the 1530s. The San Josef school specialized in teaching Native children the European mechanical arts, such as carpentry, along with basic education in reading, writing, and arithmetic. The arts were not scorned, and there were classes in music and painting. Several hundred children attended that school at any given time. The other school, in Tlatelolco, offered a European-style education in the liberal arts and sciences to the sons of the Native elite in the hope of training a Christian aristocracy. Nonetheless, by the time Vetancurt came to serve the chapel, both schools were largely forgotten and only a few children attended.[65]

The Long Seventeenth Century

In the world of art and literature, the seventeenth and early eighteenth centuries were the height of the baroque movement, which was often paired with another movement, the rococo. The baroque was a cultural phenomenon of the West (Europe and the Americas) that was characterized by exuberance and even excess in painting, sculpture, design, and literature. For scholars of literature and the fine arts, the term "baroque" helped to typify what they saw as the unique style of the period. Coming originally from a French term for irregularly shaped pearls, it came to describe works of art that were excessively elaborate and decorated. In architecture, baroque signifies an extravagant style in which decoration covers the entire surface of a facade or altar retable. In painting and sculpture, it signifies a heightened sense of the dramatic, frequently with contrasting dark and light (chiaroscuro), a sense of movement of figures in the scene, drama, and tension. In design, the baroque is highlighted by what can be seen as a fear of empty space (horror vacui). In a baroque church or altarpiece, every surface is covered not just with painting but with bas-relief made of intricately carved stucco or plaster that is then painted and gilded. An example of this is the famous Rosary Chapel in the Church of Santo Domingo in Puebla, built 1650–90.

Translated into painting and sculpture, baroque images are complex while still fully representational; the figures are twisting, turning, and grimacing, displaying in their movement, their attitudes, and the emotions that they feel. The Christ figures, especially in representations of the Passion, are bloody, broken, and twisted with pain. For the Spanish world of the seventeenth century, the epitome of sculptural expression came in the lifelike figures in scenes of the Passion that were featured in Holy Week processions. These sculptures depicted the main characters of the Passion, including Jesus and Mary, along with many of the Apostles, centurions, people of Jerusalem, and various animals, such as donkeys. These figures were arranged in tableaux to depict spe-

---

65. Gibson, *Aztecs under Spanish Rule*, 382.

cific scenes from Holy Week, such as Jesus's triumphal entry into Jerusalem on Palm Sunday, his scourging at the Temple, and his arrest, sentencing, humiliation, and eventual crucifixion. When not being used in processions, these figures were normally placed in the local church, where they could provide spiritual benefit to the devout. Thus, everyday people were quite familiar with these figures, the scenes of the Passion, and the cast of characters in that story.

In the New World, the baroque style confronted a different artistic tradition. Although much serious art was of European origin, it was frequently elaborated by Native artisans. Some scholars refer to this hybrid between European artistic traditions and Native execution as *tequitqui*, the Nahuatl word for "laborer" or "tributary." Yet Manuel Toussaint rejects the term except in cases of the true continuation of Native artistic traditions into the colonial period, preferring to call the juxtaposition of European traditions and Amerindian execution "Popular Imitation of Fine Arts."[66] More recent scholarship has argued that the term *tequitqui* is essentially racist, especially when used in conjunction with the seventeenth and eighteenth centuries, by which time many of the artisans involved had become mestizo. Moreover, the term has its origins in describing sculpture and architectural ornamentation, and thus is not particularly easily transferred to painting, either on canvas or on walls, let alone to pen, ink, and other media.[67] What most scholars agree on is that baroque art in colonial Mexico also had an important Native component that was the result of a dialogue between the European and Amerindian traditions, resulting in an impressive hybridization that made the Mexican baroque in the arts quite different from baroque art found in other regions of the Hispanic world.

The baroque also found its place in literature. Works written in this style are full of descriptive images, wordplay, and allusions. References to Greek and Roman mythology litter the page. Very arcane and exquisite words, frequently Latinisms, were chosen not for clarity or precision but for complexity. In keeping with the style's appeal to the senses, in literature the baroque came to be a highly wrought, sometimes dense style characterized by excessive description and a multiplicity of metaphors and layers of meaning.

In all genres, the baroque is a manifestation of art for art's sake. The viewer or reader is simply overtaken and overwhelmed by the multitude of appeals to the senses and emotions.

While scholars consider the period during which Vetancurt served in Mexico City to be the flowering of the baroque style, recent investigations have increasingly attempted to deepen our understanding of the baroque in the seventeenth and early eighteenth centuries. Looking at the Church and

---

66. Toussaint, *Colonial Art*, 284–97.

67. Peterson, *The Paradise Garden Murals*, 6–7.

religious expression, the idea of the baroque is attractive since so many churches were built and decorated in that style. But in understanding the history of the Church, the term is not as easily applied. It is not accurate to describe a baroque society or a political system of the baroque, since it most accurately refers to a trend in art and literature. Some have suggested that we refer to the period using the term "Counter-Reformation," certainly as it applies to Mexico and New Spain, since the region was virtually completely Catholic in its devotion. Yet that term has its drawbacks as well, since it implies that the movement was a clear reaction to the Protestant Reformation. Scholars have rightly demonstrated that not all the reforms undertaken in the Catholic world were reactive to Protestantism. Many of the changes that occurred in the second half of the sixteenth century and into the seventeenth century were rooted in trends that had begun well before the Protestant Reformation. In recognition of the fact that the Catholic Church underwent its own reorganization and reformation, culminating in and mandated by the Council of Trent, the period encompassing the period of the seventeenth and early eighteenth centuries is frequently called the Catholic Reformation.[68] Rather than necessarily being a reaction to the Protestant Reformation, many of the changes that occurred had their roots in the medieval Church and in new thinking about and approaches to issues that developed in the sixteenth century in parallel to the Protestant Reformation.

Several themes of the Catholic Reformation had an immediate impact in New Spain. Both missionary activity and higher education were important topics for the reinvigorated Church. New Spain, as a hub of missionary activity, focused not only on the missions to the Natives but also on ways of creating a deeper faith in those who were already Christian. Public displays of the most fervent side of the faith were an important tool. As such, processions and devotions involving large groups of the faithful took on a more central character. Indeed, the liturgy itself, with its vestments, pomp, and ceremony, became a central point of the expression of faith. At the same time, the development of a more personal and intimate relationship with God through private devotions, acts of charity, prayer, and meditation was embraced. These practices were in keeping with the trends that had begun in the *devotio moderna* movement nearly two centuries earlier. Education was seen as central to the Church's reform. Universities became centers for the development of a better-trained clergy. In the Spanish realms, an emphasis on education was linked with the crown's efforts to improve the quality of the clergy, using competitive exams as a way of selecting only the best qualified candidates to be parish priests.[69]

68. Taylor, *Theatre of a Thousand Wonders*, 4–7; *Directory for Confessors*, 3–5.
69. Schwaller, "The 'Ordenanza del Patronazgo,'" 253–55.

The principles of the Catholic Reformation were embodied in the canons and decrees of the Council of Trent (1545–63). They had their impact in Mexico as they were adopted and adapted for use throughout New Spain in the Third Provincial Council of Mexico, which met in Mexico City in 1585. In attendance at the council were the bishops from the Province of Mexico's various dioceses, which included the prelates of Guatemala, Michoacan, Puebla/Tlaxcala, Oaxaca, Yucatan, and Guadalajara. The Archbishop of Mexico, don Pedro Moya de Contreras, was the presiding officer. Also in attendance were the leaders of the most significant religious orders: the Franciscans, Dominicans, Augustinians, and Jesuits. Important theologians and specialists in canon law, many of them professors at the University of Mexico, served as staff to the prelates. Groups of clerics, such as the deans and chapter members of several dioceses' cathedrals, had empowered leading priests in Mexico City to represent their points of view in the discussions. The canons and decrees of the Third Provincial Council would become the basis for local canon law in these regions—spreading as far afield as Central America and the Philippines—until the nineteenth century. The decrees covered a wide range of issues confronting the Church. Nonetheless, very few of the decisions had to do with private devotions, such as the Stations of the Cross or the Rosary.[70]

While the local ecclesiastical authorities did not write about the Stations of the Cross, within the works produced by the Third Provincial Council of Mexico we can see how some of the underlying concepts and principles that are embodied in the devotion were explained and debated. In discussing the nature of religion, the bishops attending the council outlined that it had eight acts and works. Two acts are of particular interest to this discussion: devotion and prayer. According to the bishops, devotion is "Lifting the heart to God, asking for things that are appropriate for his glory and the health of our souls, as a remedy for our needs, our peace and calm, for the Christian Church."[71] Prayer, which is an act central to the Stations of the Cross, was divided into two categories: vocal and mental. The council authors saw the two types as intimately linked, since vocal prayer implies that internal prayer has already occurred. Internal prayer was linked to thoughtfulness and consideration. Since most of the decrees of the council dealt with details of canon law, there were very few other references to issues related to devotions. There were rules established to govern processions, which might have been applied to the Stations because the devotion was frequently celebrated as part of a procession from station to station. In particular, the decrees of the council refer to processions during Holy Week, which frequently were also associated with the

70. Poole, *Pedro Moya de Contreras*, 145–46; Poole, "Opposition to the Third Mexican Council," 111–13.

71. *Directory for Confessors*, 92.

Stations. These decrees mandated that processions occur only by day, never at night, nor should women whip themselves as part of the procession.[72]

Two Priests and a Nun

In seventeenth-century Mexico, the intersection of religion and the arts came to occupy a central role in the lives of the colony elite. New and impressive churches were either built in the baroque style or had important decorations added to their existing fabric. A local style developed in painting that would come to its full flower in the early seventeenth century and continue well into the eighteenth. In letters, some of the most famous authors of the colonial period produced works that continue to be read today. In addition to Vetancurt, authors like don Carlos de Sigüenza y Góngora (1645–1700) and Sor Juana Inés de la Cruz (1648–95) were publishing their writing. Both Sor Juana and Sigüenza y Góngora were born nearly twenty years after Vetancurt; don Carlos and the friar died in the same year, and Sor Juana predeceased both of them, dying five years earlier. In the *Teatro mexicano*, Vetancurt acknowledges his collaboration with Sigüenza y Góngora on a variety of topics. Most of their joint activity revolved around the natural history that Vetancurt presents in the first volume of his *Teatro*. Sigüenza y Góngora had been planning a comprehensive natural history of Mexico for several years; nonetheless, Vetancurt published his work before don Carlos was able to do so. In writing his version, Vetancurt had access to the library of the Franciscan convent in Mexico, which included the records kept by his Franciscan predecessors who were historians of the Santo Evangelio Province. Vetancurt used these resources extensively while writing his histories and chronicles in particular. He also benefited from the maps, books, and manuscripts that Sigüenza y Góngora had collected for his own study.[73] In all likelihood, Vetancurt allowed Sigüenza y Góngora access to the Franciscan papers, although the documentation of that is less definitive. Considering their works, the two men must have collaborated on several projects. If they did not truly collaborate as coauthors, they at least shared source materials and information with each other.

Sor Juana Inés de la Cruz does not seem to have had much direct contact with Vetancurt. Undoubtedly, the two knew of each other, since both published widely in Mexico during the last quarter of the seventeenth century and both were religious in the Archdiocese of Mexico. Sor Juana does not mention the Franciscan in her work. Fr. Augustín refers to Sor Juana once in his work, but only obliquely, and not because of her fame as a poet but

72. *Concilio III Provincial Mexicano*, 311.

73. Leonard, *Don Carlos de Sigüenza y Góngora*, 46–47, 81, 91n3.

because of her role in the convent where she lived.[74] However, Sigüenza y Góngora did collaborate with Sor Juana, just as he had with Vetancurt. Sor Juana and Sigüenza y Góngora had each worked on the design of triumphal arches erected in Mexico City to celebrate the arrival of the new viceroy, don Tomás de la Cerda, Third Marquis de la Laguna, in 1680.[75] Thus, Vetancurt and Sor Juana had a friend in common in Sigüenza y Góngora. What all three individuals also had in common was their Creole identity: they were all born in New Spain to Spanish parents. The seventeenth century was the period in which Creoles began to more clearly envision themselves as separate and distinct from their Iberian cousins.[76]

To better understand the relationships between these individuals and the remarkable contributions that each made to colonial New Spanish culture, we need to consider the cultural environment within which they lived. As has been noted, this was known as the baroque period in the arts and the time of the Catholic Reformation in the Church. While the period saw a flowering of the arts including painting, sculpture, architecture, poetry and even prose, it also was a time of intense spiritual devotion. As noted above, piety became very personal and very intense. While public displays of piety frequently punctuated the lives of towns and cities in processions and pageants, spirituality also became intensely personal, focused on meditation and prayer. In this atmosphere, it would seem odd that science would also make important strides. Yet in the sciences, the very first steps were taken toward empirical observation. Unique to the era, the observations were interpreted in light of Christian teachings and established concepts of nature and reality, as will be seen. Thus, scholars were unable to perceive the reality of natural phenomena they observed, preferring to interpret them through the lens of faith.

Vetancurt and Sigüenza y Góngora were eager natural scientists. Both men were Creoles from the region of Mexico City, and both chose a life in the Church and pursued their studies in Puebla. But beyond these surface similarities, the two men were more of a study in opposites. Vetancurt was twenty years the senior. He joined the Franciscan Order in his teens, taking vows in the order, and was eventually ordained a priest. Fr. Augustín became a stalwart of his order and was assigned to a series of tasks and offices of increasing responsibility, including a seat on the leadership council (*definito-*

74. Vetancurt, *Teatro Mexicano*, 2:294.

75. Curcio-Nagy, *The Great Festivals*, 19-40. While she does not include the arches erected for La Laguna, she does provide a good overview of the practice of greeting new viceroys with triumphal arches. Brading, *First America*, 362–72 does discuss Sigüenza y Góngora as a Creole patriot and author of one of the arches.

76. Creoles are individuals of pure Spanish ancestry born in the New World. Brading, *The First America*, 372–381, Brading also considers the intellectual ties among Vetancurt (whom he calls Betancurt), Sor Juana, and Sigüenza y Góngora.

rium). Sigüenza y Góngora entered the Company of Jesus (Jesuits), also in his teens. Although he was from Mexico City, he enrolled in the Colegio del Espiritu Santo in Puebla, where he took his preliminary vows for the priesthood. Unfortunately for him, he was not suited to the circumscribed life of a Jesuit priest. After a series of disciplinary actions, which some say were caused by his attraction to worldly matters, Sigüenza y Góngora was definitively expelled from the order, but only after he had been ordained a priest. He returned to Mexico City to become a parish priest (diocesan cleric) and began to pursue an academic career. He eventually won the competition to be the professor of mathematics and astrology at the University of Mexico in 1672. Even in that position, his enthusiasm for pursuits not directly related to his field of study continually diverted his attention. Thus, while he was undoubtedly a brilliant person, he was constrained by mundane matters like earning a living in his regular employment.[77]

Vetancurt and Sigüenza y Góngora wrote histories and chronicles of their time. These works provide modern-day scholars with a glimpse of the colony as seen through the eyes of its inhabitants. In their works, we also see that both men had a true devotion to the teachings of the Church and a dedication to the deeply emotional form of worship that was the essence of the era. Nevertheless, at the same time, in these works we see the beginnings of scientific inquiry, the observation of nature, and an attempt to rationally explain natural phenomena. Both men were also collectors of information in a wide and varied sense—one could say they were encyclopedists. Sigüenza y Góngora amassed what he characterized as the largest library of its time in New Spain. Indeed, the collection, perhaps even more than his published books, was the work for which Sigüenza y Góngora felt the most pride. For his part as the chronicler of the Holy Gospel Province of the Franciscans, Vetancurt supervised what was probably the largest ecclesiastical library and archive in the colony. Between the two of them, they had access to and control of materials that were both unique and essential in the study of the region's history, culture, and environment. It is this focus on the local area that many have seen as part of the spark that would help to develop a sense of Creole identity: that the Spaniards native to Mexico were a distinct population from their Iberian cousins, with their own proud and important history. And New Spain, their *patria*, was an independent and very unique part of the Spanish realm.[78]

In the specific cases of Vetancurt and Sigüenza y Góngora, these two men were part of the colony's ecclesiastical establishment, one more successfully so than the other. At the same time when they might recognize the frailty of the imperial system instituted by the Hapsburg kings of Spain, they also rec-

77. Leonard, *Baroque Times*, 195–98.
78. Brading, *The First America*, 372–381

ognized that it was based on a full embrace of Catholic doctrine. The evangelization of the Natives was what gave legitimacy to Spanish claims over the New World. Similarly, it was the defense of Catholicism against the rise of Protestantism that also defined Spain. Indeed, the version of Catholicism that gained popularity was exuberant and emotional, perhaps in contrast to more austere and reserved Protestantism of the time. The stance of Vetancurt and Sigüenza y Góngora became part of a nuanced dialogue among Creole intellectuals that focused on local pride, local history, and the unique aspects of the Creole *patria* within the larger Hispanic empire.[79]

What seems on the surface to be a tension between an emergent scientific interest in nature apparent in the natural histories developed by both authors is, in reality, a hallmark of the baroque: the piling on of information. Just as in baroque poetry and prose, where images, metaphors, and allusions are added to create an almost impenetrable text, so these scholars acquired information not to extract essential truths but to create rich tapestries of knowledge that reflected the complexity of everyday reality. One might also note that the multiplicity of sources and the depth of information also reflected well on the authors' erudition, just as obscure references to Greek or Roman mythology might reflect on a poet's sagacity. What might pass for a scientific endeavor is not a search for first principles but rather the creation of "eclectic, heteroglossic territory."[80] At the same time, there is good evidence that the dilettantish interest that Sigüenza y Góngora had for scientific investigation was, in reality, the first glimmer of a rational and dispassionate study of natural phenomena.[81]

Sor Juana was far younger than either Vetancurt or Sigüenza y Góngora; she was born after Vetancurt entered the Franciscan Order and predeceased him by perhaps five years. Like Vetancurt, however, she was born in a rural part of the southeastern Central Basin of Mexico. Her native village of Nepantla was located in the shadow of the great Popocatepetl volcano.[82] Moreover, it was about thirty kilometers, as the crow flies, from Vetancurt's home of Ayotzingo. Traveling from Nepantla to Mexico City, she might well have passed through Ayotzingo. While it is not at all clear whether Sor Juana and Vetancurt were acquainted, she did know Sigüenza y Góngora. Indeed, he is credited with delivering her eulogy.

Sor Juana and Sigüenza y Góngora, as noted, both designed arches to celebrate the arrival of a new viceroy, the Marquis de la Laguna. Triumphal entrances of viceroys into Mexico City had become important events in the

79. More, *Baroque Sovereignty*, 22–25.

80. Merrim, *The Spectacular City*, 158.

81. Bleichmar, "Science," 298–99.

82. Interestingly, *nepantla* in Nahuatl signifies an in-between place, neither here nor there but someplace in between. Karttunen, *An Analytical Dictionary of Nahuatl*, 169.

colony. The viceroys served on average some six to seven years; as a result, celebrations of the departure of one ruler and the arrival of another, while not necessarily frequent, were almost routine. Sigüenza y Góngora mentions one celebration as early as 1528.[83] Certainly in the late sixteenth century and beyond, these types of festivals, with their processions, balls, bullfights, and church ceremonies, were of tremendous importance to the colony.[84] At one of the various stops along the procession route for the viceroy's reception, Sor Juana was entrusted with the design of the arch at the cathedral. Her commission came from the priests who made up the cathedral chapter, high-ranking clerics appointed by the king to serve specific offices in that church. This was perhaps one of the highest honors the colony could afford to any creative person, male or female, and placed her squarely in the limelight. Sigüenza y Góngora received the contract for the arch at the church of Santo Domingo. Octavio Paz, in his respected biography of Sor Juana, notes that each author needed this commission to establish a solid relationship with the new viceroy. Each had a questionable past: Sor Juana suffered from a relatively unknown father and a precocious childhood. After that, she developed a problematic reputation when she left one order for being too strict and became a bit of a celebrity in another. Likewise, Sigüenza y Góngora had been expelled from the Jesuit Order and was widely considered difficult to work with.[85]

The two arches were quite distinct in theme and message. Don Carlos titled his arch the "Theater of Political Virtues That Constitute a Ruler" so that it would be a "monument to truth and the art of governing."[86] Sor Juana's arch, erected in front of the cathedral's west door, was titled the "Allegorical Neptune," which was an extended play on words. Mexico City had been built on a lagoon and was famous for its lacustrine location. At the same time, extending the play on words, the viceroy's noble title was Marquis de la Laguna (Marquis of the Lagoon). Her work was an allegorical portrait of the viceroy, equating him in power and majesty to Neptune, the Roman god of the oceans and water. Adding to her extended allusion, she used a fanciful genealogy of the gods to trace Neptune back to the concept of wisdom. All her images were deeply imbued with the baroque fondness for complexity, depth of imagery, and references to the classical past. While the arch leading into the cathedral was the physical fruit of her efforts, it was accompanied by a publication: a prose and poetry explanation of the various parts of her allegorical arch. Both the arch itself and its explanation were successful and placed

---

83. Paz, *Sor Juana*, 149.

84. The impact and importance of these processions is detailed in Curcio-Nagy, *The Great Festivals of Colonial Mexico City*.

85. Paz, *Sor Juana*, 150.

86. Paz, *Sor Juana*, 150–52.

the nun among the intellectual leaders of the colony. In keeping with more modern traditions, she also cites the sources for her ideas and thus allows readers, then and now, to glimpse into her methods of research and creativity. But, in the end, her arch and the poetry and prose that accompanied it were highlights of the baroque: "a hieroglyph, more exactly, an emblem, and enigma."[87]

Just as Vetancurt and Sigüenza y Góngora had created complex historic tapestries in their histories, so did Sor Juana use imagery, metaphor, and allusion to create her exquisite baroque poetry. If the two men explored the intersections of history, natural history, and religion, Sor Juana looked both inward and outward. Her poetry was both a commentary on the society that surrounded her and an insight into the woman herself. Her complex images, classical references, and metaphors all created a dense and sometimes impenetrable view of reality in the world in which she lived. Unable to leave the convent, not allowed to participate in the processions and parades that delighted the city, she created pageants, liturgies, and triumphal arches with her words.[88] Her works exemplify the rich and complex world that would embrace the devotion of the Stations of the Cross.

This flowering of the arts was closely linked to the central role of religion—indeed the religious fervor—in the lives of the colony's elite. Wealthy patrons commissioned paintings, sculptures, altars, and whole buildings to demonstrate their piety. In keeping with the baroque and its heightened emotional themes, a wide range of works were published that sought to deepen the emotional content of the faithful's religious experience. Christ's Passion and crucifixion, the sorrows of the Virgin Mary, and the suffering of the saints and martyrs were all widespread literary themes, and scores of books to assist the devout in their emulation of these exempla were produced. Hundreds of sermons were preached on these themes, and dozens of texts were published by the city's elite trying to capture in print the emotional content they felt upon hearing the words in church. The number of religiously themed publications grew from an annual average of thirteen (1601–1684) to thirty-six (1685–1717) to forty-five (1718–67).[89] Many of these were sermons dedicated to the praise of the Virgin Mary's various aspects: Our Lady of Sorrows, Our Lady of Mercy, Our Lady of the Pillar, Our Lady of Guadalupe, Our Lady of Suffering, and others. Mary was glorified from pulpits and in print in all her manifold facets. There was also a minor competition among the religious orders to attract the faithful. Individual characteristics of the Virgin became associated with different orders. The Franciscans embraced the

---

87. Paz, *Sor Juana*, 156, 178. The full passage was: "The arch of the *Allegorical Neptune* was in fact a hieroglyph. More exactly, an emblem, and enigma."

88. Merrim, *The Spectacular City*, 182–94; Brading, *The First America*, 372–73.

89. Taylor, *Theater of a Thousand Wonders*, 97.

Immaculate Conception among others. The Dominicans supported Our Lady of the Rosary. The Augustinians extolled Our Lady of the Pillar.

Mexico City saw a large number of construction projects in the seventeenth and early eighteenth centuries, including churches, convents, and chapels in the baroque style. This is evident to even the casual tourist in Mexico City today. Thomas Gage, a touring English Dominican friar, visited in 1625 and afterward claimed that the city boasted some fifty ecclesiastical establishments and that they had nearly infinite riches within them, consisting of altarpieces, vestments, chalices, candlesticks, and other articles used in the celebration of the Mass.[90]

This growth in urban religious establishments went arm in arm with the expansion of the number of friars and nuns entering the convents. The period between 1650 and 1730 saw a continual growth in the number of men entering religious orders in New Spain. Indeed, most of the orders reached their highest population around 1730. This same growth curve can be seen in the number of shrines and miraculous images erected in the colony. These special sites started slowly, emerging in the late sixteenth century, then continued to build throughout the seventeenth century, and reached their peak just after 1700. The eighteenth century saw a slow decline.[91]

The reasons for this growth in religious membership are varied. On a demographic level, the population of financially comfortable Creoles grew during this period, and they were the social group most likely to place their children into ecclesiastical service.[92] Spanish inheritance laws dictated that all children were to receive an equal share of their parents' wealth. Having some sons and daughters enter into the clergy diminished the attrition of family wealth from generation to generation, which was a very attractive notion to middle-class families. It was expected that some of the middle- and upper-class children (sons and daughters), because of social and economic status, would enter the convent. Increasing membership also made financial sense for the religious orders. Most orders depended on a combination of alms and investments for their financial support.[93] The investments could come from a wide variety of sources: rural agricultural estates, liens on property (both urban and rural), and rental of urban properties to mention a few. As more men and women entered the orders, there was a long-term cost to sustaining them. However, new members brought in badly needed cash and property and, per-

---

90. Gage, *Thomas Gage's Travels*, 70–71.

91. Taylor, *Theater of a Thousand Wonders*, 95–6.

92. Melvin, "Clergy," 73.

93. The Franciscans and especially the Discalced Franciscans supported themselves exclusively through alms, in keeping with the founding principles of the order, and generally did not invest money in real estate.

haps more important, connections to other comfortable and well-to-do families that might support the order in the future.[94] In a certain sense, the newcomers' donations helped to support the members already in the order.

Vetancurt, Sigüenza y Góngora, and Sor Juana were clearly products of their environment. While each reflected contemporary sensibilities in their works, they also became exemplars of their time. All three were deeply religious, although their spirituality took different forms. Sigüenza y Góngora failed to become a Jesuit, although he tried at least two times after his initial expulsion. Finally, he served as a simple parish priest in addition to his appointment as a professor at the university. Vetancurt was a highly respected member of the Franciscan Order. He eventually served in some of the most important posts in the Holy Gospel Province, although he also had pastoral duties at the chapel of San Josef de los Naturales. Sor Juana experimented with two different orders, finally becoming a member of the Hieronymite community of San Jerónimo, which was less austere than the Carmelite community where she had begun her religious career. In the Hieronymite convent she came to occupy a place of honor and consciously avoided the world so that she might better pursue her studies. Thus, while all three were clerics, they pursued very different paths. Religion provided a bulwark for their lives. For Vetancurt and Sor Juana, the religious life provided them with communities that would support them, but they had to dedicate their talents to those communities in return. For Sigüenza y Góngora, the university became his community. There, he could pursue learning while also enjoying relatively high social status. In their similarities, and even in their uniqueness, these three individuals reflected the complex world of the Catholic Reformation and the baroque.

Devotio Moderna and the Evangelization

The sixteenth-century effort to convert Natives to Christianity had born fruit by the century's end. Not only had most Natives living in the major cities and principal towns become Christian, they had also embraced many mundane aspects of the religion. Numerous commentators noted how fervently the Natives participated in processions. In addition, Natives also happily joined religious sodalities and participated in religious dramas. A cadre of Natives had been trained in Latin and Greek, were introduced to Christian theology, and were given advanced training in philosophy and the liberal arts.[95] As a result of this training, many texts were translated into Nahuatl. The most common of these were doctrinal statements and catechisms for use by local parish priests, but other works also found a small but eager audience in late

94. Melvin, *Building Colonial Cities of God*, 46–54; Lavrin, "Convent," 96.
95. Tavarez, "Nahua Intellectuals," 208–9.

sixteenth-century Mexico. Constitutions and records of sodalities were written in Nahuatl, along with more common documents such as church records of vital statistics: baptisms, marriages, and burials. On a different level, many religious plays were either written in Nahuatl or translated into the language. Several fairly sophisticated theological works also found translators and became more common among the Natives.[96]

Unfortunately, just as the various individuals who were well trained in Nahuatl were ready to tackle the work of translating important theological and devotional works, the Spanish state began to have second thoughts about the utility of having these works in a language understood by only a few Europeans. The fear was that important theological points would be erroneously translated into the Native tongue, causing possibly irreparable damage. In 1546, the Council of Trent had ruled against the translation of the Bible into common languages, requiring that the holy texts be read only in the Latin Vulgate.[97] This constrained many of the people working to provide devotional materials to the Natives. In order for any work to be published, approval was required from the local ecclesiastical and secular authorities. Vetancurt frequently served the archdiocese and viceroyalty as an official reader of Nahuatl materials submitted for publication to assure that they were theologically accurate.

One important through point connecting the Natives of New Spain with the late-medieval traditions that gave rise to the Stations of the Cross was the *devotio moderna*. One of the key texts in that tradition is the *Imitatio Christi* (Imitation of Christ) by Thomas á Kempis. In late sixteenth-century Mexico, two slightly different Nahuatl translations of this work were in circulation. The presence of this work in late sixteenth-century Mexico demonstrates how clearly the *devotio moderna* had influenced the Franciscans, the earliest missionary order to begin converting the Natives to Christianity. It also demonstrates the success of the educational efforts in training a literate group of Native intellectuals who were the intended readers for this type of work. It also underscores that the same set of influences that made the devotion of the Stations of the Cross so popular in colonial New Spain also created a broader theological discussion. Such works were frequently composed by Spaniards but with a literate Nahuatl audience in mind. The second market for these works would have been parish priests who were less than fully fluent in Nahuatl, for which the works would serve as aides providing them with basic texts.[98]

---

96. Sell, "The Classical Age of Nahuatl Publications," 1–20.

97. "Concerning the Edition and Use of Sacred Books," Second Decree, Council of Trent, April 8, 1546, http://www.thecounciloftrent.com/ch4.htm; see also Mosquera, "Nahuatl Catechistic Drama," 58–61.

98. Tavarez, "Nahua Intellectuals," 203–8, 233–35.

The Natives (and Spaniards) were not limited to translating existing texts from Spanish, Latin, or even Greek into Nahuatl. By the late sixteenth century, and certainly in the seventeenth century, many spiritually oriented texts begin to appear in Nahuatl. Perhaps the most famous of these is the narrative describing the appearance of the Virgin Mary at Tepeaca, on the northwest shore of Lake Tetzcoco, immediately north of Mexico City. The phenomenon came to be known as the Virgin of Guadalupe, named after a preexisting shrine in Spain. This narrative, called the *Huei tlamahuizoltica* (Through a Great Miracle), is extremely complex and draws on models from both the Old World and the New. Most closely related to it is the 1648 work by Miguel Sánchez, *Imagen de la virgin María*. Sánchez's work provides all the details of Mary's appearance at Tepeaca and details all the miracles associated with the apparition. For several centuries it was held as the definitive account of the miracle. Nonetheless, the Nahuatl version appeared only a year later, written by Luis Lasso de La Vega, who served the hermitage at Guadalupe. This account is also known as the *Nican mopohua* (Here Is Recounted), from the opening words of the text. Evidence points to a complex origin story for the Nahuatl version, including both official and unofficial composition strategies. It was not just a simple translation of the Sánchez text.[99]

The Lasso de la Vega account of the apparition at Tepeaca is evidence of an active world of Nahuatl religious text development. Recent scholarship has rightly questioned the authorship of various texts attributed to one historical figure or another. Many texts were supposedly written by Fr. Pedro de Gante or Fr. Alonso de Molina, for example. Both friars were known to have worked in Nahuatl, and both wrote various documented texts. But they did not write everything that has been attributed to them. Thus, one needs to question seriously Lasso de la Vega's authorship of the *Huei tlamahuizoltica*. Just because his name appears on the title page does not positively confirm his responsibility. Lisa Sousa, Stafford Poole, and James Lockhart agree that the work was probably written by him, but not by him alone. While nothing can be stated definitively, it seems most likely that the bulk of work was written by a Spaniard, probably Lasso de la Vega, but one or more native speakers must have also played an important role in its production.[100]

The publication of the *Huei tlamahuizoltica* in and of itself demonstrates that there was a market for devotional material written in Nahuatl, especially since a parallel version by Miguel Sánchez was also circulating. The Sánchez text became the more widely known version, clearly because there were fewer literate Nahuas than there were Spaniards. The publication of this work falls

99. Sousa, Poole, and Lockhart, *The Story of Guadalupe*, 1–5; Mosquera, "Nahuatl Catechistic Drama," 57–58.

100. Sousa, Poole, and Lockhart, *The Story of Guadalupe*, 43–47.

in a period of the early and middle seventeenth century, when other experiments were being conducted using Nahuatl texts, and so Lasso de la Vega's book also demonstrates that there was not just a market for books among Nahuatl readers and Spanish speakers eager for additional material in Nahuatl but that those readers sought many different types of works.

At roughly the same time, Horacio Carochi, a Jesuit priest, was engaged in an in-depth study of Nahuatl. He recognized features of the language that had been lost on previous observers. He also developed what would become the definitive grammatical study of Nahuatl, largely for use by Spaniards hoping to become more expert in the language themselves. The Carochi grammar was published in 1645 and became the definitive study of the language until the last few decades. His work was destined to be a handbook for Spanish speakers, principally missionaries, who needed a solid understanding of the language for their work. In developing the grammar, Carochi depended heavily on Native informants, as had many other scholars before him. He also had a small group of other experts whom he regularly consulted. Among these were Fernando and Bartolomé de Alva, brothers of mixed Native and Spanish ancestry. Fernando de Alva Ixtlilxochitl was the official Nahuatl interpreter for the high court of justice in Mexico City. His younger brother, don Bartolomé de Alva, was a parish priest in the Archdiocese of Mexico. Thanks to marginal notes in manuscripts written by don Bartolomé, we know that that the brothers were in frequent contact with Carochi, discussing fine points of Nahuatl grammar.[101] Another member of this group was don Carlos de Sigüenza y Góngora. In fact, some of the Alvas' books and manuscripts eventually fell into the possession of Sigüenza y Góngora. Consequently, the Alva brothers were closely allied with Sigüenza y Góngora as well.

Don Bartolomé de Alva was noted not just for his service as a parish priest but also as a well-known scholar of Nahuatl. During his life he composed a catechism in Nahuatl for use in the archdiocese, the *Confessionario mayor y menor*. But he also took it upon himself to translate several theatrical pieces from the Spanish golden age of the early seventeenth century (1580–1690), collaborating closely with Horacio Carochi.[102] While one might well imagine the writing of spiritually uplifting or practical works into Nahuatl as being routine and part of the normal process of conversion to Christianity, these theatrical pieces were only tangentially associated with conversion. Indeed, they signify a rather dramatic turn into more popular literature. They formed part of a period of creativity in Nahuatl literature that Angel María Garibay characterizes as *"el vuelo roto"* (the broken flight).[103] Garibay sees the produc-

101. Schwaller, "Don Bartolomé de Alva," 12–15.
102. Sell, "Two Eminent and Classical Authors," 26–34.
103. Schwaller, "The Brothers," 51–2; Garibay, *Historia de la Literatura*, 2:339–69.

tion of what can almost be characterized as popular literature in Nahuatl as a dramatic shift away from the very practical orientation of the early works. The story of the miracles associated with the Virgin of Guadalupe, while religious in orientation, were equally part of this new movement, but theatrical products seem to stand out as particularly unique.

While the translations of the *Imitatio christi* seem to have been accomplished by Spanish friars, Natives were responsible for composing other religiously themed works in their own language, using European models. In the realm of religious theatre, there was a fairly diverse body of materials produced by both Spaniards and Natives. The history of dramatic productions in early colonial Mexico has been well charted by several scholars.[104] Early in the evangelization, missionaries discovered that they could teach important moral lessons to the Natives through the use of plays. Miracle plays and other religiously oriented productions became standards in the missions. But in the seventeenth century, as part of the move to the baroque in the arts, drama took on an even more important role, which it would occupy for the remainder of the colonial period. As noted above, part of this effort included the translation of golden-age Spanish dramas into Nahuatl. But running alongside these translations were works seemingly written in Nahuatl as both entertaining and didactic works. Nahuatl theater was rich and varied, and much of it seems to have existed outside of excessive scrutiny by Spanish clerics. None of the works were published and thus did not require permission from ecclesiastical authorities. Local parish priests were supposed to be vigilant about works that might not be completely orthodox, but it is impossible to tell how closely they monitored the plays, let alone know how well they themselves understood Nahuatl.

Within the corpus of Nahuatl plays from the later colonial period a subgenre focuses on the Passion of Christ. These works cover many of the same themes that one can find in the devotion of the Stations of the Cross. They provided Natives with a visual experience so they could better understand and immerse themselves in Christ's agony. Approximately six Passion plays in Nahuatl are extant from the later colonial period. In addition, one play focuses on the discovery of the "true cross" by Saint Helena. These texts provide a comparison for both the content and the wording that were used in the Nahuatl version of the Stations of the Cross. There are some notable similarities between depictions of Christ's final hours in the plays and in the Stations, but there are also some significant divergences.

---

104. Louise Burkhart and Barry Sell have edited and translated four volumes of Nahuatl-language plays from colonial Mexico. The fourth volume contains Passion plays and others with distinctive Christian didactic content. Sell and Burkhart, *Nahuatl Theater*, vol. 4.

Passion plays were among some of the first productions enacted in the colonial period. They became an integral part of a series of rituals and celebrations that highlighted Holy Week. One tradition associated with Passion observances that seems to have begun in the colonial period is the creation of papier-mâché figures of Judas. These would be burned or destroyed with fireworks. Processions were also important components of Holy Week observations, drawing on some famous examples from early modern Spain. But plays depicting the events of the week were popular and seemingly widespread. Because these plays touch on matters relating to faith and morals and depicted Christian doctrine, the Inquisition frequently became involved. The number of complaints and the fact that they recurred over many decades demonstrates that merely because local ecclesiastical officials might object, or even if the Inquisition itself might prohibit certain practices, those practices did not necessarily cease. In fact, it seems that they continued as before, with perhaps a momentary lapse in one place, only to be taken up somewhere else.[105]

Although there is evidence of Passion plays in Nahuatl from the very first years of the colony, the scripts have not survived. The handful of texts that are extant all date from the eighteenth century and thus are roughly contemporaneous with the Nahuatl version of the Stations of the Cross. The largest difference between the plays and the devotional prayers for the Stations is the organizational scheme. Whereas the Stations of the Cross consists of fourteen moments during Christ's Passion, running from the condemnation by Pilate to the interment, the plays tend to include many more events and encompass a larger period.

Two published examples come from the villages of San Simón Tlatlauhquitepec and Tepaltzingo.[106] In both of these Passion plays the action begins well before the events of Good Friday. The Tlatlauhquitepec version begins just prior to Maundy Thursday, with a conversation among four Jewish leaders—Samuel, Joseph, Annas (Ananias), and Caiaphas—about the disturbances caused by Jesus since his arrival in Jerusalem. It is possible that the play actually began with events of Palm Sunday, but the manuscript was destroyed and therefore lacks both a beginning and an end. The longer Tepaltzingo play begins on Palm Sunday, with Christ calling for a donkey so that he can ride into Jerusalem in compliance with the prophesies regarding the Jewish Messiah. It then shifts to a conversation among various Jews and Caiaphas. The Tepaltzingo example ends with Jesus's death on the cross, and thus does not include the descent from the cross/pietà or the interment, which do appear in the Stations. As noted, the Tlatlauhquitepec play is incom-

---

105. Burkhart, "Pageantry, Passion, and Punishment," 8–12.

106. The texts of these two plays can be found in Sell and Burkhart, *Nahuatl Theater*, 4:126–59 (Tlatlauhquitepec), 160–241 (Tepaltzingo).

plete and ends just at the point when Jesus is condemned by Pilate, which is the first of the Stations of the Cross. Thus, the scope of the plays is quite different from that of the Stations. Only the Tepaltzingo play includes events that correspond to the portion of the Passion story that make up the Stations.

The specific sequence of events in the Tepaltzingo work follows the same general outline as the Stations but omits large portions. For instance, the Passion play moves directly from the condemnation by Pilate to Christ's meeting Veronica. This means that the play moves directly from the first station to the sixth, and it quickly moves to the crucifixion and the death of Jesus. Considering the details, the Passion play only briefly covers material in three of the stations. At the same time, there are several conversations between Jesus and his mother, Mary, that the play introduces before the sentencing of Pilate, which are very reminiscent of Jesus's meeting his mother during the Stations. Nonetheless, the plays differ markedly from the Stations of the Cross. They cover a much longer time period of the Passion, sometimes including all of Holy Week from Palm Sunday to the crucifixion. But while they begin earlier, they do not generally include the descent from the cross or the interment. The language used in the plays is, however, very similar to that used in the Nahuatl version of the Stations. The discussion of that text will occur in the next chapter.

Conclusions

Clearly, seventeenth- and early eighteenth-century New Spain experienced a time of great religious fervor and cultural change. While the transatlantic passage may have slowed communications, New Spain was fully integrated into the cultural debates throughout the larger European world. The theological discussions, sermons, and religious devotions in New Spain all had their counterparts in Europe, which they imitated and drew upon heavily. Thus, when a new concept was launched in Europe, it was only a matter of time before it spurred debates in Mexico City or Puebla. A devotion like the Stations of the Cross, which has its roots in the Passion of Christ in the Holy Land, entered New Spain in the late sixteenth century and quickly became a critically important cultural phenomenon there.

The print culture of colonial New Spain eagerly embraced small devotional handbooks. Several score of them were published each century. In many years numerous titles emerged. By and large, they reflected titles and patterns that also appeared in the Old World. Devotions like the Five Wounds of Christ or the Seven Sorrows of Mary also had adherents in New Spain. But one title emerged as far more popular than all others, a devotion of the Stations of the Cross. It was so popular that it was translated very early on into Nahuatl by Fr. Augustín de Vetancurt.

Vetancurt was a member of the Franciscan Order. He also was a Creole, a locally born Spaniard. He, and others like him, shared a love of their homeland, a deep belief in Christianity, and expansive interests that encompassed broad areas. Vetancurt, Sor Juana Inés de la Cruz, and don Carlos de Sigüenza y Góngora all manifested the complex and sometimes contradictory orientations that reflect the combination of the baroque in art and literature and the Catholic Reformation in questions of faith and devotion. The period saw a proliferation of devotions at the same time that scholars like Sigüenza y Góngora and Vetancurt were beginning to study essential questions of science, which for them was a form of natural history. The accumulation of data was not so different from the multiple levels of images and symbols that characterized the poems of Sor Juana.

At the same time that devotions were proliferating in print and poets and scholars were exploring the complexities of the baroque, in Nahuatl-speaking communities and among the priests and friars who served them, a rich and vibrant literature based on the *devotio moderna* continued to develop in New Spain. A few texts were translated from Spanish and Latin into Nahuatl, and various bilingual scholars, both Native and Creole, began to produce local devotional materials. Most of these were based on Spanish and European models, but in their translation into Nahuatl they took on a distinctive Mexican character. Especially popular were plays on a number of different themes, and Passion plays stand out as particularly resonant with the ethos of the period. They evoked a visceral response in the observer, just as participation in some of the devotions like the Stations of the Cross did. Consequently, the late seventeenth and eighteenth centuries saw a dramatic increase in the popularity of not just Passion plays but also the private and personal devotion of the Stations of the Cross, all of which were available in Nahuatl versions.

The devotion of the Stations of the Cross gained success in the colonial environment because of a confluence of two streams. On the one hand, the *devotio moderna* encouraged a more emotional and personal faith. It became part of the Catholic Reformation with its increasing emphasis on the physical manifestations of religion—processions and ceremonies. At the same time, in the world of the arts the baroque also brought an additional fascination with the emotional and even ecstatic exuberance of religion. The baroque in New Spain was then subjected to additional refinement in the hands of the Native and mestizo artisans who executed many sculptures and architectural forms. These two streams then come together in the Stations of the Cross, which can be celebrated in solitude or as a part of a larger group. It focuses on the emotional and intimate suffering of Christ and seeks to allow the penitent to walk in Christ's footsteps as he approached his death. The following chapters will continue to study the importance of the Stations of the Cross while looking at the specific elements of the Nahuatl version of the devotion published by Fr. Augustín de Vetancurt.

Chapter Four
The Texts of the Stations of the Cross

The devotion of the Stations of the Cross exists in several different forms. The principal form comprises the prayers and meditations that focus on each of the fourteen moments in the Passion of Jesus. Ideally the practice calls upon the person not only to pray and meditate but to walk and imagine one's self alongside Jesus in his Passion. Thus, the second form of the devotion involves movement: walking from station to station, bowing, kneeling, standing, and other actions. But, in addition to that, the Stations exist as paintings, plaques, sculptures, or chapels, which help the participant to imagine Jesus's Passion—to transcend time and space and take the penitent to accompany Jesus. Thus, at a minimum, the Stations exist in three forms: as a set of texts of prayers and meditations, as a set of movements between the stations and in the acts of prayer and meditation, and as decorations that denote the stations themselves. Each of these modalities becomes a text that we can read in order to understand the implications of the devotion more deeply.

Collections of prayers have a publication history dating back to the sixteenth century. The texts that accompanied the Stations, that is, the prayers and meditations, traveled to New Spain, where several became extremely popular, going through scores of publications between 1650 and 1800. These were so popular that they were also translated into Native languages, including both Nahuatl and Purépecha. Thus, the little devotional guide that forms the heart of this book was an outgrowth of this several-centuries-long period of development that began in Jerusalem and Northern Europe.

The Stations

As has been seen earlier, while there is great variation among the different devotions gaining popularity in the late sixteenth and early seventeenth centuries, the foremost model that emerged by the end of the eighteenth century and the dawn of the modern age was the Stations of the Cross as recognized by the papacy in 1731. That scheme involved fourteen stations representing the journey of Christ from the moment of his condemnation to death by Pilate until his entombment later that same day. In order to better appreciate the model upon which most devotions of the Stations of the Cross are based, we will look at the two most common Spanish-language versions from the late sixteenth and early seventeenth centuries, namely those written by Fr. Antonio de la Anunciación and Miguel Angel Candia. These versions will provide a general overview, which will then allow us to better see how Vetancurt's Nahuatl translation differs from the two and what unique qualities it brings to bear. The Candia edition is longer because, in addition to meditations and prayers, each station also includes a short poem reflecting on the themes of the station. Vetancurt used the simpler Anunciación version as the basis for his translation.

The Candia Stations of the Cross begins with a description of how it came to have been written, as discussed in the last chapter. In preparation for the devotion, the participant is asked to make the sign of the cross and then say the Act of Contrition. In general, the prayer recognizes that the penitent is sinful and wishes to stop sinful behavior and live a better life. The prayer in this version reads:

> **Candia**
> My Lord Jesus Christ, God and true man, Creator and my Redeemer, for being who you are and because I love you above all things, it weighs upon my heart that I have offended you. I propose strongly (with your divine grace) to sin no more, to confess my sins, and to persevere in amending my life. And I trust in your infinite mercy that you will have pardoned me of my faults, of giving me your grace, so that loving you in this life, then in glory I may enjoy the full fruits of your Sacred Passion. Amen.[1]

This opening Act of Contrition is followed by a short quatrain of poetry that repeats the general themes of love for Christ, repentance for sin, and the hope of redemption. It is written in a popular style (called *arte menor* in Spanish) with nine-syllable lines and consonantal rhyme.

At the conclusion of the Act of Contrition, the Candia version then indicates that the leader of the group should read the following offering prayer.

> **Candia**
> Sovereign Lord, I offer fully and completely to Your Divine Majesty all that I might meditate on and pray about in this exercise, that they might be agreeable and be of some benefit to me through your will; I also

---

1. The English translations from the Spanish will attempt to mimic the punctuation and capitalization of the original Spanish. "Señor mio Jesu-Christo, Dios y hombre verdadero, Criador, y Redemptor mio, por ser vos quine sois, y porque os amo sobre todas las cosas, me pesa de todo mi corazon, de averos ofendido, propongo firmemente (con vuestra divina gracia) de nunca mas pecar, de confessar mis pecados, y perseverar en la enmienda, y confio de vustra infinita misericordia, que me aveis de perdonar mis culpas, de darme vuestra gracia, para que amandoos en esta vida, goze los copiosos fructos de tu Sagrada Passion en la gloria. Amen." Candia, "Del Santo Exercicio," 86–87

intend to gain all of the indulgences that your Vicars on earth [the Popes] have conceded; and thus I offer everything in remission of my sins and for the Souls in Purgatory, principally [for] those of my major obligation, according to the order of charity and justice that I owe, and that it might be more agreeable to your Divine Majesty.[2]

This offering prayer has two goals. The first is to convey that the participant wishes to undergo a personal spiritual renewal. In addition to this, and central to the devotion, is the desire that through the successful completion of the Stations of the Cross, penitents will accumulate indulgences not just for themselves, but also for their departed kinsfolk. The prayer also implies that individuals participating in the devotion might do so as a group and that within the group there would be only one person who would read various prayers and meditations for all.

The opening of the Anunciación version is much more abrupt. It begins quite simply by directing the participants that everyone who wishes to follow the devotion should come together. It does stipulate that people can follow the devotion as individuals, although the implication is that generally it should be used by a group. The leader, or a member of the group who will read the devotion aloud for all, crosses himself, speaking the accompanying words out loud.[3] Then the leader says, "Through this sign," while the other participants all respond together, "of the Holy Cross, etc."[4] The "etc." in the directions indicates that the prayer is actually longer. The formula that was generally used was "By the sign of the cross deliver us from our enemies, you who are our God. In the name of the Father, and of the Son, and of the Holy Spirit. Amen."[5] The leader of the group then reads a very short offering prayer that

2. "Soberano Señor, ofrezco con todo rendimiento a tu Magestad Divina, todo lo que en este Exercicio meditaré, y rezaré, que se fuere agradable, y a mi por su voluntad, de algun provecho, tambien pretendo ganar todas las indulgencias, que han concedido tus Vicarios en la tierra; y assi se los ofrezco todo en remision de mis pecados, y por las Animas del Purgatorio, principalmente de mis mayores obligaciones, segun el orden de charidad y justicia que debo, y fuere mas agradable a tu Divina Magestad." Candia, "Del Santo Exercicio," 87.

3. That is, participants will use the right hand to make the sign of the cross on themselves: touching the head, heart (lower sternum), left shoulder, and right shoulder, saying, "In the name of the Father, Son, and Holy Spirit."

4. "Congregados todos los que huvieren de ir juntos; o si fuere uno solo a visitar estas Cruzes, se persignará uno en voz alta que será el que ha de leer las Estaciones, y dirá: *Por la senal*, y responderán todos lo mismo: *de la Santa Cruz etc.* Y luego dirá el que leyere el Ofrecimiento siguiente." Anunciación, *Luz para saber andar*, 1.

5. The Latin formula of this prayer is: "Per signum crucis de inimicis nostris libera nos, Deus noster. In nomine Patris, et Filii, et Spiritus Sancti. Amen." "Per signum Crucis: By the Sign of the Cross," Thesaurus Precum Latinarum, http://www.preces-latinae.org/thesaurus/Filius/PerSignum.html. This is a longer formula than was normally used. In general, only the second half was recited on a normal basis.

initiates the devotion.[6] The little offering prayer in the Anunciación version is just the first few lines of the much longer form that was used by Candia. The difference between the two becomes striking, then, since in the Anunciación version, the participant is engaged in the devotion purely for the benefit of spiritual renewal through prayer and meditation. The participant in the Candia version enters into a far more transactional mode: through the devotion, indulgences will be gained not just for the participant but for departed kinsfolk in purgatory. After this brief introduction, the Anunciación version presses immediately into the first station.

The First Station: Christ Is Condemned to Death

Interestingly, while the Candia edition has more detail in the overall introductory material, the Anunciación version has more detail in the introduction to each station, largely because it lacks a meditation for each station. The introductory material for each station, then, helps focus the thoughts of the penitent on the forthcoming prayer. Indeed, for Anunciación the introduction is, in effect, the meditation. In describing the first station, Anunciación provides the following:

> **Anunciación**
> This is the First Station, it is the Praetorium, and Home of Pilate, where the Redeemer of the World was rigorously whipped, by the hands of six ferocious Soldiers, with spiny rods, with knotted cords, and on them were thorns, chains, and metal hooks, that ripped out his flesh with each blow that they gave him.[7]

The details provided are both gruesome and fascinating. The enumeration of six soldiers and then their various torture methods paints a scene of cruelty. The implements have a striking resemblance to flagellation devices known in Spanish as *disciplinas.* Similar to those described here, some *disciplinas* have hooks and sharp pieces of metal, like razors, tied into knots in a cord or rope. Many paintings and other illustrations of the Passion also depict the soldiers wielding rods and sticks as they beat Jesus. In contrast to what Anunciación wrote, the Candia version merely states,

---

6. Anunciación, *Luz para saber andar*, 1

7. "Esta es la primera Estacion, es el Pretorio, y Casa de Pilatos, donde fue rigorosamente azotado el Redentor del Mundo, por mano de seis ferozes Soldados, con varas espinosas, con cordeles nudosos, y en ellos abrojos, cadenas, y garfios de de hierro, y le arrancaban la carne con cada azote que le daban." Anunciación, *Luz para saber andar*, 2.

> **Candia**
> First Station—Praetorium. House of Pilate where Jesus our Redeemer was cruelly whipped, crowned with thorns, and condemned to death.[8]

The contents for the first station, and all subsequent stations, also differs fairly significantly between the two guides. The Anunciación devotional consists of a prayer for each station. That is followed by a physical act of kissing the earth and the recitation of a short statement of contrition. For each subsequent station, Anunciación includes the number of steps it is located from the previous stop as part of the general introduction to the new station. On the other hand, the Candia guide is much more complex. It has a meditation, a short poem on the themes of the station, followed by a prayer and a short responsorial between the leader and the other penitents. Thus, the Candia devotional has briefer introductions to each station but more content overall for each one.

Looking at the prayer for the first station, the Anunciación guide has the following prayer:

> **Anunciación**
> O, Tenderest Jesus, that you wished to suffer like a slave, imprisoned and tied in chains, in the presence of the Sacrilegious People [of Jerusalem], awaiting the iniquitous sentence of death that against You was given by the Tyrant Judge [Pilate], I beseech, My Lord, that through your meekness I might mortify My pride such that suffering with humility the affronts of this life, I might remove the prison that my sins have on my soul, and be free with your grace to enjoy eternity with you.[9]

The prayer's goal is to link the imprisonment and torture of Jesus with the effect of sinfulness on the penitent. Through Jesus's meekness in the face of the unjust actions of the crowd and Pilate, the penitent might receive salvation. The language is very convoluted, with several dependent clauses all pointing back to Jesus's sacrifice and suffering. The prayer does not explicitly mention the Jewish people but refers merely to "the Sacrilegious People" (*Sacrilegio Pueblo*), with the implication that it means the Jewish people of Jerusalem. *Pueblo* is a term that can variously refer to the community (or

8. "Pretorio casa de Pilatos donde cruelmente fue azotado Jesus nuestro redemptor, coronado de espinas, y condenado a muerte." Candia, "Del Santo Exercicio," 87.

9. "O Suavisimo Jesus, que quisiste padecer como un Esclavo, con prisiones, y cadenas atado, en presencia del Sacrilegio Pueblo, esperando la iniqua sentencia de muerte, que contra Ti daba el Tyrano Juez. Suplicote, Señor mio, que por esa mansedumbre tuya, mortifique Yo mi sobervia, para que sufriendo con humildad las afrentas de esta vida, se quiten las prisiones de los pecados que hay en mi alma, y libre con gracia te goze en la eterna." Anunciación, *Luz para saber andar*, 2

town), the people themselves, or the race or nationality. Similarly, the prayer does not mention Pilate by name, but calls him "the Tyrant Judge" (*Tyrano Juez*), leaving it up to the penitent to understand the context. Of course, the sentence of death is also referred to as "the iniquitous sentence of death" (*la iniqua sentencia de muerte*) to further emphasize the injustice of it all.

The Anunciación guide, once the prayer is completed, directs participants to kiss the earth, stop for a moment, and then pray a short litany. The leader says, "Lord, I sinned, have mercy on me. We sin, and it weighs on us, have mercy on us."[10] This said, the group again kisses the earth, and then everyone says, "Blessed and praised be the passion and death of our Lord Jesus Christ, and the Clean [Immaculate] Conception of our Lady the Virgin Mary, conceived without original sin from the first instant of her being."[11] Following that brief litany, all rise and continue to the subsequent station. This litany is to be repeated after each station.

The litany, in and of itself, points to the likelihood of a Franciscan author. The Franciscan Order was a primary proponent of the doctrine of the Immaculate Conception of Mary. In modern times, the doctrine is not broadly understood by most non-theologians, but it was very widely advocated, especially by Franciscans, in the early modern period. Quite simply, Jesus was miraculously conceived by agency of the Holy Spirit; that is, Mary became pregnant with Jesus directly by God. But theologians in the Middle Ages wrestled with the problem that while Jesus was conceived through the Holy Spirit in Mary, Mary herself was conceived in the normal way, as a result of the sexual congress of her parents, who are traditionally named Anne and Joachim. This means that Mary would have carried what was seen as the stain of the original sin shared by all humanity, which was transferred through sexual relations. In Christian thinking, original sin began when Adam and Eve rebelled against God. All humans, by virtue of their descent from Adam and Eve, carry that sin. But, the theologians argued, if that were the case for Mary, then Jesus, her son, would also inherit some of that same original sin. The way to avoid the inheritance of sin, they reasoned, is that while Mary was conceived in the normal manner, God suspended any sinfulness in that act, allowing Mary to be conceived without sin. As a result, in the words of the theologians, she was immaculately conceived—conceived without stain. The doctrine did not become official Catholic dogma until 1854.[12] Some of the

10. "Señor, pequé haved misericordia de mi: Pecamos, y nos pesa, tened misericordia de nostros." Anunciación, *Luz para saber andar*, 3.

11. "Bendita, y alabada sea la Pasion, y muerte de nuesto Señor Jesu-Christo, y la Limpia Concepcion de nuestra Señora la Virgen Maria, concebida sin pecado original desde el instante primero de su Ser." Anunciación, *Luz para saber andar*, 3.

12. "Immaculate Conception," *Catholic Encyclopedia*, New Advent, http://www.newadvent.org/cathen/07674d.htm.

early advocates were Franciscans. The doctrine was also quite popular in Spain and the Hispanic world. A common greeting in the early modern Hispanic world was *Ave Maria purísima* (Hail Mary, the purest). The appropriate reply was *sin pecado concebida* (conceived without sin). Consequently, the fact that the litany proclaims the doctrine of the Immaculate Conception of Mary is a small additional indicator of a Franciscan author.

The prayer from the Candia guide for the first station is very different from Anunciación's. It was one of three elements in the commemoration of the station: a meditation, a poem, and then a prayer. Like the Anunciación prayer, it is complex and convoluted. It uses extreme language (in Spanish *-ísimo* endings translate into English as "most . . ." or "-est," e.g., "sweetest"). And it uses some of the vocabulary seen before, such as "iniquitous" and "cruel." Certainly, two of these three elements are hallmarks of the baroque in literature: complex and convoluted language and the use of extremes.

> **Candia**
> My Lord Jesus Christ, who to free me from the most just sentence of eternal death, that I have so deserved for my many faults and sins, [you] wished to be sentenced to the most atrocious death on the Cross. Concede to me, most pious Jesus, that through the admirable patience with which you accepted the iniquitous and cruel sentence, that I might be freed of the rigorous sentence of eternal damnation; and that spending all of my life in sensing and being grateful for your Sacred Passion, and I might merit, at the hour of my death, to hear from your sweetest mouth, those gracious words[:] Come blessed soul, redeemed with my blood, eternally enjoy the manifold fruits of my Redemption in glory.[13]

Just as Anunciación's guide places a small earth-kissing ritual at the conclusion of the prayer, so does Candia's. It differs slightly, however. The instructions ask that everyone say, "We adore you Christ, and we bless you, because through your cross you redeemed the world."[14] Then everyone kisses the ground as a sign of their love and gratefulness to God and to the "Holy Places" (*Santos Lugares*) where Christ suffered. Then the leader says, "Lord, I sinned, have mercy on me[;] We sin, and it weighs on us, have mercy on

13. "Señor mio Jesu-Christo, que por librarme de la justisima sentencia de muerte eterna que tan merecida tenia yo por mis muchas culpas, y pecados, quisiste ser sentenciado a la atrocisima muerte de Cruz. Concedeme piadosisimo Jesus, que por la admirable paciencia con que aceptaste tan iniqua y cruel sentencia, sea yo libre de la rigorosa sentencia de eterna condenacion; y que ocupandome toda mi vida en sentir, y agradecer tu Sagrada Passion, merezca, y en la hora de la muerte oir de tu dulcisima boca, aquellas graciosas palabras. Ven alma bendita, redimida con mi sangre, goza eternamente los copiosos fructos de mi Redempción en la gloria." Candia, "Del Santo Exercicio," 89

14. "Adoramoste Christo, y bendecimoste porque por tu Santa Cruz redimiste el mundo." Candia, "Del Santo Exercicio," 89

us."[15] This latter phrase is the same in the two versions. It is quite interesting that this particular version of prayers for the Stations of the Cross has a reference to the holy places. Clearly the devotion of the Stations had evolved to such a degree that the focus was no longer explicitly on physically re-creating Jerusalem elsewhere but in creating an emotional and spiritual landscape that would imitate Christ's.

Both of the most popular Spanish-language handbooks circulating in New Spain deal with the material that focuses on the observance of the Stations of the Cross, but they do so in slightly different manners. Quite clearly, the Anunciación version is the shorter. It includes only two elements: the description and theme of the station followed by the prayer specific to that particular station. The description of each station and the prayer offered at each station also differ between the two authors. Candia's descriptions and prayers are slightly shorter and more straightforward, but the overall content is longer because of the additional poem. Both versions feature short litanies that involve kissing the ground and a general Act of Contrition, noting that the participants are sinners, that sin troubles them, and that they ask for mercy. The important difference between the two versions is the additional poem found in the Candia version.

Looking at the first station, Candia offers the following poem, which is recited between the thematic description of the station and the prayer for that station.

> Consider, lost soul,
> that in this path so strong,
> a sentence of death was given
> to the Redeemer of life.
>
> But look that he invites you
> to contemplate his Passion,
> and that you might have contrition
> about how much you have sinned
> if you are not to be sentenced
> to eternal condemnation.[16]

Clearly the poetry continues the theme: Pilate sentences Christ to death on the cross, and through this act, Christians are redeemed and saved. Following

---

15. Candia, "Del Santo Exercicio," 89–90. The typeface makes the last line look like "We weigh and it weighs on us," as opposed to "We sin and it weighs on us."

16. "Considera alma perdida,/que ne este passo tan fuerte,/se dio sentencia de muerte,/al Redemptor de la vida:/Pues mira que te combida,/a contemplar su Passion,/y a que tengas contricion/de lo mucho que has pecado,/si no has de ser sentenciado,/a eterna condenacion." Candia, "Del Santo Exercicio," 88–89

the poem, Candia then also provides a short prayer to be said at every station following the thematic prayer:

> My Jesus, my sweet token,
> for being who you are, loved by God,
> it bothers me to have sinned
> but I propose the correction.[17]

Like other poems offered by Candia it consists of short eight-syllable lines, with aa rhyme scheme of *abba*. The tone is light and the wording is succinct. In the world of Spanish letters, poetry with eight or fewer syllables in the line is considered *arte menor* (minor art). The tone associated with *arte menor* is more popular, informal, and not suitable for serious topics. It is odd, then, that Candia would include this type of poetry in his Stations of the Cross manual. One might imagine that poetry of the more serious genre of *arte mayor* (high art, having nine to twelve syllables per line) might be more suitable for considering Christ's Passion.

The Candia version also suggests that penitents add various set prayers following the poetry and the poetic statement of contrition. In particular, the guide indicates that, at this point, the participants should meditate for a moment and then pray the following prayers: one Our Father, one Hail Mary, one Gloria Patri, and others. It does not explicitly stipulate the prayers beyond the three listed but does have an "etc.," suggesting further prayers.[18]

Looking, then, at the Anunciación version of the Stations of the Cross, one can see that each of the fourteen stations consists of an opening statement that describes the scene from the Passion and introduces the themes associated

---

17. "Mi Jesus, mi dulce prenda,/por ser quien sois Dios amado,/me pesa de aver pecado,/mas yo propongo la emmienda." Candia, "Del Santo Exercicio," 89.

18. Candia, "Del Santo Exercicio," 89. The Our Father is also known as the Lord's Prayer since it comes directly from the Gospels of Matthew (6:9–13) and Luke (11:2–4). The most common form is: "Our Father, who art in heaven, hallowed be thy name. Thy kingdom come, thy will be done, on earth as it is in heaven. Give us today our daily bread. Forgive us our trespasses, as we forgive those who trespass against us. [Although the meaning is "forgive us our sins as we forgive those who sin against us," some translations read, "For give us our debts, as we forgive our debtors."] And lead us not into temptation, but deliver us from evil." In some traditions the Lord's Prayer is concluded with a prayer called a doxology, a formulaic praise of God: "For thine is the Kingdom, and the power, and the glory, forever and ever." The Hail Mary is another ancient prayer of praise, in this instance directed at the Virgin Mary: "Hail Mary, full of grace. The Lord is with thee. Blessed art thou among women, and blessed is the fruit of thy womb, Jesus. Holy Mary, Mother of God, pray for us sinners now and at the hour of our death." The name Gloria Patri comes from the Latin form of the prayer, which means, "Glory to the Father." The prayer is a doxology. The general form is as follows: "Glory to the Father, and to the Son, and to the Holy Spirit [Ghost]. As it was in the beginning, is now, and ever shall be, world without end." Each of these prayers is concluded with the sign of agreement or assent: "Amen."

with that station. The prayer elaborates on the themes and more specifically involves the penitent who is practicing the devotion.

As noted in chapter 3, Vetancurt used the Anunciación version as the basis for his translation of the *Via crucis* and not the Candia version. The Nahuatl version is unique in the way it approaches many of the stations. The language that Vetancurt uses to describe certain features of Christianity are also, if not unique, then not very commonly found in other Nahuatl-language texts of the period. A close analysis of the material provides a better understanding of the importance of Vetancurt's Stations of the Cross.

The Nahuatl version produced by Vetancurt has devotional material for each station that includes fixed prayers and sometimes additional material of a spiritual nature, something like a small sermon or meditation, known in Nahuatl as *tenonotztlaliztli* (admonitions). These admonitions might also be called descriptions since they place the station in time and place and give a general introduction to its themes. The text of these pieces is unique in the Nahuatl version, differing in many ways from the Spanish. Nonetheless, the Spanish and the Nahuatl descriptions do have a few features in common. Just as in the Anunciación original, each of these begins with a description of the place, frequently also listing the number of steps from the last stop. The spiritual theme then follows the setting of the scene. These admonitions help participants focus on the essential elements and themes of each station. A prayer then follows each admonition. In both the Spanish and the Nahuatl, the prayer is set off with the introductory word: *Oración* (Prayer) or *tlatlauhtiliztli* (Prayer). These prayers then expand on the theme of the station and find some specific aspect that can be related to the participant's life. At the end of each station is a short litany. Each of these parts will be explored separately.

Since the devotion of the Stations of the Cross emerged at roughly the same time as evangelization began in Mexico, Vetancurt had to create a few new Nahuatl terms for his readers. One needs to recall that although Vetancurt's name appears as the author, it can be assumed that he had a group of Native informants who assisted him in his work, only one of whom has been identified. Thus, although this work will refer to Vetancurt as the author, one needs to recall that he represents a group of people who undoubtedly worked on the project. The most central term that required a Nahuatl equivalent was "station." In order to explain what a station was in this context, the friar both provided a Nahuatl description and at the same time borrowed the Spanish word. For the first station he wrote: "yn Centetli tlatlauhtiliztli netlanquaquetzalistli yn itoca EstaCion" (This is the first kneeling prayer that is called a station).[19] In some instances he chose to keep it all together as a

19. Vetancurt, *Via crucis*, 11.

single, very long word: *tlatlauhtiliztlinetlanquaquetzalistli*.[20] While this term appears at the beginning of each of the stations, later in the work, Vetancurt stopped adding the phrase *yn itoca* (its name is). Looking at the neologism for "station," it is interesting that the Nahuatl word does not necessarily designate a place. Had it done so, it would have ended in a locative such as *-pan* or *-can*. Instead, the phrase is introduced by *o*[*n*]*can* meaning "there," indicating a place.

The Nahuatl text for the description of the first station is clearly derived from the Anunciación edition of the *Via crucis* but has some significantly different elements. The Nahuatl reads as follows:

> **Vetancurt**
> Here begins a kneeling prayer called a station. It is the royal home of judgment of Pilate in the place called Praetorium. It is where and when the six soldiers beat Him to earth with lashes, thorns, and chains. [However,] just four of them repeatedly pushed Him, kicked Him and angrily whipped our beloved Savior. They repeatedly tore apart His precious body with a whip. Then Pilate sentenced Him to death, standing Him up before those who hated Him, the Jews. Very quickly they entwined a knotted whip around His neck, with which they will drag Him and with which they hurried Him along.[21]

The general structure of the Nahuatl is similar to the Spanish: the place (the Praetorian Palace), the six soldiers who beat Jesus, and his savage whipping. But the Nahuatl version provides at least one detail that is absent in the Spanish, namely that a rope or whip was placed around his neck to lead him along the route. This detail is important insofar as it appears in the illustrations that accompany the manuscript, as will be seen in the next chapter.

As was noted earlier, after the description of the station and the introduction to the themes, each of the versions (Candia's, Anunciación's, and Vetancurt's) has a prayer that collects together the themes and applies them to the participant. In English, this type of prayer is called a "collect" because it brings the various themes and ideas together. The Nahuatl prayer, as crafted by Vetancurt for the first station, is as follows:

---

20. Vetancurt, *Via crucis*, 13.

21. "Nicā pehua yn Centetli tlatlauhtiliztli netlanquaquetzalistli yn itoca EstaCion yn itetlatzontequililiztlatoCachan yn pilatos yntoCayoCan Pretorio yn canin yn iquac yn ie ihui chiquaSeme yaoquizque meCatiCa huitzitiCa teluzmeCatica tlali yc oquimohuitequilique San nahui oquimototopehuilique Oquimotetelicxilique Oquimotlahuelhuitequilique yn totlasotemaquixiticatzin OquimomeCatzazayanililique yntlasonaCayotz[in] niman oquimomiquiztlatziotequilili yn Pilatos ynmixpan oquinhualmoquechilili yntecocolicahuan yn Judiosme huel yCihui ca yquechtlantzinco OquilCatzioque yn tetetzilimeCatli yquimohuilanilizque y quimiCihuitilique." Vetancurt, *Via crucis*, 11.

Vetancurt

Alas, O completely sweet one, Jesus! You wanted them to tie you up in the fashion of one of the thieves [or] like a slave is tied up, and they sentenced You to death. May it be Your precious will, on account of Your humble patient suffering, that with Your help I govern my heart and pride. Let me free myself from my sins so that I will live happily and peacefully and so that I will enjoy pardon of sin, and afterwards in Your land of heavenly joy. So be it, Jesus.[22]

The theme of this prayer is that just as Jesus was bound and imprisoned by the Roman guards so, too, should the penitents bind up their earthly desires and prideful hearts and live without sin. This translation follows the Anunciación version quite closely with regard to the overriding themes. Nonetheless, it loses two very specific features of the Spanish. These have to do with calling the Jews a "Sacrilegious People" and referring to Pilate as a "Tyrant Judge."j Neither of these is present at all in the Nahuatl.

Following each station, in the Anunciación and Vetancurt versions, two short prayers are to be performed before moving on to the next station. The prayers also have some instructions in both the Spanish and Nahuatl versions. They are quite similar between the two languages:

Anunciación

Lord, I have sinned; have mercy on me. We have sinned and it weighs on us, have mercy on us.

Blessed and praised be the Passion and death of our lord Jesus Christ, and the Pure Conception of our Lady the Virgin Mary, conceived without original sin from the first moment of her being. Amen.[23]

Vetancurt

O our Lord, O God, I have greatly sinned; pardon me. We have greatly sinned; pardon us. For I very much regretted [the sins I committed] in Your presence.

Perfectly praise the suffering and precious death of our beloved honored Savior Jesus Christ and His pure birth from the royal virgin Saint Mary whom original sin never reached. So be it, Jesus.[24]

---

22. "yio CenquizCatzopeliCatzintle Jesus Ca ticmonequiliti yn iuh Seme ychteque omitzimomayilpilique yn quename tlahcohtli mayilipilos yhuan omitzmomiquiztlatzōtequililique Auh ma xicmotlasonequiltitzino ynpāpatzincao yn mocnotlapaCayiohuilitzin ynic motepalehuiliztiCatzinco nicpachoS yn noyolo yn nonepoalis ma yitechcopa ninotoma yn notlatlacolo ynic paca yocoxca ninemiz ynic nicnomasehuiz yn tetlapopolhuilistli Satepan yn motlaltzinco yn ilhuiCac papaquilistli ma yhui mochihuan Jesus." Vetancurt, *Via crucis*, 12.

23. "Señor, pequé haved misericordia de mi: Pecamos, y nos pesa, tened misericordia de nosotros. . . . Bendita, y alabada sea la Pasion, y muerte de nuestro Señor Jesu-Christo, y la Limpia Concepcion de nuestra Señora la Virgen Maria, concebida sin pecado original desde el instante primero de su ser." Anunciación, *Luz para saber andar*, 3. From this point forward, all Spanish quotations are taken from this Anunciación text.

Aside from a few turns of phrase and items that were implied in the Nahuatl, this is essentially a direct translation. The instructions that accompany these brief prayers are especially evocative on several different levels. In the Spanish and the Nahuatl, the faithful are instructed to kiss the ground, stop as a group for a few moments, and then say the first prayer. Following that, the participants are to kiss the ground again and then read the next prayer aloud. Following the closing prayer, the participants are to rise (one assumes from a kneeling position) and walk to the next station.

Kissing the ground is not currently a common action for Christians, although in recent decades several popes have kissed the ground upon landing in a new country. In the Middle Ages and early modern period it was not uncommon.[25] In the devotion of the Stations of the Cross, we might think that kissing the ground is a reminder that the Way of the Cross is a sacred route, and thus kissing the ground would signify that one is walking on holy ground. For a seventeenth-century Nahua, the ritual might have been perceived as curious, indeed. The Spanish instructions read, "Upon saying this, they will kiss the earth, and everyone will stop for a bit. . . ."[26] In Nahuatl it is "Niman otennamiquiztlalli . . ." (Then the earth is kissed). And then, following the first prayer, the Spanish instructions indicate, "This said, they will kiss the earth again," and in Nahuatl, "occepa otenamiquiztlalli," (Again the earth is kissed).[27]

In the pre-Hispanic world of the Nahua, a very common gesture of greeting and showing respect for a lord or an important place was to touch one's fingers to the dirt and then put them in the mouth, seemingly eating dirt. The small ritual was known as *tlalcualiztli* (the eating of dirt/earth).[28] In the early years of the evangelization of the Natives, the missionaries became aware of pre-Hispanic traditions that had cognates in Christian practice. Generally, the friars tolerated those that could be modified easily to Christian practice,

---

24. "toteCuioe Diose Ca CenCa huel onihueytlatlaco ma xinechmotlapopolhuilitzino Ca CeCa huel otitlatlacoque ma xitechmotlapopolhuili Ca CenCa huel oninoyolotequipacho mixpantzinco . . . ma CenquisCayectenehualo yn itlayiohuilitzin yhuan yntlasomiquilitzin yn totlasomahuiztemaquixitiCatzin JesuChr[is]to yhuan ychipahuaCatlaCatililoCatzin yn tlatoCaychpochhtli Santa maria ynnayc ytetzinco oaCic yn tlatlacolpeuhCayotli." Vetancurt, *Via crucis*, 12–13.

25. This might have its origins in Scripture, specifically in Isaiah 49:23. The prophet foretells the savior, saying, "Kings shall be your foster fathers, and their queens your nursing mothers. With their faces to the ground they shall bow down to you, and lick the dust of your feet."

26. "Dicho esto, besarán la tierra, y se pararán todos un poco." Anunciación, *Luz para saber andar*, 2

27. "Dicho esto, besarán la tierra otra vez." Anunciación, *Luz para saber andar*, 3. Vetancurt, *Via crucis*, 12–13.

28. Sahagún, *Primeros memoriales*, 71.

such as infant baptism. But in other instances, the missionaries were very wary of Native customs. Examples of this wariness were prohibitions against the consumption of sacred foods like amaranth, which was used to make divine images that were later eaten, sometimes with the local fermented beverage, known in modern times as pulque. This ritual was simply too close to the Christian sacrament of the Eucharist. Thus, it is surprising to find included in the Stations of the Cross what could easily be interpreted as a pagan ritual: kissing the dirt in the manner of the old *tlalqualiztli* ritual.

The Second Station: The Cross Is Laid upon Him

The second station focuses on Christ's taking up the cross on the road to Calvary. According to the descriptions, it was located twenty-one steps from the Praetorian Palace where Jesus was condemned. The themes of the station focus on the weight of the cross and Jesus's difficulty in carrying it. There are also references to the guards mocking Jesus: stripping him of his garment, dressing him in robes, stripping him again, whipping him, and placing the crown of thorns on his head. Anunciación offers this description:

> **Anunciación**
> This is the second Station, that consists of twenty-one steps, that the Lord walked from the Praetorium of Pilate to the place where they put the serious weight of the cross, on which he was to be Crucified, on the wounded shoulders of our most beloved Lamb Jesus. In order to lay it on him, they stripped him of his old and torn clothing, that they had placed on him in jest and derision, when they crowned him with thorns, having removed this Crown from him with cruelty [to lay the cross on him], they put it on him again with intense pain.[29]

As with all the descriptions in the Spanish version, Anunciación outlines the themes of the station and places it geographically within the Passion's route. Some of the important details include the fact that the cross was laid on Jesus after he was stripped of the royal robes that the guards used to mock him. Traditionally Jesus was then dressed again in his own robe, although this particular description is somewhat confusing in that regard (this robe will reappear later in the devotion). Lastly, central to the station is the act of put-

29. "Esta es la segunda Estacion, que consta de veinte y un pasos, que anduvo el Señor hasta ella, desde el Pretorio de Pilatos y el lugar donde a nuestro amantisimo Cordero Jesus le pusieron en sus lastimados ombros el grave peso de la Cruz, en que havia de ser Crucificado; y para ponersela, le desnudaron de la vestidura vieja, y rota, que le pusieron por burla, y escarnio, quando le coronaron de espinas, haviendole quitado para esto la Corona con crueldad, y se la bolvieron a poner con inmenso dolor." Anunciación, *Luz para saber andar*, 3.

ting the crown of thorns on Jesus in mockery of the title "the King of the Jews," which had been popularly given to him by virtue of his reception as the Messiah or Savior.

Vetancurt, in the Nahuatl version of this station, focuses on the same themes but with some notable exceptions:

Vetancurt
The second place of kneeling prayers called a station. Our beloved Savior was walking about; it was twenty-one steps. Here is where they put on the neck of our beloved Savior Jesus Christ the very heavy crossed sticks, the cross. In order to properly set it on Him they first put on Him a garment, then they adjusted it on Him. They put the red worn-out blanket on Him when He was being made sport of. Finally, they again put His garment on Him and again on top of His head they laid sticks and thorns, a round crown of thorns. These thorns painfully and repeatedly entered in many places, causing His blood to flow forth.[30]

As will be discussed below, in this instance Vetancurt uses the neologism for the Cross: *Cuauhnepanoli Cruz* (Crossed wood, Cross). While the Spanish version describes Jesus being stripped of his robe, here a tattered red robe is put on him, again to mock his kingly reputation. The description gets confusing regarding taking clothes off and putting clothes on. The Spanish version strips him of his old robe, implying that he carried the cross stripped down. But the Nahuatl version clearly has him donning an old tattered robe again. This, too, is in keeping with iconography of a robed Jesus carrying the cross, as will be seen. In many paintings, engravings, and sculptures of Christ on the road to Calvary, he is depicted as wearing a robe, while other images also present him as stripped down.

Anunciación offers up the prayer associated with this station so that the penitents might internalize the experience and heighten their personal identification with it.

Anunciación
Oh Supreme King of the Heavens, that you suffered having been handed over to the will of the Jews, in order to be cruelly tormented, and you

30. "ynic OC Can tlatlatlauhtiliznetlaquaquetzaliztli yn itoca estaCion Cenpoalli yhuan Se y tlacxineanaliztli Ca monenemilititia yn totlasotemaquixitiCatzin niCan Cani yn oquimoquechpanolltilique yn totlasotemaquixtiCatzin Jesu Chr[i]sto yn CenCa yetecCatzintli Cuauhnepanoli Cruz Auh ynic quiyectlalilizque achtopa oquimoquitililique yn tlaquentzin ye niman oCaquilitique yn chichilitic tilimasoli oquimoquentilique yn iquac yhCatzinco omahuilitequi Auh yequene oc Cepa oquimoquentilique yn itlaquentzin yhuan oc Cepa ycpactzinCo oquimomanilique yn tlacotli yn huitzintli yn tepeyotli yn xocohuitzyahuali cexna huel tecocoCayotiCa miecca oCaCallactia yni huitzintli ynic omeyancuinli yn iEsnoquihuilitzin." Vetancurt, *Via crucis*, 13–14.

> received the grave weight of the Cross on your wounded shoulders, hearing the rabid voices of your enemies, I beseech you, Lord of my soul, that with your grace I might resign my will to yours and that happily I might take up the Cross of penance, such that doing it truly for my sins I might see you always in Heaven.[31]

This prayer repeats word for word some of the themes of the description, specifically receiving the "serious weight" of the cross on his "wounded shoulders." While in the previous station reference was made to the people of Jerusalem as a "Sacrilegious People," in this prayer they are clearly identified as Jews and then, a bit later, as enemies with rabid voices. This anti-Semitism was a component of many Passion-related texts well into the twentieth century. In the prayer, the penitent is asked to consider penance as the equivalent of Jesus's cross: an unpleasant obligation.

The Nahuatl version of this prayer parallels the Spanish edition quite closely. As was seen above, it uses the neologism of "Crossed wood" to describe the cross. The prayer asks that the penitents be allowed to complete the devotion to better prepare themselves for the penance needed to take up the burden of a godly life in order to reap the benefits of heaven:

> **Vetancurt**
> Alas, O only God, O Master of Heaven, O precious ruler Jesus! You wanted to cast Yourself into the hatred of the scoundrel-like Jews who took You into custody and loaded onto Your shoulders the crossed sticks of wood, the very heavy cross. I implore You: Help me so that I will bring to a [successful] conclusion and will patiently receive penance so that I will take on the burden of the proper life of heaven as You wish. And with You, afterwards, You will give me heavenly joy. So be it, Jesus. O our Lord God.[32]

While the Nahuatl does describe the Jews as "scoundrel-like," it lacks some of the more negative descriptions of the Spanish version, which also harkens

31. "O Rey Supremo de los Cielos, que sufriste ser entregado a la voluntad de los Judios, para ser cruelmente atormentado, y recibiste el grave peso de la Cruz sobre tus lastimados ombros, oyendo las rabiosas vozes de tus enemigos: Ruegote, Señor de mi alma, que con tu gracia resigne mi voluntad en la tuya, y que tome gustoso la Cruz de la penitencia, para que haciendola verdadera[mente] por mis pecados, te vea siempre en el Cielo." Anunciación, *Luz para saber andar*, 4.

32. "iyo ySeltzin teotzintle ylhuicacqueCatzintle tlasotlatohuane JeSuS yn oticmonequilitin yn ipan timomayahuitzinoz yn iteCayecocoli yn tlahueliloque Judiosme yn omitzmomaylPilique yhuan Omitzmamaltilique yn quauhnepanoli CenCa yetecatzintli Cruz niiehmitznotlatlauhlitla ma xinechmopalehuilitzino ynic nictzioquixitiz nicpaCaseliz yn tlamaCehuiliztl ynic nicnomamaltis ylhuicac yecnemiliztli yn iuh ticmonequilitia Auh satepan motlaqmrtzinco tinechmomaquiliz yn ilhuicac papaquiliztli ma y mochihua JeSuS t[o]te[Cuioe] D[io]se." Vetancurt, *Via Crucis*, 14–15.

to the "rabid voices of your enemies." But just as in the Spanish, the basic theme of the prayer, and the station in general, is that as the faithful go through life, they, too, carry a burden, just as Jesus carried his cross. This sentiment harkens to a passage from the Gospel of Matthew in which Jesus admonishes his followers to practice abstinence and shoulder their own personal burdens in order to follow him. "If any want to become my followers, let them deny themselves and take up their cross and follow me." In this prayer, Vetancurt follows a well-established tradition of using the word *ilhuica* to signify "heaven." This word originally simply signified the sky, but it was chosen in the sixteenth century to serve as a stand-in for the Christian heaven.[33]

The Third Station: His First Fall

The first of the three falls is the topic of the third station. Just as the first station's introduction and prayer focus on the weight and burden of the cross, this station continues to elaborate on that theme. Similarly, Christ's wounds also remain a focus throughout the devotion and are mentioned in this station. The Anunciación version describes the scene in this manner:

> **Anunciación**
> This is the third station, that consists of eighty steps, that to there the Lord Jesus walked. It is the place where his Divine Majesty, walking with his Holy Cross on his back, moaning and sighing, almost without being able to move his feet because of the great weakness that he carried because of the great speed, with which that vile infamous scoundrel tormented him. He fell to earth under the Holy Cross, and, with the strength of the blow that it gave him, opened again his sores and wounds [with] much blood flowing from them with the greatest of sorrows and pains.[34]

The passage is a bit obscure, since it is not entirely clear who the "vile infamous scoundrel" is. Looking at other devotional handbooks for the Stations, one can conclude that Anunciación was probably referring to one of the guards who accompanied Jesus. Other versions also note that Jesus had a rope tied around his neck. The Nahuatl version, for instance, calls it a whip tied about his neck. Whip or rope, it was useful to make Jesus keep up the

33. Schwaller, "The *ilhuica* of the Nahua."

34. "Esta es la tercera Estacion, que consta de ochenta pasos, que hasta ella anduvo el Señor Jesus: es el lugar donde caminando su Divina Magestad con la Santa Cruz acuestas, gimiendo y suspirando, sin poder casi mover los pies, por la flaqueza grande que llevaba con la grande prisa, que aquella vil, infame canalla le atormentaba, cayo en tierra, debajo de la Santa Crtuz, y con la fuerza del golpe que dio, se abrieron de nuevo las llagas, y heridas, corriendo mucha sangre de ellas, con grandisimos dolores, y penas." Anunciación, *Luz para saber andar*, 4.

pace. Anunciación also suggests that this was one of the causes of the fall. The Candia text makes it even more explicit. It begins in a manner similar to the Anunciación version, but at the fall explains,

Candia
[A]nd His Divine Majesty, not being able to stand because of the many sorrows and weakness, the cruel and rabid ministers [guards] pulled on the rope and beat and wounded him again, saying many expletives and blasphemies.[35]

Vetancurt translated the third station following the Anunciación model fairly closely. Both locate it at eighty steps from the previous stop. Jesus moans and sighs in both. Being exhausted, he falls. The guards in the Nahuatl version are referred to as "those who hated Him."

Vetancurt
The third place of kneeling prayers [called] a station. Our God was walking around; it was eighty steps. Here is where with weeping and sighs our Savior bears the cross on His shoulders. He could absolutely no longer raise it so that He completely fainted, for those who hated Him drove Him on until He fell to the earth at the foot of the cross. He firmly fell to earth, His flayed [skin] opened, and His precious blood repeatedly poured out.[36]

The prayer in the Anunciación version that follows this description makes a connection between Christ's fall to the earth and his lifting up the sins and troubles of the world. It also contrasts the harshness of Jesus's treatment with the softness of the "fruit of the Cross," which is a metaphor for salvation. Thus, in keeping with baroque artistic sensibilities, there are contrasts of up and down, harsh and soft, light and dark, all expressed through the somewhat gruesome matrix of the descriptions of Christ's sufferings.

Anunciación
O most beloved Jesus, who, tired with the cross, [which] made you fall to the earth with its weight, in order that we might know the gravity of

---

35. "Y no pudiendose levanter su Divina Magestad, por los muchos dolores, y flaqueza, los crueles, y rabiosos Ministros, le tiraban de la soga, le daban nuevos golpes, y heridas, diciendole muchos improperios y blasfemias." Candia, "Del Santo Exercicio," 92.

36. "ynic yexCa netlaquaquetzialistli tlatlatlauhtiliztli EstaCion yn ohualmonenemilititia yn toteotzin Nauhpohuali ychixineanaliztli niCa Cani choquiztiCa elCiCihuiliztica quimimamalia yn Cruz yn totemaquixiticatzin Auh Ca huel ÇenCa acmo quimehuilia ynic CenCa ye omosotlahualtitzino ynic quimototoquiliaya yntecocoliCahuan asta tlalpa omohuetzitin ytzintlan yn + Cruz huel chiCahuac Omotlahuitectzino yc Çenohuian omoya[Catia?] omotlatlapo yn ixipehualitzin huel CenCa yc ohualnonoquiuhtia yn itlasoyesiotzin." Vetancurt, *Via crucis*, 15.

our sins, represented in this beam. I beseech your Divine clemency that with the help of your grace blame be raised from me and that firm and stable in the fulfillment of your Commandments, I will not stop the mortification of my body, such that forever loving you in life I might enjoy the soft fruits of the Cross in your Glory.[37]

The Spanish word choice and syntax reflect the baroque. The syntax is very broken, with multiple clauses that add layers of description. Similarly, in referring to the cross, the text calls it a "beam." The word Anunciación uses is *Madero*. In the masculine, the word means "a squared and worked piece of wood." The feminine form of the word in Spanish, *madera*, is the generic term for "wood."

The cross figures as the focal point for the translation of the prayer in the Vetancurt version. The relationship between the heavy cross and the weight of sins is made explicit in the Nahuatl version. It closely follows the Spanish but has some unique differences.

Vetancurt
Alas, perfectly lovable Jesus! So that we would recognize the heaviness of our sins (for the very heavy cross You bore on Your shoulders because of us is just a stand-in for them) You fell because of Your weariness at the foot of the holy cross. I implore You: with the help of Your precious firm will, Your grace, may I quickly rise so that Your divine will shall be realized. Here I will live in the penance You want until I enjoy the final fruits of the holy Cross You revealed to me, [i.e.,] heavenly joy, glory.[38]

Perhaps the most striking feature of the prayer is that it does not end with the traditional closing phrase of "So be it Jesus," or simply "So be it" (*Ma yuh mochihua*). In this prayer he uses a very different phrase, "māchā ma cenquizca totecuioe diose" (Perfectly praise, O Our Lord God). In this phrase, the copyist or Vetancurt has contracted a long phrase into just a few syllables. *Cenquizca* is not used grammatically here, indicating that something might

37. "O Amantisimo Jesus, que fatigado con la Cruz, te obligó a caer en tierra con el peso de ella, par que conociesemos la gravedad de nuestros pecados, figurados en ese Madero: Ruego a tu celemencia Divina, que con el auxilio de tu gracia, me levante de la culpa; y que firme, y estable en el cumplimiento de tus Mandamientos, no dexe jamas la mortificacion de mi cuerpo, para que firme siempre en amarte en la vida, goze los frutos suaves de la Cruz en tu Gloria." Anunciación, *Luz para saber andar*, 5.

38. "yio CenquizCatlasotlani Jesus moCiahuizticCatzinco ytzintlan otimohuetziti yn santa Cruz ynic tiquiximatizque yn ietiliz yn totlatlacoll Ca san quixiptlayotia yn CenCa yeteCatzintli Cruz yn topampatica oticmomamaltitzinno nimitzinotlatlauhtilia ma ytepalehuiliztica yn motlasochiCaliztlanequilitzintli yn moGraCiatzin ma yhuan ninehuantiquetzi ynic neltiz yn moteotlanequilitzin niCa ye ipan ninemiz yn ticmonequilitia yn tlamaCehualiztli ynic ixquichiCa nicnomasehuiz yn itzōpeuCa yn itlaquilotzi yn santa Cruz ynnotinechmonextilili yn ilhuiCac papaquiliztli yn la gloria," Vetancurt, *Via crucis*, 16.

be missing, especially since the *ma* indicates an indirect command. In all likelihood it is *ma cenquizcayectenehualo*, making it something like "May our Lord God be perfectly praised."[39]

The Fourth Station: He Meets His Blessed Mother

Jesus's meeting with his mother was the theme of the fourth station. It became an extremely popular moment in early modern devotions despite lacking a solid scriptural basis. The paragraph that sets the scene describes Jesus and Mary almost like lovers. Like other meditations, it is filled with the use of superlatives. Lastly, it states that Mary then followed her son all the way to Calvary. The scriptural sources do indicate that Mary appeared later at the crucifixion, but there is nothing to indicate whether she followed Jesus or took a different route or arrived later. The description reads,

> **Anunciación**
> This is the fourth station, which consists of sixty steps that to reach there the Lord walked. It is the place where our Most Innocent Lamb going with the Most Holy Cross on his back, met his Most Holy Mother, sad and afflicted. And seeing those two fine lovers, their hearts transposed by sorrow and anguish. And with this pain the Lady went behind her beloved Son all the way to Calvary, not losing sight of him with great pain in seeing him so despised.[40]

The prayer that accompanies the station also focuses on Mary. It has references to the symbolism of the Seven Sorrows. The prayer specifically refers to the "cruel bolts [arrows] of sorrow."[41] The iconography of Our Lady of Sorrows (Nuestra Señora de los Dolores) frequently depicts Mary having seven arrows or swords piercing her heart. Thus, the prayer provides a link between the Stations of the Cross and the competing devotion of the Seven Sorrows of Mary. As noted earlier, seven is a common and powerful number in the Judeo-Christian tradition. In Christianity, in addition to the Seven Sorrows of Mary, there are also the seven deadly sins and seven cardinal virtues.

---

39. My thanks go to Louise Burkhart, who assisted me with this and made this suggestion. Personal communication, January 14, 2021.

40. "Esta es la quarta Estacion, que consta de sesenta pasos que hasta ella anduvo el Señor; y es el lugar donde yendo nuestro Innocentisimo Cordero con la Santisima Cruz acuestas, encontró con su Santisima Madre, triste, y afligida; y mirandose aquellos dos amantes, quedaron sus corazones traspasados de dolor, y angustia; y con esta pena se fue esta Señora tras su Hijo amado hasta el Monte Calvario, no perdiendole la vista, con grande pena de verle tan despreciado." Anunciación, *Luz para saber andar*, 5.

41. "[C]rueles saetas de dolor." In Spanish *saeta* refers to the arrow shot from a crossbow, which in English is more specifically called a bolt. In Spanish, a *saeta* is also an ejaculatory song in praise of the Virgin or Jesus performed during Holy Week processions.

And, as was seen, there was a competing devotion of the Seven Falls of Jesus. This station also highlights some of the rhetorical tools common of baroque literature. One of these is the piling up and adding on of descriptors. It also demonstrates another hallmark of baroque literature, which is a series of parallel constructions describing a single event. The prayer is as follows:

> **Anunciación**
> O, mother, the most afflicted of all women, through the cruel bolts of sorrow that pierced your heart, gazing on Jesus, your Son, the light of his eyes eclipsed, his Face uglied, his Body denigrated, his Divine Head with thorns wounded, his bones from the hard weight of the Cross tormented, by the Jews reproached, by men disgraced: I beseech thee, Afflicted Mother, that I was the cause, with my sins, of your sorrows, that I cry bitterly such that purged with confession and penance, I might be admitted into the Realm of Glory.[42]

This translation into English focuses on the parallels, although it does not scan fluidly. Nonetheless, it is clear that the prayer includes a series of seven sufferings that Christ endured using the past participles: eclipsed, uglied, denigrated, wounded, tormented, reproached, and disgraced. It is probably not a coincidence that the prayer has a series of seven assaults. It is also notable that Anunciación uses the phrase "Realm of Glory" in order to refer to heaven, literally the "Fatherland of Glory." In the seventeenth century the idea of fatherland, *patria*, was intimately linked to one's home and family roots. The expression personalizes heaven.

A feeling for the differences in translation between the Nahuatl and the Spanish can be seen in the introduction for this station.

> **Vetancurt**
> There is where His weeping mother Saint Mary and her afflicted beloved son recognized themselves on the road and met face to face. How they mutually loved each other! Darkness broke, like a big thorn that quickly pierced through her heart; it was a great affliction of the heart. Even though she did not wipe His face, she follows Him with weeping until He reaches the top of the mountain [called] Calvary.[43]

---

42. "O Madre la mas afligida de las mugeres, por las crueles saetas de dolor, que traspasaron tu corazon, mirando a Jesus tu Hijo, eclypsada la luz de sus ojos, afeado su Rostro, denegrido su Cuerpo, atormentados sus huesos con el duro peso de la Cruz, baldonado de los Judios, y hecho oprobio de los hombres: Ruegote, Madre afligida, que pues fui la causa, con mis pecados, de tus dolores, los llore amargamente, para que purgados con la cenfesion, y penitencia, sea admitido en la Patria de la Gloria." Anunciación, *Luz para saber andar*, 6.

43. "Ca ye niCan ynic nauhCan netlaquaquetzaliztli EstanCion ohualmonenemilititia yn totlasotemaquixtiCatzin yepohuali yhuan matlactli tlacxineanaliztli ōCan Cani omixi-

Clearly the sentiments of the introductions are nearly identical, focusing on the relationship between mother and son. They differ from one another in only the smallest details. The Nahuatl adds an environment of darkness and notes that Mary did not wipe her son's face. On the other hand, the Spanish notes that Mary felt anguish at seeing her son despised. Vetancurt might have selected the detail about wiping his face in order to heighten the effect of the sixth station and Jesus's encounter with Veronica whose peculiar role in the Stations of the Cross is to wipe his face with her cloth.

The Nahuatl version of the prayer for the fourth station also focuses closely on Mary and her reaction to seeing her child tortured and abused by the punishment meted out on him. There is a very interesting play on the theme of darkness in that darkness was on him and his face was blackened:

> **Vetancurt**
> Alas, O merciful precious honored mother, O poor Saint Mary! You surpassed absolutely all women in weeping and heartfelt bitterness when you saw your youngest child, your only child, darkness on Him, His honored face blackened, His fresh body ripped to shreds, thorns piercing His head and His bones going numb with the great weight of the holy cross! And when the Jews dishonored Him, the people of the earth idly laughed. He became our God. O my beloved mother, since I have pained you with my sins may it be your precious will (because of what you suffered) that as your sadness pained you, may likewise my sins worry me so that I will merit and enjoy confession and pardon of sin; thus I will be purified here on earth and afterwards over there in heaven, the place of eternal riches, glory.[44]

The references to blackness and darkness are ways to parallel in Nahuatl the ugliness and disfigurement described in the Spanish version. But the Nahu-

---

matque OtlicCa omixinamictzinoque yn ichoquiznatzin santa maria yhuan yn itonehuiliztlasoconetzin Auh yn queni Omonepantlasotlatzinohuaya ytlapantzinco otlayohuac yn iuhqui Cenhueyhuitztli Onalquiztiquiz yn iolotzin yn huey yolopatzimiquilitzin Auh yn maCihui ynnamo oquimixipolihui Ca choquiztica oquimotepotzitolitia yn no quixquichCa maxilititiuh yn tepeticpac y CallVaro." Vetancurt, *Via crucis*, 17.

44. "iyo ycnohuatlasomahuizchoquiznatzine Santa mariatzine chOquiztzicA yolchichiCaliztica ynnotiquinmopanahuili yn Cenmixiquichitin yn Cihuan yn iquac oticmotili yn moxocoyotzin yn moCenteconetzin ynpantzinco otexyoatiquiz ynic otlitliehileuehtia yn imahuizxayaCatzin Otziatzayantia ynCeliCatlanaCayotzin onanalquiztia y huiztli yn itech ytzinotecontzin oÇeÇepoCatia yn iomiotzin yn iCa yn huey yetiliz yn sa[n]ta Cruz Auh ynic oquimahuizpoloque yn Jodiosme yn mahttizhuilihuetziquiz yn tlaticpac tlaca Omochihuitzino yn toteotzin ô notlasonantzine Canel Ca nehuatli yn notlatlacolltiCa ônimitzinoyoltonehuili ma xicmotlasonequiliti ypāpatzinco ynnoticmiohuilititzino yn queni omitzymoyoltonehuili yn moyoltequipacholiztzin ma Sa no yuhqui nechtequipacho yn notlatlacoll ynic nicnomaÇehuiz yn neyolcuitiliztli tetlapopolhuiliztiCa ynic niChipahualoz y niCan tlalticpac Auh satepan yn onpalhuicac neÇetlamachtoloyan yn gloria ma yUh mochihua," Vetancurt, *Via crucis*, 17–18.

atl does not provide the sevenfold description of Jesus, limiting it to just four: face blackened, body ripped to shreds, thorns piercing his head, and bones going numb. One phrase in the Nahuatl that particularly stands out is "yn mahttizhuilihuetziquiz yn tlaticpac tlaca" (people of the earth idly laughed). This creates a powerful contrast between Jesus, who is hideously disfigured and sorely treated, and the people who laugh in a carefree and idle manner.

The Fifth Station: Simon of Cyrene Is Made to Bear the Cross

The meeting with Simon of Cyrene is the theme of the fifth station. Unlike many of the stations, there is biblical evidence for the encounter. All three of the Synoptic Gospels (Matthew, Mark, and Luke) have accounts of Simon being forcibly recruited by the guards to help carry the cross for Jesus. This is an important moment in the Passion both because it is grounded in the Bible and also because an outsider was forcibly made to help Jesus. Again, the guards are anonymous in the description of the station. They are merely present in the fact that the verbs are plural. In this sense, it closely parallels the third station in that the forces of evil are nameless and faceless and thus very menacing.

> **Anunciación**
> This is the fifth station, which consists of sixty one steps, that to it the Lord walked, and it is a place where they enlisted Simon of Cyrene that he might help carry the Cross for our Savior, not moved by piety that they had for his Majesty, but fearing that he not die on the road, because they saw him inclining to earth because of the great weight of the Cross, with his swollen eyes, and blind from tears and blood, [with a] slow step because of weakness, and with knees trembling, following the two Thieves who were judged with his Majesty.[45]

The nameless guards are depicted as cruel. They force Simon of Cyrene to carry the cross, not out of altruism towards Christ, but rather out of self-interest to the guards: they did not want Jesus to die along the way.

The Nahuatl version of the encounter with Simon of Cyrene also closely parallels the Spanish. They clearly differ in the number of steps. A discussion

45. "Esta es la quinta Estacion, que consta de sesenta y un pasos, que hasta ella anduvo el Señor, y es el lugar donde alquilaron a Simon Cyrineo, para que ayudase a llevar la Cruz a nuestro Redentor, no movidos de piedad, que de su Magestad tuvieron, sino temiendo no se les muriese en el camino, porque le veian, que caminaba con el Cuerpo muy inclinado a la tierra, por el peso grande de la Cruz, con los ojos hinchados, y como ciegos de lagrymas, y de la sangre, el paso lento, por la flaqueza, y con las rodillas temblando, siguiendo a los dos Ladrones, que ajusticaron con su Magestad." Anunciación, *Luz para saber andar*, 6–7.

of Nahuatl and numbers will be found later in this chapter. Clearly, in Nahuatl the locative name "of Cyrene" is partially phonetically rendered as "Cixineo." Nahuatl does not have the sound of the letter *r*, and the sound value of the *x* in Nahuatl is *sh*. Thus, the Nahuatl would be pronounced "see-she-NAY-oh."

> **Vetancurt**
> The fifth place of kneeling [prayers called] a station. Our beloved Savior was walking about; it was seventy-one steps. Here is where they lifted the body of Simon Cixineo [Simon the Cyrene] so that He will help our Savior. He is the first. They were not compassionate; the laborer did it just because of his fear that He would not suffer from faintness on the road. Because He showed the heaviness of the cross to others it is as though He was about to suffer. His face greatly swells up with His tears and His blood, His eyes completely blind. [?] and they came to severely judge Him; the two thieves next to Him will be judged [too].[46]

The Nahuatl is especially complicated because Vetancurt wanted to show both Jesus's divine and human natures. As God, he was omnipotent and capable of enduring any suffering. But as a human, he was subject to all human frailty. To bridge this theological gap, Vetancurt had phrases such as: "Because He showed the heaviness of the cross to others it is as though He was about to suffer." On the other hand, Simon acted because he was ordered by the guards, but also because he feared that Jesus might faint. In both the Spanish and Nahuatl accounts, the result of the torment was purely human and physical: Jesus's face swelled; tears and blood from the crown of thorns blinded him. Lastly, both sources mention the two thieves that traditional sources recount were crucified with Jesus. The theme of thieves appears in the prayer for the first station and reappears in the twelfth station describing the actual crucifixion. While the Synoptic Gospels mention the two thieves, it is only at the actual crucifixion. There is no indication that they might have accompanied Jesus in his walk.

The Spanish prayer corresponding to this station makes the point that Simon's example of helping Jesus during his Passion can serve as an example to Christians of all eras. Simon was, in effect, a representative of all who would

46. "ynic maCuilCan netlaquaquetzaliztli EstaCiOn ohualmonenemilititia yn totlasotemaquixiticatzin yepoali yhuan matlatli oCen = tlacxineanaliztli niCan cani oquitlaquehueuhque yn Simon Cixineo ynic quimopalehuiliz yn totemaquixiticatzin ynic Çe amo teyxnoytaliztli ynnoquichiuhque San imauhCaCopa yn milichiuhqui ynnotetlaCamac ypāpan Amo otlica mosotlauhCamiquiliz yeiCa quimotililiaya yn ietiliz yn santa Cruz ynuhquima ye moÇiauhcopanaltiznequi ye huel opoposahua yn ixayaCatzin yxayotica yhuan yestica yn ixitelolotzin huel ye mioCahualtitihui ye mohuihui Oquilitinelan yhuan yn mohuicatihuitzie quimotequitziotoquilitihuitzie Omentin yn ichteque ynahuactzinco tlatziôntequililozque." Vetancurt, *Via crucis*, 19.

seek to help Christ. Specifically, the prayer likens Simon's assistance to the devotion of the Stations of the Cross itself.

> **Anunciación**
> Most Loving Jesus, that with your burning charity you carried along the road to Calvary the very heavy cross on your fatigued shoulders, and you wanted that in the person of the Cyrene, we would help you to carry it [the Cross], such that through this means we might participate in these treasures that are encompassed in the exercise of the Holy Cross. I beseech you, Lord, that with enflamed devotion and with a fervent spirit, you sear me with the cross of my denial of myself and take me away from my vicious customs so that by following your steps I might achieve the eternal pleasures of Heaven"[47]

The Spanish version presents a series of images based on heat. Phrases such as burning charity, enflamed devotion, fervent prayer, and sear all convey notions of heat and passion. This might well be in contrast with the pleasant notion of heaven, where there is no pain or suffering.

A comparison of the Nahuatl and Spanish versions shows that while they end in very similar phrases, the opening lines differ. The two also elaborate different themes.

> **Vetancurt**
> Alas, O You completely loving one, Jesus! It is just because of Your loving charity that You wanted to go carrying on Your shoulders Your entirely heavy crossed sticks of wood, this holy cross which made Your precious shoulders black and blue and inflicted burning pain on them. And You wanted with the image of Simon Sixineo that we will help You so that we will merit and enjoy what You revealed to me here, the very high value of the cross. O my God, let it be Your precious will. I will enter from below into penance and despise the evil life. Let me just occupy myself in following after You here on earth so that I will merit and enjoy heavenly joy. So be it.[48]

---

47. "O Amantisimo Jesus, que con tu ardiente caridad llevaste por el camino de el Monte Clavario, la muy pesada Cruz sobre tus muy fatigados ombros, quisiste, que en persona del Cyrineo, te ayudasemos a llevarla, para que por esto medio se nos participase de los tesoros, que están encerrados en el exercicio de la Santa Cruz; Suplicote Señor, que con encendida devocion, y con ferviente espiritu, me abrese con la cruz de la negacion de mi mismo, y me aparte de mis viciosas costumbres, para que siguinedo tus paso, consiga los eternos gozos del Cielo." Anunciación, *Luz para saber andar*, 7.

48. "iyo in tiÇequizcatlasotlallonitzontle JeSuS san ipampatzio yn motetlasotlalitzi oticmonequilititzinno y topapatica yn yn ticmoquechnoltitias yn CenquizCayetec yn moquauhnepanoltzin ynyn santa Cruz yn oquixoxohuili ynnoquitotoneuh yn motlasoacollotzi yhuan oticmonequilititzino yxipitlayotica yn Simon Sixineo ynic timitztopalehuilizque ynic tictomasehuizque yn nican otitechmonextilili yn CenCa tlasotli ypatiuhtzin yn Cruz

What is most striking is that the Nahuatl text has the more descriptive passages referring to Jesus's suffering. Vetancurt describes the "black and blue" shoulders with "burning pain" inflicted on them. Rather, the Spanish versions uses these types of descriptions later in the prayer, praying about "enflamed devotion" and "sear me with the cross." In both prayers, Simon becomes a representative or stand-in for all of humanity, assisting Jesus in his Passion.

The Sixth Station: Christ's Face Is Wiped by Veronica

As noted above, the sixth station is traditionally dedicated to Veronica. Veronica does not appear in the Gospels, but hers is a pious legend that accreted to the Passion story. According to the legend, a woman took pity on Jesus. Seeing that his face was covered with blood and grime, she took a cloth and wiped his face. In the end, the image of Jesus's face appeared miraculously imprinted on the cloth. While the story refers to biblical times, all versions of the legend date from after the thirteenth century. Descriptions of a miraculous image are somewhat earlier, dating to as early as the eleventh century.[49] In English the cloth is referred to as the Veil of Saint Veronica, while in Latin it is known as the Sudarium. The rise of the Cult of Saint Veronica's Veil coincides roughly with the development of the devotion of the Stations of the Cross. The presence of Jesus's encounter with Veronica in the Stations of the Cross undoubtedly helped to further the popularity of both Veronica and the Stations.

The Spanish introduction to the encounter with Veronica mentions her by name and describes the general outlines of the meeting. It is fairly short, but does exhibit the baroque tendency to add descriptors on top of one another:

> **Anunciación**
> This is the sixth station that to it the Lord walked with one hundred and ninety-one steps, and it is the place where to our most pious Jesus that holy Woman, Veronica, emerged and seeing his Majesty so sweaty, and so fatigued, and his Most Holy Face obscured with sweat, bruises, dust, saliva, slaps, and blows that they had given him, that, moved by piety, she removes a cloth with which she cleaned him, and in three places his Most Holy Face remained imprinted.[50]

---

ma xicmotlasonequilititzino noteotzine yny no ytlanpa niCalaquiz yn tlamasehualiztli yhuan nictelchihua yn aqualli nemiliztli ma Sa niq[ui]xCahuiz y nimitzomotepotziotoquiliz y nican tlalticpac yn inic nicmasehuiz yn ilhuicac papaquiliztli," Vetancurt, *Via crucis*, 19–20.

49. Kuryluk, *Veronica and Her Cloth*, 122–24.

50. "Esta es la sexta Estacion, que cuenta de ciento y noventa y un pasos, que hasta ella anduvo el Señor, y es el lugar donde a nuestro piadoso Jesus le salió aquella santa Muger Veronica, que viendo a su Magestad tan sudado, tan fatigado, y su Santísimo Rostro obsurecido con el sudor, cardenales, polvo, salivas, bofetadas, y golpes que le dieron, movida a

The listing of descriptors includes repetition of closely associated words, such as *bofetadas y golpes*. Both of the words refer to hits and blows but have slightly different deeper meanings. *Bofetadas* specifically means "slap," while *golpes* is a more generic word for any blow. Also of interest is that in describing the image that was miraculously imprinted on Veronica's cloth, the author carefully notes that Jesus's face appeared three times on it. Most depictions relate only one image. But in some places, there was an image of the Trinity in which the same face was depicted three times, side by side.[51] The statement that the image was repeated three times might possibly imply this image.

The Nahuatl translation of the text is even simpler that the Spanish, not engaging in the multiplication of adjectives and descriptions. Nonetheless, it is equally emotive, using constructions to engage the reader in the action.

> **Vetancurt**
> The sixth place of kneeling [prayers called] a station. It was ninety-one steps; our God was walking about. Here is where the honored person named Veronica encountered our Savior on the road. When she saw Him His precious face was greatly swelled up, very blackened and bruised. What a state His eyes were in! Then she quickly pulled out for Him a thin white honored cloth with which she wiped His tormented face. A very great miracle occurred, so that in three places where the cloth was covering [Him], the precious face of our Savior was copied in [those] three places.[52]

Immediately one notices that the distance listed in the two versions is quite different. The Spanish says that it was 191 steps while the Nahuatl has only 91. As will be noted, this can be attributed to difficulty translating numbers from Spanish to Nahuatl since the two cultures used different number systems.[53] In the statement, "What a state His eyes were in!" could also read, "What a state His face was in!" since in Nahuatl the word for "face" and "eye" is the same.

---

piedad, se quito un lienzo con que limpió, y quedo estampado en tres partes su Santisimo Rostro." Anunciación, *Luz para saber andar*, 7–8.

51. Later this depiction of the Trinity was declared heretical by Pope Benedict XIV. Panofsky, "Once More 'The Friedsam Annunciation and the Problem of the Ghent Altarpiece,'" 433n66.

52. "ynic chiquaSeCa netlaquaquetzaliztli EstaÇiÔn Nauhpohualli tla yhuan matlactli OCe ycxineanaliztli omonenemilititia yn toteotzin niCan Cani OtliCa oquimonamiquilico <21> yn totemaquixticatzin yn mahuiztlaCatzintli ytocatzin Veronica yn quac oquimotili huel Çenca Opoposaahauh huel otlitlileuh oxoxohuixi yn itlasoxayaCatzin ôyeyez tien yn ixtelolotzxin nimân ôquimoquixitilitihuetzi yn iztaCanahuac yn tilmatzintli yniquimixpopohuiliz yntonehuilizxayaCAtzin AUh CenCa huey tlamahuisoltican omochiuh ynic yexCanpa cuell pachiuhtiCa yn tilmatli OmoyexCâCopintzino yn yn itlasoxayaCatzin yn totemaquixtiCatzin." Vetancurt, *Via Crucis*, 20–21

53. As will be seen, while Europeans used a decimal system (base ten) the Nahua, and most Native peoples of Mesoamerica, used a vigesimal system (base twenty).

Nahuatl word choice also figures as an issue in this station. Writing about the cloth that Veronica used to wipe the face of Jesus, Vetancurt chose to use the word *tilmatli*: "yn iztaCanahuac yn tilmatzintli yniquimixpopohuiliz." *Tilmatztintli* means "honored" or "revered cloth." The word can be used to signify a wide range of cloth items. In general, it refers to a mantle or cloak, but in other contexts it can refer to clothing more generally. Using it to describe the cloth that Veronica used to wipe Jesus's face implies a much larger object than usually depicted in Western art. At the same time, the word had an important cultural context in the minds of listeners in late seventeenth-century Mexico. In Mexican ecclesiastical history, the most famous *tilmatli*, or *tilma*, was the cloak worn by Saint Juan Diego. When he saw the Virgin of Guadalupe, according to the pious legend, she filled his garment (a cape worn knotted over the shoulder) (or bag, depending on the version) with flowers. When he presented the cloth to the bishop, the flowers had miraculously imprinted the image of the Virgin on the cloak.[54] Thus, in the period in which Vetancurt was active, the best-known *tilmatli* was that of Juan Diego, which was taken to be the true image of the Virgin.[55] Similarly, the face that emerged on the cloth of Veronica was believed to be the true image of Christ. The Natives of Mexico might have been more familiar with their own pious legend of Guadalupe. Vetancurt might have used the term *tilmatli* to draw a parallel between the two events. Other texts from slightly later than the Vetancurt *Viav crucis* also use *tilma/tlamahtli*. The Passion play from Tepaltzingo also chose to use the word, calling it a *tilmatzin*, "honored cloak."[56]

The Spanish prayer does not mention Veronica by name but merely refers to her as "that pious woman." The conclusion of the prayer is the most commanding. Just as Jesus imprinted his image on Veronica's cloth, so might he imprint the grace of his image on the soul of the penitent. It continues the use of some less common words and phrases such as "uglied" and "furious waves of torment." There is an odd juxtaposition in the Spanish version in that Anunciación combines the use of "imprint" with "brush." Rather than "painting your image on my soul with the brush of your grace" or "imprint your image on my soul with the press of your grace," he mixes the media.

---

54. Two words are used for the garment, *cuexanitl* (a bag) and *tilma* (the possessed form of *tilmatli*). The cloak upon which the miraculous image of the Virgin was impressed is known most commonly as the *tilma*. Generally the term *cuexanitl* is used early in the story, when the flowers are collected. *Tilma* becomes more common as the miracle is displayed. Sousa, Poole, and Lockhart, *The Story of Guadalupe*, 78–79, 82–83.

55. Poole, *Our Lady of Guadalupe*, 27–28, 118.

56. Sell and Burkhart, *Nahuatl Theater*, 4:236–37.

Anunciación
Most Beautiful Jesus, when your face was most uglied with countless spits, injured by the affronts, and fatigued by the furious waves of torments, that pious Woman alleviated you of part of your suffering, cleaning the sweat of your Face with the cloths of her head covering, and [it] remained imprinted on them. I beseech you, My Lord, that with your brush of grace you imprint the image of your most Holy Face on my soul, and do me the favor that thus, present it in the Court of glory.[57]

The Nahuatl version of this prayer is quite similar but uses slightly different phraseology. While the Spanish addresses "Most Beautiful Jesus," the Nahuatl calls upon the "perfectly beautiful one, Jesus." Perhaps most important is that, unlike the Spanish, the Nahuatl prayer does mention Veronica by name. Just as in the Spanish text, supplicants ask that Christ's image be copied onto their spirit, or soul, in order to receive joy in heaven.

Vetancurt
Alas, O perfectly beautiful one, Jesus! How Your precious face suffered, how they struck you in the face! They dirtied You when they spat in Your face. You received the help of the lady Veronica when she wiped Your precious face with a soft cloth. May it be your precious will that through Your help, Your precious face is copied onto my spirit so that there I will eternally honor You and so that I will obtain and enjoy heavenly joy. O our Lord, O God.[58]

Consequently, the prayer makes the association between the penitent's soul and Veronica's veil in that the image of Jesus is to be imprinted—that is, made permanent—on both. In this way, the image of Jesus and his suffering will always be a part of the participant's life.

---

57. "Hermosismo Jesus, que quando mas afeado tu Rostro con las innumerables salivas, injuriado con afrentas, y fatigado con las furiosas olas de trabajos, te alivió parte de las penas aquella piadosa Muger limpiando el sudor de tu Rostro con las tocas de su cabeza, y quedo impresso en ellas. Suplicote, Señor mio, que estampeme mi Alma con le pinzel de tu gracia la imagen de tu Santisimo Rostro, y me de tu favor para que asi la presente en la Corte de la gloria." Anunciación, *Luz para saber andar*, 8.

58. "iyo CenquizCaquallnesCatzintle Jesus Ca yniquixototoneuhticatCa yni motlasoxayatzin ynic Omitzinmixitlatlatzinilique omitzmocatzahuilique yruc mixtzinco ochichaque oticmoÇelili yn itepalehuiliz yn Cihuatzintli VeroniCa yn yamanqui tilmatican ynnoquimopopohuili yn motlasoxayacatzin ma no xicmotlasonequilititzino yn iCa yn motepalehuitzin yn motlasoGraCiatzin ma ytech noyolia mocopintzino yn motlasoxacatzin ynic onCa ÇenmiCac nimitznomahuiztililiz ynic nicnomasehuiS yn ilhuiCac papaquiliztli." Vetancurt, *Via crucis*, 21–22.

The Seventh Station: His Second Fall

Jesus's second fall is the theme of the seventh station. As noted earlier, the falls are not part of the Gospel accounts, but were added as part of the medieval and early modern devotions that grew up around the Passion. Most of the themes are repetitions from the third station, the first fall. They include the weight of the cross, the damage done to Jesus by the soldiers and guards who beat him and by the wounds that he suffered. The distance from the previous station to this is one of the longest in the devotion, 336 steps. This must have also been considered as a contributing factor to his fall as the stations were developed. The location of the fall was traditionally placed near the Gate of Justice or Gate of Judgement in Jerusalem, perhaps to emphasize what Christians felt was the injustice of Jesus's punishment. Pious legends hold that Jesus's death sentence was posted on this gate. The Spanish version reads as follows:

> **Anunciación**
> This is the seventh station, which lies three hundred thirty-six steps, that to there the Lord walked; and it is the place of the Gate of Judgement, where after having taken our Redeemer, with the Holy Cross bearing down on his shoulders through the public streets in order to offend him even more, he fell a second time to the earth for lack of energy, because the weight of the Cross had made one large wound on his shoulders from all the others, which pained him greatly.[59]

The image of the many wounds on Jesus's back coalescing into one massive laceration is particularly gruesome. It is in keeping with the baroque period's fascination with the morbid and extreme.

The Nahuatl description of the station completely lacks any reference to the Gate of Justice, but instead describes the scene as the entrance to a palace. The change is somewhat curious because the Mexica did have several discrete gates to the city of Tenochtitlán and certainly to the sacred precinct at the center of the city.[60] Mostly curiously, the Nahuatl clearly notes that it was here that Jesus fell to earth for the first time, *yc cepa tlalpan*, while the station commemorated the second fall.

---

59. "Esta es la septima Estacion, que consta de trecientos y treinta y seis pasos, que hasta ella anduvo el Señor, y es el lugar de la Puerta Judiciaria, donde despues de haver llevado a nuestro Redentor con la Santa Cruz acuestas por todas las calles publicas, para mayor afrenta, cayó segunda vez en tierra, por faltarle ya las fuerzas; porque con el peso de la Cruz, se le havia hecho en le ombro, de todas las heridas una muy grande, que lastimaba demasiado." Anunciación, *Luz para saber andar*, 8–9.

60. Mexica is the appropriate term with which refer to people commonly known as the Aztecs.

Vetancurt
The seventh place of kneeling prayer [called] a station. Our beloved Savior was walking about; it was three hundred thirty-six steps with which He arrived [here?]. Here is where He was taken out from a house. It was the entrance of the palace [where] He fell to earth for the first time and there [where] His strength was completely spent with the weight of the holy cross. How He fainted with a great flaying. The precious shoulder of our beloved Savior Jesus Christ greatly swelled up and ached.[61]

The copy of the Vetancurt *Via crucis* studied here exhibits many revisions in this particular station. Several words were written and then crossed out, indicating that the scribe who copied the text was also confused. Vetancurt seems to have had difficulty describing the Gate of Justice mentioned in the Spanish version. At the same time, in the Nahuatl, Jesus seems to almost be going out and coming in at the same time. The Nahuatl also lacks the detail of the many wounds becoming a single large one. Instead, the wounds are described as becoming a "great flaying," *huey xixipehualiztli.*

The prayer associated with the seventh station focuses entirely on the wounds from which Jesus suffered, his weakness, and the heaviness of the cross, not unlike the prayers for the third station. It also shows many of the same baroque tendencies, such as the use of superlatives. Of particular interest is the contrast between Jesus's "delicate" body and the rough and heavy cross.

Anunciación
O Most Delicate Jesus, you were carried with such ignominy to your majesty by the fatigue of your delicate Body that you fell for the second time with the Beam of the Cross, I beseech that you illuminate my understanding that I might know the immense weight that the sins that I have committed have. Give me your grace that they [my sins] might not drag me to eternal punishment but rather that the desire to serve you might live in me.[62]

---

61. "ynic chicōCa netlaquaquetziallizfli tlatlauhtiliztli EstaCion yni Omonenemilititia y totlasotemaquixitiCatzin Caxtoli oÇe pohualli yhuan Caxtoli oÇe ycxinmamaltzin ynic Omaxillitico ynic ma xilli yn totemaquixiticatzin ye niCan yn Cani ynic Callpan omoquixititzino tlahtoCaCallquiyahuac[t]enco yc cepa tlalpan omotlahuitectzino yhuan CenCa ônCan nepoliuhCa yn ichiCahualliztzin yCa yn ietiliz y Santa Cruz ynic huel omosotlahualtitzino ycCa Çe huey xixipehualiztli CenCa opoposahuac ototoneuh yn itlasoacolltzin yn yny totlasotemaquixitiCatzin Jesu Chr[i]sto." Vetancurt, *Via crucis*, 21–22.

62. "O Suavisimo Jesus, pues fuiste llevado con tanta ignominia de tu Magestad; y por la fatiga de tu delicado Cuerpo, caiste segunda vez con el Madero de la Cruz: te suplico, alumbres mi entendimiento, para que conozca el inmenso peso, que tienen los pecados que cometo. Dame tu gracia, para que no me arrastren a la eterna pena, mas antes viva en mi el deseo de servirte." Anunciación, *Luz para saber andar*, 9.

The prayer, again, equates the weight of the cross that Jesus had to bear with the spiritual weight of sins carried by the penitent.

In the Nahuatl version of this prayer, again the guards play a more active role. While not mentioned or referred to in the Spanish, in the Nahuatl they are called scoundrels, *tlahueliloque*:

> **Vetancurt**
> Alas, O completely honorable Jesus! You wanted this. With dishonor they accompanied You. Those scoundrels greatly worked at Your death so that with fainting and numbness Your precious body, You, fell to the ground. Help me so that I will relieve the heaviness of my sins, so that I will no longer bear on my shoulders the burden of my sins. Give me my strength [back?] so that [?] in the place where He was condemned. Especially let the service concerning Your work touch me in passing. So be it, Jesus.[63]

The Nahuatl version also gives a certain degree of agency to Jesus. It states, "You wanted this," *oticmonequilititzino*. At the same time, the prayer also puts blame on the guards who became the proximate cause for Jesus's weakness and suffering. Just as in the Spanish, there is a comparison of the physical weight of the cross and the spiritual weight of sins borne by the penitent. Although it is a bit confusing, the prayer asks that Jesus, through his work of saving grace, might relieve the penitent of sin.

The Eighth Station: He Meets the Women of Jerusalem

The eighth station features Jesus's encounter with the women of Jerusalem. As noted earlier, this is one of the few events for which there is some scriptural evidence. Nonetheless, the event is mentioned only in the Gospel of Luke, with no parallels in the other Synoptic Gospels (Luke, 23:27–31). According to Luke, a group of men and women began to follow Jesus after Simon of Cyrene was forced to help carry the cross. These people were mourning Jesus and crying out against his punishment. Jesus turned to the crowd but only addressed the women, saying:

63. "iyo CenquizCamahuiztililoni Jesus ynin oticmonequilititzino yn temahuizpoliztiCa yn mitzinmohuiquilizque ynic Çenca omitzmomiquiztequipannilihuiquetiaque yn tlahueliloque ynic sotlahualiztica osesepocatia yn motlasonaCayotzin ynic opa tlalipa otimohuetziti otimotlahuitectzino ma xinechmopalehuitzino ynic niquixitiz ynietiliz yn notlatlacoll ynicCacmo nicnomamaltiz yn itlatlacoll ma xinechmomaquili y[?] notechiCahualitzin inicamo [?]tiliztzaz imiquiztetlatziontequililoyan ylhuiSe ma notech quisan yn tetlayecolltiliztli ytechpa yn motequipanollCatzi = ma yuh mochihua Jesus," Vetancurt, *Via crucis*, 23.

Luke 23:28–31
Daughters of Jerusalem, do not weep for me; weep rather for yourselves and for your children. For look, the days are surely coming when people will say, "Blessed are those who are barren, the wombs that have never borne children, the breasts that have never suckled!" Then they will say to the mountains, "Fall on us!"; to the hills, "Cover us!" For if this is what is done to green wood, what will be done when the wood is dry?

Much about this passage is enigmatic. It is among the various apocalyptic prophesies attributed to Jesus. For many early Christians, Jesus's death inaugurated the beginning of the end. At some point in the near future, the world would end. Jesus would return to earth and establish his kingdom. But before that time, the unrighteous would suffer. Thus, in this saying, Jesus foretells a time of suffering that will usher in the final judgement.

The Spanish version of this station draws upon this scriptural passage, incorporating part of it. It also paints the women of the crowd in a sympathetic manner, crying and grieving for Jesus in his suffering:

Anunciación
This is the eighth station, which lies at three hundred forty-eight steps, that to there the Lord walked, and it is the place where some pious Women, seeing our most innocent Jesus in such a miserable form, since they took him publicly to crucify, made an abyss of sorrow, ignominy, and affronts, when just before he had been acclaimed by the Public for his miracles, they wept bitterly; and the Lord turned to them, consoling them by saying: "Daughters of Jerusalem, do not cry over my death, rather cry for yourselves and your children."[64]

The direct quote from Scripture differs slightly from the standard version in that in the introduction Jesus asks them to not lament his death, while Scripture is more general, admonishing the women simply not to weep over Jesus. The introduction also focuses on the contrast between Jesus having been hailed as a miracle worker and praised on Palm Sunday to having been condemned to die shortly after. These extremes of emotion and pathos fit well into the general baroque style.

In this station, the close relationship between the Nahuatl and Spanish versions is manifest. The Nahuatl introduction for the eighth station also

---

64. "Esta es la octava Estacion, que consta de trescientos y quarenta y ocho pasos, que hasta ella anduvo el Señor, y es el lugar donde unas piadosas Mugeres, viendo a nuestro Innocentisimo Jesus en tan miserable forma, pues le llevaban publicamente a crucificar, hecho un abysmo de dolores, ignominias, y aftrentas, quando poco antes le havian visto aclamado del Pueblo, por sus milagros, lloraban amargamente; y el Señor buelto a ellas, las consolo diciendoles: *Hijas de Jerusalem, no lloreis mi muerte, sino llorad sobre vosotras, y vuestros hijos.*" Italics in the original. Anunciación, *Luz para saber andar*, 9–10.

diverges from Scripture in that Jesus asks that the women not weep for his death. However, in the Nahuatl version, the language does not make distinctions between males and females, as is almost required in Spanish. The Nahuatl introduction is more gender neutral than the Spanish mostly because in Nahuatl most expressions are simply not gendered. Nonetheless, the introduction does translate the address to the women of Jerusalem in a manner very similar to the Spanish.

> **Vetancurt**
> The eighth place of kneeling prayers [called] a station. It was 308 steps; our God was walking around. Here is where the compassionate women of Jerusalem were when they saw sinless Jesus in the place of crucifixion not long [after] the city had honored Him because of all the miracles He had wrought; everyone had wept for Him. But our Savior gazed at the women, saying to them: You are the children of Jerusalem. Do not weep for My death. Cry more especially for yourselves and weep because of your children.[65]

The word used, *pilli*, is a gender-neutral term for "children,"or in this context "you [plural] are children," *ynnamopilhuan*. We can compare this to a scene from the Passion play produced somewhat later in Tepaltzingo. In the play, the author has Jesus address the women first in the gender-neutral manner, but then he clarifies that they are the women of Jerusalem: "You children of Jerusalem, you dear women."[66] Vetancurt also implies that the whole community has honored Jesus and his actions by explicitly using the Nahuatl term for a precontact city-state, *altepetl*.

The Spanish prayer associated with the eighth station draws a parallel between Jesus's addressing the weeping women of Jerusalem and the tears shed over sinfulness by the penitent:

> **Anunciación**
> O Sovereign Teacher, that walking to that rocky Mount Calvary, in the midst of immense pain, you taught those pious Women pained by your

65. "ynic chiCuexCan netlaquaquetzaliz tlatlatlauhtiliztli estaÇiÔ Caxtolli poalli yhuan ChiCuey ycxineanalliztli ynnomonenemilititia yn toteotzin niCan Cani yc no aCaCi Cihuatzintzintin Jerosale yn iuhCatzintli ynnoquimotilique ynnamo tlatlacolleCatzintli Jesus mamasohualtiloyan quimohuiquilia CenCa temauhCatzitzinti ynic motonehualtitiuh ynnayamo huehCahuis yn quimomahuisoltiliyaia ynnah ynnaltepetli ypampa yn ixichi yn itlamahuisolotlachihualtzin oquimochihuilitzinno yn ixiquich tlaCatli yCatzinco omochoquillique Auh yn totemaquixitiCatzin ynhuiccopa omotlachialti yn Cihuatzintzintin oquinmolhuilin ynnamopilhuan Jerosalen maCamo Ximochoquilican NomiquiliztiCa ylhuise Sannapampa xichoCaCan yhuan ynpampa ynnamopilhuan XimochoquiliCan." Vetancurt, *Via crucis*, 24–25.

66. "Yn ampilhuan yn JeroSalen yn aSihuatzintzinti." Sell and Burkhart, *Nahuatl Theater*, 4:236–37.

> labors, they should cry for themselves, and for their faults. Concede to me my Master, that with fervent tears of contrition, I cry my sins, and wash with them [tears] the many [sins] that my Soul has incurred through sinful works, that with my spirit mortified, I might always be in your friendship and grace.[67]

In the prayer, Anunciación makes clear that Jesus admonishes the women of Jerusalem, that they should cry for themselves specifically because of their own sinful behavior. This seems to be somewhat different from the original scriptural admonition that the tears should come from the realization of the trials and adversities of the end times. It moves the focus from the general context of the end times to the specific state of the women. The prayer begins with the invocation of "O Sovereign Teacher." The Spanish *O Maestro Soberano* might be translated as "Sovereign Master." But in Spanish the term *maestro* more commonly refers to a teacher. In this instance, the prayer specifically refers to Jesus teaching the women of Jerusalem, and thus the translation of "Teacher" is more accurate. This is confirmed in Vetancurt's choices when translating the prayer into Nahuatl.

Vetancurt, in translating the prayer, changed the meaning in a subtle way. He emphasized that even during the Passion, Jesus was involved in teaching about the Gospel. The Nahuatl prayer ends up showing that even in the midst of suffering, Jesus could be engaged in a teachable moment with the women of Jerusalem.

> **Vetancurt**
> Alas, O heavenly teacher! Even though You follow with torment Your road of suffering, You did not abandon Your task of teaching, with which You revealed to me how sins will make [one] cry. Also show and teach me how with weeping, tears, and sadness, all my sins with which I blackened and dirtied my soul made me cry; let me wash and purify it with my tears. Let me occupy myself in loving You so that I will earn and enjoy Your instrument of sadness, [i.e., Your] grace.[68]

---

67. "O Maestro Soberno, que caminando a aquel fragoso Monte Calvario, en medio de aquella inmensidad de penas, enseñaste a las piadosas Mugeres, que se dolian de tus trabajos, que llorasen por si, y por sus culpas: Concedeme Maestro mio, que con fervorosos lagrymas de contricion, llore mis pecados, y labe con ellas los muchos en que ha incurrido mi Alma con obras pecaminosas, para que mortificado mi espiritu, ete siempre en tu amisatad, y gracia." Anunciación, *Luz para saber andar*, 10.

68. "Iyo ylhuiCaC temachitiCatzintle maCihuin tonehuiliztiCa yn no ticmotoquilitia yn motlayohuilizohuitzin Ca amo oticmoCahuili yn motemachtiltequitzin ymc otiquinmonextilili yniquename quichoquiltiz quenyn itlatlacollo Auh mano nehuatli Xinechmonextilili Xinechmomachtili yn quenin choquiztiCa yxayotica yolotequipacholiztica nechoctiz yn ixquichi yn notlatlacoll yni onictlilehui onicCatziahui yn noanima ma yc nicpahca yc nicchipahua yn nixayo ma niquixCahui ynic nimitznotlasotlitiliz ynic nicnomaSehuiz yn motequalltiayatzin yn GraCia ma yuh mochi." Vetancurt, *Via crucis*, 25–26.

The prayer, in both Spanish and Nahuatl, completely loses sight of the women of Jerusalem and focuses almost entirely on tears: tears shed because of sin and tears that might be the agents of purification and redemption. Indeed, there is no specific reference in the prayer to the women, but only to issues of sin, weeping, and purification.

The Ninth Station: His Third Fall

The third fall provides the situation for the ninth station. Having exploited most of the clear themes related to the falls in the first two instances, authors frequently merely expand on meditations, admonitions, and prayers from the two previous falls in this one. In his introduction, Anunciación further develops ideas already seen in the two earlier falls.

> **Anunciación**
> This is the ninth station, that lies one hundred sixty-one steps, that to it the Lord walked, and it is the place where our Sovereign Redeemer, bleeding out and losing strength, fell for the third time to the earth with the Holy Cross, even to have his Holy Mouth reach the soil, bathing it completely with blood, and wanting to rise, could not. Before returning to fall again, his Sacred Person was wounded in many places, such as his arms, hands, and knees by the many sharp stones that there were in the road.[69]

In this introduction, Anunciación focuses on blood and the soil, rocks and stones. Jesus is so bloodied by this point that as he falls to the earth; a great pool of his blood is left on the spot. In the prayer for the previous station, Calvary is described as rocky or craggy, *fragoso*. In this introduction, the reader is informed that the road itself is littered with sharp stones ready to wound hands, knees, and feet. The image of having Jesus fall down so far that his mouth nearly touches the ground surely created a moment of pathos for Spanish readers.

If the Spanish reader might have been saddened that Jesus nearly landed with his face in the dirt, the Nahuatl-speaking readers might well have been confused. The Nahuatl translation seems to be avoiding having Jesus's lips touch the earth, perhaps in avoidance of anything resembling the ancient ritual of *tlalcualiztli*, kissing or eating dirt, seen above. While the Spanish version

---

69. "Esta es la novena Estcion, que consta de ciento y sesenta y un pasos, que hasta ella anduvo el Señor, y es el lugar donde nuestro Soberano Redentor desangrando, y faltando las fuerzas, cayó tercera vez con la Santa Cruz en tierra, hasta llegar con su Santo Boca en el suelo, bañandola toda de sangre, y queriendose levantar no pudo, antes bolviendo a caër de nuevo, se hirió en muchas partes de su Sagrada Persona, como en los brazos, en las manos, y en las rodillas, que en aquel camino havia." Anunciatión, *Luz para saber andar*, 10–11.

has Jesus's lips almost touch the soil, the Nahuatl does not mention the holy mouth nearing the earth. On the other hand, the fall is so powerful that he hits his face on the ground.

Vetancurt
The ninth place of kneeling prayers [called] a station. It was [three hundred?] steps; our God was walking around. Here is the third time our Savior fell to the ground. Moreover His precious blood was very much spilling so that His strength was entirely spent, because when He would have gotten up He was no longer able to do it, He again fell to the ground and His elbows and His face and His hands and His feet vehemently hit the ground. [He/His body] was hurt in many places because [He was] badly [injured] on the road.[70]

Clearly Vetancurt chose to translate this in a manner that conveyed the same ideas without mentioning Jesus's mouth. Instead, his face hits the ground, vehemently, along with his hands and feet. The word used in the description is *xayacatl*, which means either "face" or "mask." Another common word for "face" was *ixtli*, which also means "eye." At the same time, the very notion that the Christian God might be so punished as to even seem to be engaged in a pagan ritual of kissing the ground might in itself have provided a shock to Natives hearing the meditation. In the Nahuatl, the theme of blood is clearly present, but not as much in Anunciación's image of a pool of blood forming were Jesus's face nears the earth. The Nahuatl also notes that Jesus wants to get up but completely lacks sufficient strength to do so. This detail is not explicit in the Spanish.

The prayers associated with the ninth station also focus on the action of Jesus falling and the patience that he exhibits in facing his tormenters. In the Spanish version, Anunciación is critical of the Jews whom he associates with the guards who accompany Jesus. The two phrases used are "furious rage" and being "trampled," both of which are linked to the Jews.

Anunciación
O Most Benign Jesus, who suffered to be carried along with furious rage, and have your Divine Person be trampled by the Jews, with the shoves that they gave you, with which they made you fall for the third time to the

70. "ynic chicnauhCan netlaquaquetzaliz tlatlatlauhtiliztli estaCiô Caxtilco poallianpa omomopohuilli ycxineanaliztli omonenemilltitia yn toteotzin yn niCan Ca yc yexpa omohuetzinti yn totemaquixitiCatzin yCa yCamachlltzin yc Omotlahuitectzinno Auh yequeni huel CenCa ononoquiuhtia yntlasoyesyotzin ynic huellopolihuiCa yn iChiCahualitzin yehiCa yn iquac omoeUatzinnozquiaya ayocmo omohuelitilitzinno San no Sepa Omotlallhuitectzinno yhuan tlalliitech Omotzotzonate ynnimolictzin yhuan yxayaCatzin yhuan ymatzitzin yhuan ycxixitzitzin miyeCannomococotzinno Ca nozo huel CenCa tetetlan ynnotliCa." Vetancurt, *Via crucis*, 26–27.

earth with the weight of the Cross. I beseech you, my God, that I might suffer the restraints of my enemies, that, through your love I deny myself, so that having patience in [my] works, I enjoy you in eternal content.[71]

The prayer also obliquely compares the torments that Jesus suffers to the enmity and criticisms that the penitents might feel from their enemies. This seems to be a somewhat false analogy.

The Nahuatl is shorter and simpler than the Spanish. It omits any references at all to the Jews. Rather, the prayer refers to the guards as "enraged workers of death," *tlahuelmiquiztequipanoque*.

Vetancurt
Alas, O perfectly compassionate Jesus! You [suffered/paid the price to?] the enraged workers of death; they flayed You so that You fell to the ground [a third time]. May it be Your precious will that with Your help I will conquer those who hate me, in this fashion doing penance to You. Afterwards I will earn and enjoy happiness, [i.e.,] glory.[72]

Furthermore, as opposed to the Spanish version that equates suffering derision and opprobrium at the hands of others as an earthly penance somehow parallel to Jesus's suffering, in the Nahuatl translation the penitent merely requests assistance to conquer one's enemies. This defeat of one's enemies somehow constitutes a penance in this context. Neither the model offered by the Spanish-language version nor that offered in the Nahuatl approaches the model set forth in the Lord's Prayer: that penitents might be forgiven by God to the degree that they forgive those who have harmed them. Indeed, one of the core teachings of Christianity is what is popularly called the Golden Rule, namely the instruction to act toward others in a manner in which we would like to be treated ourselves, although it is framed in the reverse in the Lord's Prayer in terms of sin and forgiveness: forgive me my sins as I forgive the sins of those who sin against me.

---

71. "O Benignisimo Jesus, que sufriste ser llevado con furiosa rabia, y ser atropellada tu Divina Persona de los Judios, con empellones que te daban, con que te hicieron tercera vez caër en tierra, con el peso de la Cruz: Suplicote, Dios mio, que sufra Yo las mesuras de mis enemigos, y que por tu amor me níegue â mi mismo, para que teniendo paciencia en los trabajos, te gozen en los contentos eternos." Anunciación, *Luz para saber andar*, 11.

72. "Iyo CenquizCa tetlaocoliayanie Jesus ynin ticmopayohuititzino yn tlahuelmiquiztequipanoque omitzmoxixipehuilique ynic yexpa Otimotlahuitectzinno ma san xicmotlasonequiltitzino ynic motepalehuiliztiCatzinCo ynic nicpahuiz yn notecocoli-Cauh yn iuh mohuictzinco nitlamahSehuaz Auh satepan nicnomasehuiz yn papaq[qu]liztli yn Gloria." Vetancurt, *Via crucis*, 27.

The Tenth Station: He Is Stripped of His Garments

In the introduction for station ten (He Is Stripped of His Garments) the two versions manifest some significant differences. The introduction focuses on Jesus being stripped of his clothing, degraded, and offered wine mixed with bitter herbs. These details come from the scriptural accounts of the crucifixion. The Synoptic Gospels all mention that the crucifixion occurred on the hill known as Calvary in Latin, Golgotha in Greek. The stripping is inferred rather than stated in the Gospels, since all mention that guards gamble with one another over who might win the discarded clothing. The Gospels concur that some mixture of wine and bitter herbs is offered, but only Mark and Matthew note that he refuses it; Matthew adds that Jesus tastes it and then refuses.[73] These details all form the basis of the introduction in the Spanish version.

Anunciación
This is the tenth Station, which lies eighteen steps that to there the Lord walked. This is where having arrived our pious Redeemer to Mount Calvary, they removed his Royal Vestments, with the atrocity and fierceness that on other occasions they had done, and removing them they again renewed all of his wounds, and sufferings; and they gave him wine mixed with bitter herbs: where you can consider, how would it be that this Divine Lord [would be] trembling with cold, and with the shame of seeing himself naked in the presence of all the People.[74]

Vetancurt's Nahuatl translation is much shorter but covers all the essential details. Wine was not a drink that was known to Nahuatl speakers. They had their own mildly intoxicating beverages but nothing that approximated wine. In light of this, Vetancurt refers to the drink as a "bitter potion," *ChiChic patli atli.*

Vetancurt
The tenth place of kneeling prayer [called] a station. It was eighteen steps; our Savior was walking around. Here is where he reached Skull Rack Mountain Place, Calvary. There they disrobed Him; there they laid

73. Luke 23:34–36; Matthew 27:34–36; Mark 15:23–24.

74. "Esta es la decima Estacion, que consta de diez y ocho pasos que hasta ella anduvo el Señor, y es lugar donde haviendo llegado nuestro piadoso Redentor al Monte Calvario, le desnudaron de sus Reales Vestiduras, con la atrozidad, y fiereza que otras vezes lo havian hecho; y quitandoselas, se le bolvieron a renovar todas sus llagas, y dolores; y le dieron â beber vino mezclado con hiel: adonde puedes considerer, qual estaría este Divino Señor, temblando de frio, y con la verguenza de verse desnudo en presencia de todo el Pueblo." Anunciación, *Luz para saber andar*, 11–12.

> on all the lashes until they [removed] His garment from Him. Again, with torment the spilling of His blood was renewed and [with] all His flaying and because of His bloody fainting He asked them for a small bit of water. Likewise, they angrily gave him a bitter potion [as] a drink; with it He just fainted. It is very necessary for us to go about sadly remembering when our beloved Savior thus [went]. He was naked in public—How ashamed He was! For truly His precious body was shamefully naked before all kinds of people.[75]

While the two versions are remarkably similar, there are subtle differences. In the Nahuatl, the guards seem to be whipping Jesus to remove his garments. In Spanish his garment is explicitly called "his Royal Vestment." In the Nahuatl, Jesus asks for water and is given wine and bitter herbs, whereas in the Spanish, no request for water appears. Lastly, in the Nahuatl the admonition to the reader to consider Jesus's situation is much longer, "It is very necessary for us to go about sadly remembering when our beloved Savior thus [went]," whereas in Spanish it is simply "you can consider."

The prayers associated with the station focus to a great degree on Jesus's nakedness. Stripping a person naked was generally seen as more than just an embarrassing form of public punishment. It symbolically degraded the person, reducing them to mere flesh and blood, stripping them metaphorically even of their personhood. Both versions of the prayer, in Spanish and Nahuatl, also focus on the role of the Jews in the crucifixion as the principal witnesses of Jesus's nakedness. The prayer also asks that just as Jesus refused the wine mixed with gall, the penitent might reject the worldly delights that would be mixed with sin and suffering.

> **Anunciación**
> O Most Patient Jesus, who tolerated, when in the presence of the Jews, that they remove your garments, reopening your wounds, leaving you completely naked. I beseech you, Lord, for these sorrows, and for that which you felt when they offered wine mixed with gall to you, that I might not drink the delights mixed with the gall of blame that the Devil

---

75. "ynic mahtlaCan Netlaquaquetzializtlatlatlauhtiliztli estaCiOn CaXtoli Omey poalli yicxineanaliztli omonenemilititia yn totemaq[ui]xitiCatzin y niCan Cani Omaxilitico yn tziōpantepec CalVaro Auh Ca onCan oquimopetlahuilique enCan yXiquichi asote oquimotlalilique asta oquimotlahuelquitililiquetzin yn tlaquentzinn oc Cepa tonehuiliztiCa OmoyaCuilitia yn iesnoquihuilitzin yhuan yn ixiquichi yxixipehualitzin <29> yiesSotlahualiztiCatzinco Oquimitlaniliaya tepitzon atzintli San no quimotlahuelmaquilique ChiChic patli atli Sa yc OhualmoSotlahualtitzino Auh Ca huel toteChi monequi tictlaocollylnamictinemizque yn iquac yuhCatzintli Omotatzinno yn totlasotemaquixitiCatzin teyxipan OmopetlahuititiCatca quexquichi yPinahuiztzin Ca ye neli pinahuiliztica OpetlauhtimoCauh yn itlasonaCayotzin yn mixipan yn nepampa tlaca." Vetancurt, *Via crucis*, 28–29.

offers me, rather before stripping my soul naked to myself, I might follow him who was stripped for me on the holy Beam of the Cross.[76]

The Nahuatl version of the prayer is longer and more focused on the bloodiness. In both prayers and the introduction, it is noted in passing that by stripping Jesus, the guards also open up wounds that had begun to scab over as a result of the clothing. Removing the clothing disturbs the scabs and opens the wounds.

Vetancurt
Alas, O perfectly and completely peaceful Jesus! You patiently suffered Your shameful nakedness before the perverse Jews. They undressed You so that the spilling of Your blood was renewed. May it be Your precious will because of all Your burning, aching blood, all Your painful, exhausted blood. For truly it is on our account that with Your joyful mouth You drank the first bitter liquid. But as for me: Your precious will be done, that I will no longer drink or take for myself something which perverts people, the various earthly things which are the hateful instruments of my perverted enemies. Let me not [erase?], let me not [soil?] so that I will leave myself entirely in Your hands, the reason being because You remained naked and died on the cross.[77]

There are some significant differences between the Spanish and Nahuatl. Perhaps most arresting is that the Nahuatl refers to Jesus drinking the mixture of wine and gall with a "joyful mouth," *CamonepapaquiltizCamactzin*. This differs significantly from the biblical accounts, which have him refusing the liquid. The latter part of the prayer, then, asserts that the penitent will desist from sinful behavior and not take the bitter wine, placing their trust in the Lord. Some of the beauty of Nahuatl exposition can be seen in the couplets

76. "O Pacientisimo Jesus, que toleraste, quando en presencia de los Judios, te quitaron las testiduras, renovando tus llagas, y quedaron todas tus carnes desnudas: Ruegote, Señor, por estos dolores, y por el que sentiste, quando te ofrecieron el vino mezclado con hiel, que no beba Yo los deleytes, que mezclados con hiel de culpas me ofrece el Demonio; sino antes desnudo del amor de mi mismo, siga al que se desnudó por mí en el Madero santo de la Cruz." Anunciación, *Luz, para saber andar*, 12.

77. "Iyo CenquizCa tlapaCayeliz ehCatzītle JeSuS ynnoticmopaCayohuilititzinno yn mopetlahualitzin pinahuiliztica ynmixipan yn tlahueliloque JuDiosme omitzinmopetlahuilique ynic OmoyanCuiltia yn moyesnōq[ue] huilitzin ma xicmotlasonequiliti ypapatzinco yn ixiquichi moyestonehuilitzin yn ixiquich moyeschichinaquilitzin Ca neli yc CamonepapaquiltizCamactzin ynic Ca topāpatica yc ce ticmititzinno yn chichiC atli Auh ne yn nehuatli ma san xicmotlasonequilititzino maCacmo niquiz maCacmo nicnomaCaS ynta yhuin yn teyolmalaCacho yn nepapan tlalticpac tlaelhuiloni ynitetlapololtiliz ynoteyauohu yn tlahueliloc ma yc niquixipehui ma yc niCatzelhui ynic mosemactzinco ninoCahuas ynic ypampatiCa petlauhCatzītli otimoCauhtzino Cruztitech Otimomiquilitzino." Vetancurt, *Via crucis*, 29–30.

talking about Jesus's loss of blood: "all Your burning, aching blood, all Your painful, exhausted blood," "yn ixiquichi moyestonehuilitzin yn ixiquich moyeschichinaquilitzin." In classical Nahuatl, repetitive descriptions were frequently piled on one another to create extremely complex images. Some of these include diphrases in which two unrelated nouns are juxtaposed to create a third meaning. The best example is of the term *altepetl*, which signifies a city-state. It actually consists of two words, *atl* meaning "water" and *tepetl* meaning "hill." But combined or juxtaposed together they mean city-state. In other instances, descriptors are merely added to emphasize a characteristic. In another stylistic vein, frequently the words for "feather" (*quetzal*) and "jadestone" (*chalchihuitl*) were added to descriptions to convey the notion of precious things. Thus, this doubling up of descriptors having to do with blood is very typical in Nahuatl. In the European tradition, the use of multiple images as descriptions is also a very common poetic construction in baroque literature.

The Eleventh Station: He Is Laid on the Cross and His Crucifixion

The eleventh station focuses on the crucifixion itself. Clearly, all the Gospels describe the crucifixion, since it is an act that is central to Christianity. The cross itself is the symbol of the religion, and the crucifix, the depiction of Christ on the Cross, is also central to Christian iconography and found in nearly all Christian churches. The Spanish introduction to the station is full of the symbols used to describe the crucifixion in art and sculpture.

> **Anunciación**
> This is the eleventh station, which lies twelve steps that to there the Savior of the World walked, and place where our pious Jesus was hung on the holy Tree of the Cross, and was nailed to it in his Feet and Hands, where his Holiest Mother hearing the first blow of the hammer was as if dead from sorrow. And it was such a great cruelty that those who crucified him again placed on him the Crown of thorns, pushing it down so that the thorns reached his divine eyes, filling his eyes, beard [or chin], and mouth with blood.[78]

---

78. "Esta es la undecimal Estacion, que consta de doze pasos, que hasta ella anduvo el Salvador del Mundo, y lugar donde â nuestro piadoso Jesus le tendieron en el Arbo[l] santo de la Cruz, y fue clavado de Pies, y Manos en ella, en donde oyendo su Santissima Madre el primer golpe del martillo, quedó como muerta del dolor, y fue tan grande la crueldad de los que le crucificaron, que le bolvieron â poner la Corona de espinas, apretandosela, hasta que las espinas llegaron â sus divinos ojos, llenandole con la sangre, ojos, barba, y boca." Anunciación, *Luz para saber andar*, 12–13. In Spanish, *barba* can refer either to the beard or metaphorically to the chin.

In the iconography of the crucifixion, in addition to the cross itself, other common symbols include the hammer and nails and the crown of thorns. Other items include the pincers used to hold the nails in place, the ladder used to bring the body down after death, dice used by the guards to gamble for Jesus's robe (seen in station ten), and even the winding cloth used to eventually wrap the body. Thus, this description calls forward several of the most common elements of the crucifixion iconography. This description also uses a poetic form of the word "tree" (*arbol*) symbolically to refer to the cross.

The Nahuatl translation provided by Vetancurt follows the Spanish model fairly closely, allowing for differences of expression between the two languages. Vetancurt labored over the right word for the cross, as will be seen below, and also for nails, since metal objects were still new to many Nahuatl speakers. Rather than describe the crucifixion workers as cruel or even enjoying their torture of Jesus, Vetancurt merely notes that they were not sad.

> **Vetancurt**
> The eleventh [place] of kneeling [prayers called] a station. It was twelve steps with which our Savior arrived. Here is where on the crossed sticks, the cross, they laid down Jesus, our beloved God [and where] His precious hands were nailed down. They repeatedly crossed Your precious feet over one another, [hammering them down] with metal nails. And when Your beloved mother heard then right away on His account [?] she weepingly fainted. The workers of death were not sad in the least, but again laid on top of His head the round thing of thorns. They were unable to see where His eyes ended, right where the thorns ended. His eyes and His mouth were very [filled with blood].[79]

Throughout the work in describing the cross, Vetancurt frequently provides both a neologism and a borrow word. In most instances he states, *quauhtlanepanoli Santa Cruz*, "crossed wood Holy Cross," or *quauhnepanoli Santa Cruz*, "the crossed pieces of wood Holy Cross." The Nahuatl expressions literally mean "wood placed on wood" or "crossed wood." Seldom does Vetancurt just use the neologism, so the two terms become a pair tied together, almost like a bilingual diphrase. The neologism appears in a few

---

79. "11ynic matlactli oCe Netlaquaquetzaliztli estaCiOn y matlactli omeyme ycxineanaliztli ynic omaxilitico yn totemaquixitiCatzin y niCan Cani ypan quauhnepannoli Cruztzin no quimotequilique yn totlasoteotzin JeSuS oncan ohualteposquauhmiminaloc yn itlasomatzin tepostlaxichtiCa ynnoquihualmonenepanilihuique yn motlasoyecycxitzin Auh yn iquac OquimoCaquin ynimotlasonātzin yn tepostehuilonitzitzinCatiCa Ca Sa niman ypāpatzinco otlaoana [?] ynic Omochoquizsotlahuiltitzino Auh yni miquiztequipanoque niman amo omotlaocoyalitique Sannoc Cepa ycpactzinco Oquimomanilique yn tetepeyotli y tlacotli yn xocohuitziyahualli ynnahuelloquitilique yn campa tlami yn ixitelolotzin huellopā otlatlamito yn huitzitli huel CenCa yc Ohualyeyesten yn ixitelolotzin yhuan yCamachtzin." Vetancurt, *Via crucis*, 31–32.

works by other authors.[80] But in many instances, Vetancurt uses the Spanish borrow word *cruz* as if it were a Nahuatl morpheme. In the introductory matter he wrote: *Cruztitech omomiquilitzino*, "on the Cross he died." In this instance, Vetancurt adds the postposition *-itech* (upon) to the word *cruz* using a *ti-* ligature. In this prayer, he has chosen to use his bilingual expression *quauhnepannoli Cruztzin*, "crossed wood honored Cross." In this instance, depicting the serious and holy nature of the act of crucifixion, he chose to place the Nahuatl honorific *-tzin* on the borrowed Spanish word *Cruz.*[81]

Another of the curious words used to describe the crucifixion is the term adopted for "crown of thorns," *xocohuitziyahualli.* This term was used by other authors as well to signify the crown of thorns. In a passion play dating from roughly the same period from Tepaltzingo, the same word, with a slightly different spelling, was used: *xocohuetzyahualli.* The *xocohuiztli* was a type of thorny plant common in central Mexico.[82] The resulting construction means "a round thing of thorns." It also can be translated as a "circlet of thorns."

In both instances where Vetancurt discusses the nails, he uses a word that describes them as metal objects. This is done through the inclusion of the word *tepoztli*, which became a colonial calque to signify any object made of metal.[83] The specific words used are *ohualteposquauhmiminaloc* and *tepostlaxichtiCa.* The first word means something along the lines of "there pushed a metal dart into wood." It combines root words for "metal," "wood," and the verb "to throw an arrow, dart, or crossbow bolt." The neologism of "metal arrow" was common for nails in mid-colonial Mexico. The second word simply means "a thing made of metal" and could be used in a variety of manners for metal objects, alone or in combination with other words.[84] Another neologism for "nail" combines words for "thorn" and "metal": *tepozhuiztli.* In the one known instance where this term was used, it was pluralized in the Nahuatl manner. This is curious because in Nahuatl the only

80. Sell and Burkhart, *Nahuatl Theater*, 4:280, passim. This usage dates from the early eighteenth century. Burkhart points out that in the morality play about the discovery of the true cross by Saint Helen, Emperor Constantine calls the cross by the Nahuatl neologism until he becomes a Christian, and then he uses the borrow word (33–36).

81. James Lockhart called this stage 2 in the development of colonial Nahuatl, when Spanish nouns were incorporated into Nahuatl and treated as Nahuatl morphemes. It began in the late sixteenth century. Lockhart, *The Nahuas after the Conquest*, 284–304.

82. Sell and Burkhart, *Nahuatl Theater*, 4:180–81. Burkhart, *Holy Wednesday*, 224–27.

83. The Nahua had metals, copper, gold, and silver, but these were relatively soft. *Tepoztli* has a literal meaning of "capable of breaking stone." It is a combination of *poztequi*, "to split or break lengthwise," while *tetl* signifies "stone." Karttunen, *An Analytical Dictionary*, 205, 232.

84. Burkhart, *Holy Wednesday*, 230.

words that received plural endings were considered animate. Either the Nahuatl author, in that instance, had begun to apply pluralization in the Spanish style while using Nahuatl forms or the author wished to convey something about the animacy of the nails.[85]

With such rich symbolism available, one expects that the prayers offered for the eleventh station will be similarly rich and textured. Anunciación offers a fairly simple prayer.

Anunciación
O Most Gracious Jesus, that with immense love that burns in your divine breast, you suffered to be spread out on the Cross, dislocating your extremities, your Feet and Arms nailed to it. I beseech you, my Lord, through your ineffable charity, that I not extend my feet and hands into any evil, but rather that after my heart is infused with your love, I live crucified to your service with the favor of your grace.[86]

In this prayer, the penitent again attempts to draw a parallel between what is happening to Jesus and some aspect of their life. In this instance, the forcible placement of Jesus on the cross is compared to the penitent's taking on of evil things. It also calls on the penitent to become a living sacrifice in service to and love for Jesus. It is remarkable in its simplicity and avoidance of most of the possible symbols that the crucifixion offers. Yet some of the terms used are not common and serve to heighten the effect of the description. For example, *descoyuntados*, is a clinical term that means "dislocated," which heightens the effect of Jesus being spread on the cross. It paints a picture of Jesus being splayed out so far that his joints have been dislocated.

Vetancurt, in his Nahuatl translation, opted to use some of the rich symbolism offered by the language. We can note the use of the neologism for nails, *tepozmimitica*, "metal darts."

Vetancurt
Alas, O compassionate Jesus! You dearly wanted through Your loving charity to suffer on the cross. They crucified You, piercing each of Your precious hands and feet with metal darts. O my Lord: I pray and implore You, just because of Your perfectly great loving charity I not spread [?] my hands and feet so that I will sin. May I not take [even] a handful of the evil life for myself. Let me, through my compassionate

85. Sell and Burkhart, *Nahuatl Theater*, 4:308–9n97, 309n99.

86. "O Clementisimo Jesus, que con el amor inmenso, que en tu pecho divino ardia, sufriste el ser estendido en la Cruz, desconyuntados sus membros, calvados tus Pies, y Manos en ella: Ruegote, Señor mio, por tu inefable caridad, que no estienda Yo mis pies y manos â la maldad; sino antes traspasado mi corazon con tu amor, viva crucificado en tu servicio con el favor de tu gracia." Anunciación, *Luz para saber andar*, 13.

offerings and with Your help, [i.e.,] grace, bring my life of penance close to me.[87]

The prayer in Nahuatl is more evocative than it is in Spanish. The impact is that one can see the penitent reaching out and spreading his hands to grasp evil, just as the prayer asks that that not happen. But, again, with so much potential symbolism, the prayer is relatively simple and straightforward and a close approximation of the sense provided in the Spanish version.

The Twelfth Station: The Crucifixion and His Death Upon the Cross

Christ's death on the cross is the theme of the twelfth station. Accordingly, the introductions are relatively short in both Spanish and Nahuatl.

Anunciación
This is the twelfth station that includes fourteen steps, and it is the place where this Lord, already crucified on the Holy Cross, was carried by a squad and they let it drop suddenly into the hole in the rock. With the blow his entire Most Holy Body shuddered, and his pious Mother, seeing him so mistreated, fainted, as if dead, with the great pain that the vision caused her.[88]

The motion of the introduction draws the reader into the scene. One can imagine a small squad of men lifting the cross, with Jesus on it, carrying it the few yards, and then dropping it precipitously into the hole. Anunciación might be playing with two similar but unrelated words. In describing the hillside into which a hole was carved, Anunciación uses the word *peña*, which means "rock" or "crag." It is similar enough to the word for "pain" or "sorrow," *pena*, that appears a few lines later to unconsciously connect the two sections of the introduction. One should also note that Anunciación inserts the Virgin Mary into many of the stations where she

87. "Iyo ycnohuaCatzintle JeSus yn San motetlasotlaliztiCatzinco ynnoticmotlasonequilititzinno yn Cruztitech timoCiauhCopinalititias omitzmomamasohualtilique tepozmimitica omitzimococoyonilique yn motlasomatzin yn mocxitzin nimitznotlatlauhtilia NoteCuiotzine ma San ipampatzinco yn CenquizCahuey motetlasotlalitzin maCamo nima[na]loa [?] yn noma yn nocxih ynic nitlatlacoz maCamo nicCuic nicnomatziololotiz ynnaqualli nemiliztli ma San nicnoyolmanaliztiCa notech nicpachoz yn notlamaCenhualiz nemiliztli yn iCa yn motepalehuilitzin yn GraCia." Vetancurt, *Via crucis*, 32–33.

88. "Esta es la duodecima Estacion, que consta de catorze pasos, y es el lugar en donde ya crucificado este Señor en la Santa Cruz le llevaron de tropa, y le dexaron caër de golpe en el agugero de una peña, con el qual golpe se estremeció todo su Santisimo Cuerpo; y viendole tan maltradado su Madre piadosa, quedó desmayda, y como muerta, con la grande pena que le causó su vista." Anunciación, *Luz para saber andar*, 13–14.

was not generally known to have been present. Most accounts, do, however, place her at the crucifixion, although none provide an insight into her reactions to the events.

In translating this introduction, Vetancurt closely follows the model provided by the Spanish. There are a few changes, mostly as a result of Nahuatl syntax and constructions, which provide a slightly different overall vision.

Vetancurt
The twelfth [place] of kneeling prayers [called] a station. It was fourteen steps with which our Savior arrived. They quickly raised Him up there [in the place full of people's bodies?] They angrily abandoned Him; they despisingly rejected Him. His body relapsed into sickness with His fall to the earth; again, His precious earthly body suffered with what was another [punishment]. And His beloved sorrowful mother Saint Mary was [in] such [a state] when she saw her beloved son! Right then her precious heart was anguished [to the point of] fainting.[89]

The Nahuatl does not explicitly include the guards who carried the cross, with Jesus on it, to the place it was erected. Nonetheless, the Nahuatl does describe them as angrily abandoning, *OquimotlahuelmaCahuilique*, and "despisingly" rejecting, *Oquimotlalhuitequilique*, Jesus. Again, this is an interesting pair of descriptive verb phrases. As noted above, this was a very common rhetorical device in Nahuatl, especially in elevated speech. It was an indicator of elevated speech when using in succession two or more words or phrases, each having a slightly different meaning from the last, to develop a complex description.

The prayers for this station add detail to the picture painted in the introduction. In particular, they mention the two other convicts, usually called thieves, who, tradition holds, accompanied Jesus at his crucifixion. This prayer asks that the penitent might die to the world just as Jesus died on the cross.

Anunciación
O Divine Jesus, although crucified on that beam between two Thieves, you were raised to the view of the whole World and endured insufferable torment. I beg you, my Lord, that you cure the illness of my Soul, and that stepping on the Earth and its vanities, you raise my spirit to the con-

89. "ynic matlatli omome Netlaquaquetzaliztlatlatlauhtiliztli eSTaCiOn matlatli onnahui ycxineanaliztli ynic omaxilitico yn totemaquixiticatzin Auh Ca ye onCa ôquimehuatiquechilique tetlaCayoCo OquimotlahuelmaCahuilique Oquimotlalhuitequilique AUh Ca yCa yn itlalhuitequilitzin omoCaxanitzinno yn inaCayotzin oc Cepa yc oce Cepo Catca omoCiauhcopinni yn itlasotlaltzin Auh yn itlasochoquisnantzin Santa maria yn iuhcatzintli yn oquimotili yn itlasoConetzin Auh San niman omosotlauhpātzimiquititia yn itlasoyolotzin." Vetancurt, *Via crucis*, 33–34.

templation of and desire for eternal things. And only You do I love, and You I want. Through your love, I die to the world and to myself.[90]

The Synoptic Gospels and John all mention the two convicts who were crucified alongside Jesus. Both Mark and Matthew narrate the same scene. In those Gospels the thieves join the crowd in taunting Jesus, saying that if he could destroy the Temple in three days, as he had claimed, why could he not save himself now?[91] The Gospel of Luke develops the theme further and has the two criminals take opposing sides in the argument, leading to the tradition of the "good thief" and the "evil thief." After the guards taunt Jesus, asking why he does not save himself if he really is the King of the Jews, one of the convicts joins in and says that if Jesus were the Messiah, he should save himself, and them too. The other criminal then criticizes the guards and his fellow criminal, noting that they were condemned for actual crimes, whereas Jesus has done nothing wrong. The second convict, the "good thief," then asks Jesus to remember him when he enters into Glory. Jesus replies that indeed he will, and that they will be together in paradise.[92] Given this rich material about repentance immediately before death, it is odd that it is not included either in the introduction or, to a greater degree, in the prayer associated with the station.

Vetancurt does not change the sentiment of this prayer in his translation. The general arc of the prayer is essentially the same as the Spanish version.

Vetancurt
Alas, divine being, Jesus! On the cross in the middle of the two thieves, You wanted various torments so that You would die in public. I pray and implore You: Cure me of the sinful sickness of my spirit so that right at my feet I will cast earthly confusions. And as for my eyes and heart, my sight and my will: may I alone want for them the things of heaven. (See p. 220 below.)

This prayer does an excellent job of conveying the same general meaning as the Spanish version, but in a simple manner. The only item of note is that Vetancurt, in the Nahuatl, implies that Jesus desired his own death and the torture that it included. This is not orthodox thinking within Christian communities. Indeed, the Gospels portray Jesus as strongly conflicted over his impending death. The most famous instance of this is a prayer when Jesus

90. "O Divino Jesus, que crucificado en ese Madero entre dos Ladrones, fuiste levantado â vista de todo el Mundo, y padeciste tormentos insufribles: Te ruego, Señor mio, que sanes las dolencias de mi Alma; y que pisando al Mundo, y sus vanidades, se levante mi espiritu â la contemplacion, y anehol de las cosas eternas, y solo â Ti ame y â Ti quiera, y por tu amor muera al Mundo, y a mi mismo." Anunciación, *Luz para saber andar*, 14.
91. Mark 15:27–32; Matthew 27:38–44.
92. Luke 23:35–43.

asks God to "take this cup from me," meaning he wants God to relieve him of the torture and pain of his imminent death. That particular phrase appears in one form or another in all the Gospels, including John.[93]

The Thirteenth Station: His Body Is Taken Down from the Cross (Deposition and Pietà)

The thirteenth station commemorates Jesus's body being taken from the cross. In art, the scene is frequently referred to as the "descent from the cross" or the "deposition." In Anunciación's Spanish version of the Stations of the Cross, the introduction places Mary at the center of the scene, holding the body of her dead son in her arms. In sculpture and painting, this image is frequently called the pietà.

Anunciación
This is the thirteenth station and the place where our Lord Jesus Christ was lowered from the Cross and placed in the arms of his Holiest Mother, where you will contemplate how much sorrow the Most Holy Virgin would feel seeing in her arms her Most Holy Son completely broken, covered with wounds, and undone, and the great affliction of having to give that rich treasure of the world in order to place him in a tomb.[94]

Perhaps the most surprising element of the introduction is when the author switches to the second person to directly address the penitent. Rather than remain aloof as a third person narrator, in this passage Anunciación directly addresses the readers and charges them to contemplate the scene that has been painted. He next calls on them to imagine Mary's sorrow in handing her son, the treasure of the world, over for burial.

In dealing with the translation of this text, Vetancurt changes the impact slightly. Rather than address the readers, Vetancurt switches into the first-person plural ("we will go about remembering") to include the reader with himself. The e mphasis on the Virgin's sorrow is central in the translation as well.

Vetancurt
The thirteenth [place] of kneeling prayers [called] a station. Here is where they lowered our Savior into the lapfolds of [and], laid Him down for, His weeping mother Saint Mary. We will go about remembering with

93. Mark 14:36; Matthew 26:42; Luke 22:42; John 18:11.

94. "Esta es la decima tercia Estacion, y el lugar donde nuestro Señor Jesu Christo fue baxado de la Cruz, y puesto en los brazos de su Santisima Madre: donde contemplarás quanto dolor sentiría la Santisima Virgen, viendo en sus brazos â su Hijo Santisimo, todo descoyntado, acardenalado, y deshecho; y en la afliccion tan grande de haver de dar aquel rico tesoro del Mundo para ponerlo en el sepulcro." Anunciación, *Luz parta saber andar*, 14–15.

sad weeping her anguish, for she was very hurt in her heart when she saw her only child. Her heart and honor blackened and numbed, she cried right out [because?] His precious body no longer appeared human. And He also was very anxious: How sad my mother is! For He was given to her so that He was left locked up in His sepulchre.[95]

Jesus is clearly dead, the Nahuatl version recognizes that as a divine being, he could continue to observe what was occurring. Thus, the narration observes, "He also was very anxious: How sad my mother is!"[96] Lastly, the Nahuatl observes that Jesus was placed in the "lapfolds," *yCuixantzinco* (spelled *cuexantli* in standard orthography,) of Mary. This was a specific anatomical place for Nahua speakers. It refers to carrying objects in one's skirts, but it also describes the region between the waist and the lower thighs.[97]

The prayers for this station are addressed directly to the Virgin Mary. The penitents implore her assistance in gaining the glory of heaven.

Anunciación
Most Pure Mother of my Most Gracious Jesus; I beseech you, Lady, through the pain that you felt when having held in your arms your beloved son for the last time, you had to place him in the tomb, reach down to me from your majesty. I fully appreciate his and your sorrows so that his passion might be my antidote, his wounds become my food, his blood dew, his death life, and his Cross glory, that I might walk through this [world] to that [i.e., Heaven] with your favor to see him eternally.[98]

The prayer is very much in the baroque style and also reinforces certain aspects of the Catholic Reformation. The opening invocation addresses the

95. "ynic matlactli omey netlaquaquetzaliztlatlauhtiliztli eStaCioñ Ca ye niCa yn Canin oquimotemohuilique yn totemaquixitiCatzin yCuixantzinco Oquimotequililique ynchoquiznantzin Santa maria tlaocollchoquiliztiCa ticlnamiquiztinemizque yn inetequipacholtzin Ca CeCa omoyolotoneuhtzino yn iquac oquimotili ynCenteconetzin Otlitlileuh oCeCepoliuhtia yn yolotzin yn imahuizyotzin huellotzatzantia yntlasonaCayotzin ayocmo motlaCaneXititzinoa Auh Ca Oc no <36> CenCa no huel omotequipachotzinoaya ynic notlaocollnantzin Ca oquimotemaquili ynic quimoCalltzaCuilitihue ynin imiquiztepetlaCaltzinco." Vetancurt, *Via crucis*, 35–36.

96. It could also be an issue of spelling, since the third person would be *motlaocollnantzin*, rather than *notlaocollnantzin*.

97. Kartunnen, *An Analytical Dictionary*, 71.

98. "Madre Purisima de mi Clementisimo Jesus: Suplixote, Señora, por aquella pena que sentiste, quando haviendo tenido en tus brazos â tu amado Hijo, ultimamemte, te lo quitaron para ponerlo en el Sepulcro, me alcanzes de su Magestad, aprecio tan grande de sus dolores, y los tuyos, para que siendo mi antidoto su Pasion, manjar sus llagas, rocio su Sangre, vida su Muerte, y gloria su Cruz, camine por esta, â aquella, con tu favor, â verle eternamante." Anunciación, *Luz para saber andar*, 15.

"Most Pure Mother of my Most Gracious Jesus." As noted, the use of superlatives is an important hallmark of the baroque. In this case, the superlatives accompany fairly strong adjectives such as "pure" and "gracious." The closing phrases are evocative of the baroque in that there is the play of opposites, a list of divine characteristics that the penitent hopes will become routine and assurance that Christ's passion will become the antidote to the sins of the world. Furthermore, the prayer goes on to ask that Jesus's wounds might become like food and his blood like the dew. Then the oppositional comparison emerges: through Christ's death the penitent enjoys life such that the Cross will become glory, in other words, like heaven. The intercession of the saints was one of the areas which the Catholic Church wished to emphasize in opposition to Protestant denominations' saints. Protestants, in general, believe that prayers should be addressed only to God. The Catholic Church continues to teach that the saints in heaven can act as intermediaries and intercessors for the faithful. Thus, the fact that this prayer is addressed to Mary, and not to God, emphasizes that it is Catholic.

This extremely complex prayer clearly posed challenges to Vetancurt and his team when it came time to translate it. Many of the concepts are unique to Christianity and clearly stood as obstacles to translation.

> **Vetancurt**
> Alas, O our beloved honored mother, O perfectly merciful one, beloved honored mother of my beloved Savior Jesus Christ! It was just on account of His very anguished death that Your precious heart suffered burning pain when you saw that they laid Him down in the tomb. Let me be helped with your strength. I will place and copy the torment of my beloved Savior on my heart. Let me regard His torment as a medicinal plant. Let His honored flaying be my food, my proper deportment will be His precious blood. Let His precious death become my life. Let His cross be my vow so that I will eternally serve Him until I go to see Him in heaven.[99]

The prayer follows the Spanish fairly closely until the play of opposites and divine characteristics. At that point, Vetancurt opts to translate the prayer

99. "Iyo totlasomahuiznatzine CequizCatetlaocollti Catzintle ynnitlasomahuiznatzin yn notlasotemaquixiquetiCatzin JeSuChr[i]Sto nimitzinnotlatlauhtilia ma San papatzīco y moYolopatzinmiquilitzin ynic Otoneuh yn motlasoyolotzin yn iquac oticmottili yn motlasonConetzin ynic quimotequilitihueh ynnoztoc tepetlaaCallco ma moChiCahualiztiCatzinco nipalehuilo yeh ytechi nictlaliz ytech niccopinaz y noyolo yn itonehuitzin yn notlasotemaquixitiCatzin ma yehuatzin yn ipan nicmatiz yn teuhuitzitzilipātli yntlayohuilitzin ma notlaquall yes yn ixixipehualitzin <37> y nonemachis yes yn itlasoyesyotz ma noyoliliz mochihuas yn itlasomiq[ui]litzin ma nonecuillnetoll yes yn iquauhnepanolltzin ynic ma semiCaC ninotlayecolltiz yn ixiq[ui]chiCah nicnotiliztiuh yn ilhuiCatl itehc." Vetancurt, *Via crucis*, 36–37.

focusing more on the sense of the passages rather than the literal meaning of the words. Vetancurt achieves some eloquent passages in this translation. For example, rather than saying that Jesus's blood is like dew, Vetancurt translates the passage to read, "my proper deportment will be His precious blood." The friar also reverses the order of the attributions. In the Spanish, a feature of Jesus is transformed into something positive for the penitent. In the Nahuatl phrase, however, something laudable for the penitent represents something of Jesus's passion.

In other instances in this prayer, Vetancurt opts for what seem to be distinctive translations. In the prayer we find the expression "Let His honored flaying be my food," "ma notlaquall yes yn ixixipehualitzin." It is clear in the context of the whole prayer that the suffering of Christ is to serve as medicine for the soul and food for the spirit. But a close reading of the Nahuatl opens up several levels of meaning. In all likelihood, the prayer refers to the Eucharist in which the bread and wine become the body and blood of Christ. Yet using this particular word (*ixixipehualitzin*) implies that the flayed skin of Jesus is to be consumed as food. The Spanish version is slightly different, and although the construction is complex, the meaning is straightforward: "Your wounds [are] my food."[100] The words in Spanish are descriptive simply of the wounds, *llagas*, and of generic food, *manjar*. There is an important difference between being flayed (having skin removed) and being wounded. This is especially true when one considers ancient Nahua tradition. The Mexica deity associated with rebirth and springtime was Xipe Totec (Our Lord the Flayed One). Some of the rituals associated with his cult included the flaying of a sacrificial victim. A priest would then wear the skin for various periods of time. In certain ceremonies the flayed skin was consumed. For example, in the month of Tlacaxipehualiztli (the Flaying of Humans) the victim was flayed, and then his flesh was ritually eaten, perhaps including some skin. We should not assume that because the *Via crucis* was written more than a hundred and fifty years after the conquest the old ways had been completely forgotten. In a roughly contemporary play, one of the characters boasts that he will kill his enemies, flay them (*nicynxipehuaz*), and wear their skins.[101] Given this continuing knowledge of the old tradition, the choice of *xipe* in discussing the wounds of Jesus is distinctive. It might well point to a high degree of sophistication. By using the word for flayed skin, Vetancurt might well have been clearly indicating the true presence of Christ's body in the Eucharist.

Nonetheless, looking more closely at other places in the Nahuatl version of the Stations of the Cross, Vetancurt frequently uses words built on, *xipe*,

100. "Manjar sus llagas." Vetancurt, *Via crucis*, 15. "Manjar" in this period signified food in a very generic sense.

101. Sell and Burkhart, *Nahuatl Theater*, 4:286–87.

to describe Christ's wounds. In the introduction of the third station, the first fall, the Spanish reads: "He fell to earth under the Holy Cross, and with the force of the blow it gave Him His wounds opened again."[102] In this instance, Vetancurt again uses a word formed with *xipe* to refer to the wounds: *yn xipehaulitzin*. In his dictionary, in the Spanish-to-Nahuatl section, under "wound" (*llaga*), Alonso de Molina lists various words for things such as a "new wound with blood," a "wound with matter," and a "large wound." One of the words, among others, that Molina lists as a root is *chipeuiliztli*.[103] At this distance it is hard to tell whether that word is just a phonetic variant of *xipehualiztli*. Nonetheless, the data indicate that there are two distinct root words, one having to do with a wound, the other related to flaying. Certainly, in Nahuatl, especially in middle-colonial texts having a *ch* replaced by an *x* is not out of the question. Nevertheless, because of all the pre-Hispanic associations of the root *xipe*, it seems extremely odd that of all the Nahuatl words at his disposal, Vetancurt chose *xipehualiztli* rather than something based on the verb "to hurt or wound," *huitequi*.

The Fourteenth Station: He Is Laid in the Tomb (Interment)

The final station is the burial of Jesus in the tomb. Again, Anunciación devotes most of the introduction to this station to the Virgin Mary. The pathos of the mother viewing the corpse of her son figures as the central theme.

Anunciación

This is the fourteenth station that lies thirty steps, in contemplation of the Solitude of our Lady at the foot of the Cross, and it is the place of the Holy Sepulchre of our Redeemer Jesus Christ, where after having been in the arms of the Most Holy MARY, his Mother, that Sacred Cadaver, and having been anointed with many fragrances and wrapped in a very clean Cloth, they put it with much reverence in the Tomb, and closing the door with a large stone, which was to put it on the heart of the Virgin MARY; and so great was the sorrow that this Lady felt in seeing herself now without the presence of Jesus her SON, which exceeded all the other [sorrows] that she had suffered until then.[104]

---

102. "Cayó en tierra, debajo de la Santa Cruz, y con la fuerza del golpe que dió, se abrieron de nuevo las llagas." Anunciación, *Luz para saber andar*, 4.

103. Molina, *Vocabulario castellana y mexicana*, folio 79. This might also be spelled *chipehuiliztli*.

104. "Esta es la decima quarta Estacion, que consta de treinta pasos, en contemplacion de la Soledad de nuestra Señora al pie de la Cruz; y es el lugar del Santo Sepulcro de nuestro Redentor Jesu-Christo, donde despues de haver estado en los brazos de MARIA Santisima,

The focus of this introduction places the sorrows of Mary foremost. Among them is the solitude of Mary as she realizes that her son has died. Both of these aspects of Mary became important cult figures in the Christian world. Our Lady of Sorrows (Nuestra Señora de los Dolores) is a very popular aspect of Mary that gave rise to the name Dolores in many Hispanic families. Similarly, Our Lady of Solitude (Nuestra Señora de la Soledad) is a common aspect of Mary throughout the Hispanic world. The Virgin of Solitude has some resonance with the Franciscan Order. It is the advocation for one of the chain of missions that the order established in California, Soledad. The introduction to station fourteen repeats specific details of the biblical accounts of the entombment, and later discovery of the empty tomb on Easter, including wrapping the body in a new cloth, using fragrant oils (Gospel of John), and rolling a stone over the mouth of the tomb.[105]

Vetancurt chooses to keep much of the focus in this introduction on Mary, following the Spanish version. Again, certain details are difficult to render into Nahuatl, and the translation shows where Vetancurt has to use neologisms and circumlocutions to convey the message of the Spanish.

> **Vetancurt**
> The fourteenth place of kneeling prayers [called] a station. Here is what is called His stone burial house, the grave of our beloved Savior. With loving charity He was [covered] with flower water that was like [the extract of a] medicinal plant. His precious dead body was dressed in a new, white, soft covering. Then they laid Him in a tomb. They covered up the entrance of the cave with a big stone. But when His beloved mother saw Him she wiped the face of her beloved child and youngest child. She suffered beyond all [others] when they spread out a big covering stone on Him. Then a great affliction [darkened] [her face] Let us piteously call to [Him?].[106]

---

su Madre, aquel Sagrado Cadaver, y de haverlo ungido con muchos olores, y embuelto en una Sabana muy limpia, le pusieron con mucha reverencia en el Sepulcro, y cerrando la puerta con una loza muy grande, que fue ponerla sobre el corazon de la Virgen MARIA; y fuè tan grande el dolor, que sintió esta Señora de vérse yá sin la presencia de Jesus su Hijo, que excedió â todos los que hasta allí havia padecido." Anunciación, *Luz para saber andar*, 15–16.

105. Matthew 27:59–61; Mark 15:45–47; Luke 23:52–54; John 19:39–42.

106. "ynic tla matlatli onnauhCa netlaquaquetzaliztlatlauhtiliztli estaCion Auh Ca ye niCan yn motenehuan yn inetoquiliztepetlaCalltzinco yn SepullCrO yn totlaSotemaquixitiCatzin yn Cani yeh iuh tetlasotlaliztiCa huitzitzilipatli yuhqui quename xochiatli yc o[?]ui ma matelloquen Yc oquimomeCatla tlapachilihuique Çe yztac yanCuiC yamãqui tlachpachiuhcayotli yc oq[ui]miloloc yn itlasomiquiliztlactzin niman oquimotequilique yn miCaoztoctecochoCon Çe huey ixitlapalli tetl yC oquixitlahpachoque ynnoztoCalltentli Auh yn iquac Oquimotili yn itlasonantzin ye q[ui].mixipolluia yn itlasoConetzin yn ixocoyotzin oquiCenpanahui yn ixq[ui]chi ynnoquimiyohuilititzino yn ipatzinco oquiteCaque yn huey yn tlapalltetli Auh niman ypantzinco otlxyoatia ynnica yolopatzimiquilitzin ma no tictotlaoCollnochilliCa ma timochintin tictotlatlauhtiliCan." Vetancurt, *Via crucis*, 37–38.

The anointing of bodies with fragrant oils seems not to have been commonly practiced in mid-colonial Mexico. As a result, Vetancurt has to use a circumlocution to describe it as best he can. But he comes up with the phrase "flower water that was like [the extract of a] medicinal plant," "huitzitzilipatli yuhqui quename xochiatli." In describing Mary and her son, Vetancurt chooses to call him her "youngest child," *ixocoyotzin*. In precontact times, many children had names that referred to birth order, although this was more common among females than males. But to call Jesus her youngest causes the reader to ponder the idea that he had older siblings. This, of course, runs counter to Catholic theology, which holds that Jesus was Mary's only son.[107]

The prayers associated with the last station conclude the whole devotion, although both the Spanish and Nahuatl versions have supplementary materials, including additional closing prayers. The Spanish version of the prayer for the fourteenth station asks the Lord to assist penitents in ridding their lives of sin to prepare themselves for receiving the holy sacrament of the Eucharist and to prepare for their eventual death.

> **Anunciación**
> O Divine Lord, that after you suffered so many affronts on Mount Calvary you wished that your Sacrosanct Body be interred with all decency and veneration, placed in a new Tomb in which no other body had ever been interred. I beseech you, my Lord, through the merits of your Most Holy Passion that (with your grace) my Soul be cleansed of all blame and that it be purified in such a manner, with your love, that it seem to have never entered into the death of sin, so that thus I might receive you in the Most Holy Sacrament of the Altar, in which with us you attend until the end of the World.[108]

Some of the details elaborated in the prayer are central to some of the beliefs and tenets of Christianity. One of these is that the tomb in which Jesus was placed was a new one, having never been used before. Three gospels refer to the tomb as a new one. Mark does not clearly indicate one way or another,

---

107. Some in the early church proposed that Joseph was a widower and that he had children by his first wife. In this way, Jesus could have had older brothers. Catholic teaching holds that the brothers and sisters mentioned in the Bible are cousins and that Mary's virginity was perpetual. "The Blessed Virgin Mary," *Catholic Encyclopedia*, New Advent, https://www.newadvent.org/cathen/15464b.htm.

108. "O Divino Señor, que despues de tanta afrenta como padeciste en el Monte Calvario, quisiste que tu Cuerpo Sacrosanto fuera sepultado con toda decencia, y veneracion, colocado en un Sepulcro nuevo, en el qual no havia sido enterrado otro cuerpo alguno: Suplicote, Señor mio, por los meritos de tu Pasion Santisima, que (con tu gracia) limpie mi Alma de toda culpa, y la purifique de tal manera, con tu amor, que parezca no haver entrado en ella la muerte del pecado, para que asi te reciba en el Santisimo Sacramento del Altar, en el qual con nosotros asistes hasta el fin del Mundo." Anunciación, *Luz para saber andar*, 16.

but points out that it was a tomb owned by Joseph of Arimathea. Matthew mentions its ownership and adds that it has not been used. Both Luke and John put emphasis on the fact that it has never been used before.[109]

In the Nahuatl version, Vetancurt also notes that it was a new grave. When he describes the suffering of Jesus, he uses a common rhetorical device, Nahuatl repetition of similar concepts. The sufferings fall into two groups: insults and assaults, verbal versus physical. The insults on Jesus were "unspeakable, immeasurable, and diverse." While the assaults that were specifically included: "pains, torments, dishonors, and sufferings."

> **Vetancurt**
> Alas, O Deity Who is perfectly worthy of love, O God! You thus suffered all the unspeakable, immeasurable, and diverse pains, torments, dishonors, and sufferings! But afterward You wanted Your dead body to be buried with honor, also in a new grave. I pray and implore You: just because of Your tormented passion may You purify my spirit. Renew me so that I will receive Your precious esteemed body, the Most Holy Sacrament [as] You are seated until the world will come to an end, with purity of heart.[110]

The translation follows the Spanish model fairly closely, expressing that Jesus had himself desired the honorable burial. It also looks for Jesus to be with the penitent until the end of time, as does the Spanish, but it especially aims to prepare the faithful person to receive the holy sacrament of the Eucharist, called the "Sacrament of the Altar" in the Spanish version and the "Most Holy Sacrament" in the Nahuatl.

The Spanish-language Anunciación version and Vetancurt's Nahuatl version both have distinct content after the prayer for the fourteenth station. In the Anunciación handbook, there is a litany that recounts the attacks and insults suffered by Jesus during the Passion. At the conclusion of each of these, the penitents are asked to respond with "Blessed and praised be forever such a great Lord." For example, the first insult is "For the Agonies of the Garden, and imprisonment of the Lord, Blessed and praised be forever such a great Lord."[111]

---

109. Mark 15:45–46; Matthew 27:58–60; Luke 23:50–53; John 19:38–41.

110. "Iyo Çenquizcatlasotlaloni yCeltzin teotli Diose yn ye uh oticmonequilyohuilititzino yn ixquich amoyhtolon ynnamo tamachiuhqui ypapan tecoco <39> tetoneuh emahuizpolo tlayohuiliztli Auh satepan oticmonequilititzino mahuizyotiCa motoCatzinoz yn momiquiliztlactzin yn no çan yāCuiC tecochco nimitzinotlatlauhtilia ma san ipapantzinco yn motlayohuilizpanSSiontzin ma xinechmochipahuilili yn noyolia ma xinechimoyanCuilili ynic noneyollchipahualiztica nicnoCeliliz yn motlasomahuiznaCayotzin y SantiSSimo SaCramento yn timehuilitítiCa yn ixquichca tzonquizaz yn Çemanahuactli." Vetancurt, *Via crucis*, 38–39.

111. "Por las Agonias del Huerto, y prisiones del Señor: Bendito y alabado sea para siempre tan gran Señor." Anunciación, *Luz para saber andar*, 17–18

Each of these insults is then listed in chronological order from the Garden of Gethsemane, to the trial before Pilate, through the way of the cross, ending with the interment. At the very end of the entire work, Anunciación places a prayer and response:

> **Anunciación**
> [Pray aloud] Blessed be forever such a great Lord, who wished to suffer for us such an immensity of pains, and because our sins were the cause of so many censures, and affronts, we all say the Act of Contrition with great sorrow and repentance for having offended such a pious Lord, . . .[112]

Thus, the Spanish version ends much as it began, with the formal prayer known as the Act of Contrition. After that, the author or the publisher merely places the words *Laus Deo*, "God be praised," in Latin to conclude the work. This short section is translated by Vetancurt quite directly:

> **Vetancurt**
> Let us perfectly praise Him with all our heart [and will?] Such are You, God of Love! He wanted through His loving charity to save us, so that on our account He suffered everything. But if truly we will thank Him, let our sins make us cry, let us vow before Him, [let?] us say our words of heart-felt affliction, let us cry before Him.[113]

The Vetancurt translation, or at least the copy that we have, also closes this call with the Act of Contrition. In the Nahuatl, the closing Act of Contrition is quite long and differs from the prayer used at the opening of the devotion of the Stations of the Cross. Of interest in this prayer, Vetancurt has the penitents call out that they have been manifold sinners, sinning many times. In Nahuatl this becomes "having sinned four hundred times," *ônoÇentziontlahuellilitic*. For the Nahua, the number four hundred represented a very large number.

But the Vetancurt devotion then continues for several more pages. In particular, the next section details the counting of many things associated with the Passion and redemption. Among these are the number of indul-

112. "Bendito sea para siempre tan Gran Señor, que quiso padecer por nosotros tanta inmensidad de penas, y pues nuestros pecados fueron la causa de tantos oprobrios, y afrentas, digamos todos con gran dolor, y arrepentimiento, de haver ofendido â tan piaposa Señor, el Acto de Contrición." Anunciación, *Luz para saber andar*, 18.

113. "AUh ma tictoÇenquizCayectenehuiliCa moch iCa yn toyolo ynCiahuiliz yn iuhCatzintli y yn titlaÇotlalizteotli yCa ytetlaSotlalitzin Oquimonequilititzino yn techmomaquixitilitzinnoz ynic topapatiCa yn ixiquichi oquimiyohuilititzino Auh yntlanell tictlasoCamatizque ma ma [te]chocti yn totlatlaColl ma yxpantzinco titonenetolotiCa ya tiquitoCan yn toyolochichinaCaliztlahtolitzin ma yhxipantzinco timochoquiliCan." Vetancurt, *Via crucis*, 39–40.

gences gained and the number of sinners to be redeemed from purgatory by saying the prayers. Following this, the Vetancurt edition becomes somewhat morbid and begins to enumerate the drops of blood shed by Jesus and other similar points of suffering. The participants recall the blows and injuries, false testimonies, whippings, blasphemies, and other torments of Christ in the rest of the litany, with the same response after each. This litany is no longer a standard part of the Stations of the Cross devotion, but there are similar litanies circulating, such as a "Litany of the Passion," which can be found in several places.[114]

In some of the other devotional works from seventeenth- and eighteenth-century Mexico, there were similar passages that recited the number of blows and other offences against Jesus. For example, something very similar appears in a section of the work known as the *Cadena de oro*, from the pen of María de la Antigua. In several of the printed copies of this work there is a section entitled "Recopliacion de los Dolores de N[uest]ro Redentor" (Compilation of the Sorrows of Our Redeemer). In one example of this book the numbers describing the affronts to Jesus have been blacked out, and in another copy the entire section has been cut out and removed. Some examples of sufferings include "The [blows] on his arms were sixty two; the drops of blood that he shed were 730,500; the tears that he shed for us sinners were 700,200."[115] As noted earlier, the blacking out of numbers appears in yet another devotional. In a copy of the *Via dolorosa* of Nicolas de Espindola, someone even blacked out the number of falls that Jesus suffered in the Passion.[116] Clearly, at some point in the eighteenth century, an injunction was issued against considering the number of sufferings that befell Jesus in the Passion.

Nonetheless, a unique version of this litany of suffering appears in Vetancurt's Nahuatl translation. It describes all the affronts to Jesus in terms of very large numbers, using what can only be described as a variant of the normal Nahuatl counting system. Each of the sufferings is described in exquisite detail: "144 kicks, 120 times they stoned him, 102 slaps in the face, . . . 28 times they struck his chest with stones, . . . 80 times they mistreated him, . . . 77 times they whipped his neck, . . . 350 times on a stone base, . . . 70 times on a stone column, . . . 4,800 times they tore his precious body with a whip." Other fantastical numbers include his paying for our sins 130,000 times with

114. "Litany of the Passion," Catholic Online, https://www.catholic.org/prayers/prayer.php?p=466.

115. Antigua, *Cadena de oro*, 58–59. "Los que dieron en sus brazos fueron sesenta y dos. Las gotas de sangre que derramo fueron setecientas mill y quinientas. Las lagrimas que por nuestros pecados lloró fueron setecientos mil y docientas." Antigua, *Cadena de oro*, 58–59. The copy in which pages were removed is held in the John Carter Brown Library, BA745 .A629c, after p. 60.

116. Espindola, *Via dolorosa*, 11, 18, 20. JBL, BA761 .E77v

his blood; 16,200 dripping tears; 5,475 flayings (wounds?); and 384,060 drops of blood.[117] The presence of these indicates that the printed edition might well have had such details, appearing as it did in the late seventeenth century. Later printings in Spanish seem to lack the section, probably in response to an injunction.

To understand how unique this section is, one needs to know a bit about the Nahuatl number system. The Nahua, like most Mesoamerican groups, used a vigesimal number system, unlike the decimal system currently used by a majority of countries. The decimal system counts by integers, tens, hundreds, and so on. The Nahua counted by integers, twenties, four hundreds, eight thousands, and so on. For example, in Nahuatl one hundred is expressed as five twenties, *macuilpohualli*. One thousand was stated as two four hundreds plus ten twenties, *omtzontli ihuan mactlacpohualli*. In general, in English we do not use a number higher than nine in any given place (integers, tens, hundreds, etc.) in formal situations. For example, we do not say "thirty-four teens." The "teens" go up only to nine. In common speech, we do say things like "fifteen hundred," but English speakers know that it signifies "one thousand five hundred." Similarly, in Nahuatl, there should be no multiplier higher than nineteen in any place category. Yet in these fantastical numbers, Vetancurt has been very creative and violated these basic numerical rules. The best example of the violation of this rule is found in the huge number: "onpoalli yhuan macuilli xiquipilli yhuan yheipoallitziontli yhuan yehpoalli," "two twenties and five [i.e., forty-five] eight thousands, and three twenties [i.e., sixty] four hundreds, and three twenties." This clearly breaks the basic rules by having multiples over nineteen in any given level (i.e. integers, twenties, four hundreds, eight thousands). It violates this by having thirty-five in the eight thousands group and sixty in the four hundreds group.[118] The explanation for this odd occurrence is twofold. On the one hand, the author is attempting to give the impression of the innumerable wounds and indignities suffered by Jesus during his Passion. In a similar manner, in English we might say "a gazillion" or "eleventy-seven thousand," made-up numbers to convey something very large or extraordinary. On the other hand, to this day in Nahuatl-speaking regions, one sign of one's command of the language is the ability to express large numbers. In the example of the *Via crucis*, Vetancurt, in going beyond expressing large numbers according to the regular conventions, begins to simply make them up.

---

117. Vetancurt, *Via crucis*, 43–45

118. It is difficult to determine what the correct version of this would be in Nahuatl, because most sources have the system ending with the eight thousands, *xiquipilli*. This number would require two (one hundred sixty thousands), eight *xiquipilli* (four hundreds), and three *poalli* (twenties).

Additional Observations on the Nahuatl

Looking at the Nahuatl version as a whole, several of Vetancurt's word choices stand out.[119] Just as we have seen the use of the Nahuatl root *xipe* that might have elicited unwanted comparisons to precontact traditions, and *tilma* might evoke the legend of Guadalupe, there are other word choices in the text that stand out because of pre-Hispanic traditions. Vetancurt's choice of words to discuss Calvary, also known as Golgotha, raises some questions. One of the clearest instances of Vetancurt's decisions regarding this word appears in the introduction for station ten. In that station, Vetancurt uses both a neologism and a borrow word in his discussion. It reads: "NiCan Cani Omaxilitico yn tziōpantepec CalVario" (Here is where he reached Skull Rack Place, Calvary).[120] Here Vetancurt juxtaposes the Nahuatl neologism with the Spanish word. In both Greek (Golgotha) and in Spanish (Calvario), the place name means "Place of the Skull." Rather than just let the Spanish word stand alone, as with Jerusalem and other place-names, Vetancurt has chosen to translate it into Nahuatl. Indeed, in several other places he just uses Calvario rather than attempting a translation. For example, in the introduction for the fourth station (Jesus Encounters His Mother) Vetancurt writes *yn tepeticpac CallVaro* (On the top of Mount Calvary).[121] But at station ten, the Nahuatl word that he chooses is unexpected. Rather than simply saying "skull hill/mountain" in Nahuatl, which could be *tzontepec*, he chooses "Skull Rack Hill," using the term *tzompantli* as the base. In pre-Hispanic times, the Mexica used to display the skulls of their sacrificial victims precisely on the *Tzompantli*, "Skull Wall or Rack." It was a constant reminder of the power and terror of the Mexica deities. Thus, the term carried with it a large number of pre-Hispanic associations that must not have been lost on the Natives who used this devotion. There were two other words that perhaps might have served Vetancurt better. The more common word for the skull was *cuaxicalli*. A slightly more precise term for the head, once separated from the rest of the body, was *tzontecomatl*.[122] At the same time, other colonial authors used *tzontepec* for the translation of Calvary.[123]

---

119. In the following discussion, it is assumed that the word choice and even orthography reflect Vetancurt's text. Unfortunately, the manuscript is a copy of a printed text. While it is unlikely that the scribe inserted different words, it is quite possible that spelling changes might have emerged as part of the copying process.

120. Vetancurt, *Via crucis*, 28. The word *tziōpantepec* is curious on its own, as will be seen. The macron over the *o* signifies the presence of an '*n* that is not written. Vetancurt (or the copyist) also has a tendency to insert the letter *I* where it would not normally occur. For example, in constructions that contain the syllable *-tzon-* Ventacurt writes *-tzion-*.

121. Vetancurt, *Via crucis*, 19.

122. Karttunen, *An Analytical Dictionary*, 67, 317, 318.

123. Vetancurt is not the only author to use *tzonpantepec*. Louise Burkhart provides the following citation for another: "La passion de n[uest]ro Señor Jesu christo," Berendt-

While Vetancurt and his team made certain notable and curious word choices in Nahuatl, he also crafted some truly lovely and moving phrases in that language. Some of these manifest a sensitive control of the language as well as profound sentiments. In the prayer for the eighth station (Jesus Meets the Women of Jerusalem), Vetancurt introduces some lovely turns of phrase. "Ca amo oticmoCahuili yn motemachtiltequitzin ynic otiquinmonextilili yniquename quichoquiltiz quenyn itlatlacolo Auh ma no nehuatli Xinechmonextilili Xinechmomachtili yn quenin choquiztiCa yxayotica yolotequipacholiztica nechoctiz."[124] This translates to "You did not abandon Your task of teaching with which You revealed to me how [one's] sins will make [one] cry. Also show and teach me how with weeping, tears, and sadness, all my sins with which I blackened and dirtied my soul made me cry." In this passage there is a wonderful parallelism using the words *temachtia*, meaning "to teach something to people," and *nextia*, meaning "to reveal or describe something."[125] In the first phrase, the subject of the verb is Jesus, who does the teaching and revealing. In the second, placed in the imperative, the person praying asks that God teach and reveal to them. For Nahuatl speakers, wordplay like this would have been an indication of serious writing since in classical Nahuatl, the use of slight modifications to words and phrases to introduce new meanings was an essential part of rhetoric. Indeed, this type of construction demonstrates a very high level of sophistication in the language.

Conclusions

There is little doubt that the Anunciación text of the Stations of the Cross, known as the "Luz para saber andar" formed the basis for the Vetancurt Nahuatl version. Looking closely at the two texts, half of the meditations are fairly close translations of the Spanish. In three instances the Nahuatl is more extensive, and in four the Spanish is more extensive or there are other differences between them. With regard to the prayers, six are clearly close translations, three are slightly different, and four more have some noticeable differences. There is some variability in the translations and their length and complexity. The Nahuatl prayer is much shorter and simpler than the Spanish for station fourteen, while in station four it is longer and more complex.

In the case of the prayers some very similar patterns emerge. Many of these are clearly translations of the Spanish. But a few are quite different from one another. In the case of the prayer for station three (His First Fall), the Nahuatl is somewhat different from the corresponding Spanish version.

Brinton Linguistic Collection, item 200, folio 33v. The line is "quihuicasque in onpa tzompantepec quithocayotia Calvario."

124. Vetancurt, *Via crucis*, 25.

125. Karttunen, *An Analytical Dictionary*, 171, 221.

Vetancurt
Alas, perfectly lovable Jesus! So that we would recognize the heaviness of our sins (for the very heavy cross You bore on Your shoulders because of us is just a stand-in for them) You fell because of Your weariness at the foot of the holy cross. I implore You: with the help of Your precious firm will, Your grace, may I quickly rise so that Your divine will shall be realized. Here I will live in the penance You want until I enjoy the final fruits of the holy cross You revealed to me: heavenly joy, glory.[126]

Anunciación
O Most Loving Jesus, who tired from the Cross that obliged you to fall on the earth from its weight, so that we might know the gravity of our sins, figured in that Wood; I beg your Divine clemency, that with the aid of your grace, raise me from the blame, and that firm and stable in the fulfillment of your Commandments, of my body, such that being firm in loving life, I enjoy the soft fruits of Your Cross of Glory.[127]

Clearly, in this instance a direct translation would not have been as clear to the Nahua penitent as a slightly more descriptive prayer. The Nahuatl is much more detailed than the Spanish in order to better explain what the fall signified. It is also important to notice the other slight differences. In the Nahuatl, the invocation is to "Perfectly lovable Jesus." This has roughly the same meaning as the Spanish "Most Loving Jesus." Similarly, at the conclusion the Nahuatl refers to "final fruits of the holy cross," while the Spanish has "soft fruits of Your Cross of Glory." The Nahuatl offers "heavenly joy, glory," while the Spanish does not, having already equated glory with the cross. The Nahuatl has the penitent "quickly rise," as if they have fallen as well or are rising from a kneeling position. When we consider the exact text, significant differences appear, while at the same time the overall thrusts of the prayers are quite similar.

While the meditations and the prayers are generally anti-Semitic, in one meditation the Nahuatl adds extra material against the Jews, but in another prayer, they are not mentioned at all. Perhaps the most interesting difference

126. "yio CenquizCatlasotlani Jesus moCiahuizticCatzinco ytzintlan otimohuetziti yn santa Cruz ynic tiquiximatizque yn ietiliz yn totlatlacoll Ca san quixiptlayotia yn CenCa yeteCatzintli Cruz yn topampatica oticmomamaltitzinno nimitzinotlatlauhtilia ma ytepalehuiliztica yn motlasochiCaliztlanequilitzintli yn moGraCiatzin ma yhuan ninehuantiquetzi ynic neltiz yn moteotlanequilitzin niCa ye ipan ninemiz yn ticmonequilitia yn tlamaCehualiztli ynic ixquichiCa nicnomasehuiz yn itzōpeuCa yn itlaquilotzi yn santa Cruz ynnotinechmonextilili yn ilhuiCac papaquiliztli yn la gloria." Vetancurt, *Via crucis*, 18.

127. "O Amantisimo Jesus, que fatigado con la Cruz te obligó a caer en tierra con el peso de ella, para que conociesemos la gravedad de nuestros pecados, figurados en ese Madero: Ruego a tu clemencia Divina, que con el auxilio de tu gracia, me levante de la culpa; y firme, y estable en el cumplimiento de tus Mandamientos, no dexe jamas la mortificacion de mi cuerpo, para que firme siempre en amarte en la vida, goze los frutos suaves de la Cruz de Gloria." Anunciación, *Luz para saber andar*, 5.

occurs in the prayer for station 6 (Christ's Face Is Wiped by Veronica). While the Spanish does not mention Veronica by name, the Nahuatl does. In Spanish the critical passage reads, "That pious woman alleviated part of your suffering cleaning the sweat from your Face with the towels from her head."[128] On the other hand, the Nahuatl is much more explicit: "You received the help of the lady Veronica when she wiped Your precious face with a soft cloth."[129]

One of the more notable features of the devotion is the notation of how many steps each station is from the previous one. By and large, the distances coincide fairly closely between the Nahuatl version and the Spanish of Anunciación. The only discrepancies appear in the fourth, sixth, eighth, and fourteenth stations. The ninth station might be a case apart. For the fourth station, for example, the Spanish reads: "This is the fourth station which consists of sixty-one steps that to there the Lord walked."[130] The Nahuatl reads very much the same: "Here is the fourth place of kneeling [called] a station. Our beloved Savior was walking around; it was seventy steps."[131] The text initially said sixty steps, but the copyist put "and ten" between the lines, as opposed to "and one."

Several of the discrepancies seem to result from the Nahuatl author's inability to convert from decimal numbers to vigesimal numbers. For example, in the fourth and fifth stations, the Spanish distances are sixty and sixty-one steps, respectively. Yet the Nahuatl ends up with seventy and seventy-one. Many non-native speakers of Spanish have difficulty hearing the difference between sixty and seventy in the language: *sesenta* and *setenta*. Frequently, even native speakers of Spanish need to emphasize the different sound. In the sixth station, the Spanish gives the distance as 191 steps, while the Nahuatl simply gives ninety-one, accidentally dropping the hundred. For the ninth station, in Spanish the distance was 161 steps, but in Nahuatl it is not at all clear, since there has been an erasure. Lastly, in Nahuatl there are no distances listed for the fourteenth station, while the Spanish provides the nominal distance of thirty steps.

It is clear that Vetancurt did not write new prayers and meditations for his version of the Stations of the Cross. Rather, he translated a very popular devotional book that was widely available at the time. What is remarkable is that the Nahuatl version was published only ten years after the first known edition in Spain. This is an extremely rapid transfer of intellectual property

---

128. "Te alivió parte de las penas aquella piadosa Muger, limpiando el sudor de tu Rostro con las toallas de su cabeza." Anunciación, *Luz para saber andar*, 8.

129. Vetancurt, *Via crucis*, 21.

130. "Esta es la quarta Estacion, que consta de sesenta pasos que hasta ella anduvo el Señor." Anunciación, *Luz para saber andar*, 5.

131. Vetancurt, *Via crucis*, 17.

for the early modern period. The Nahuatl version was, however, just one of more than a score of other published versions of essentially the same work. In the long century from 1680 until 1800, a new edition of a devotional guide to the Stations of the Cross came out on average every five years. That publication history puts this particular book, and the genre as a whole, among some of the best-best selling from the colonial period.

The Vetancurt *Via sacra* must be considered an independent creation of the friar and his team. Obviously, he drew heavily on the Anunciación version, but the two are dissimilar in many ways. Vetancurt had to rewrite large portions of the work to make it intelligible to his Native audience. In translating and modifying the text, he also frequently changed the meaning. Beyond changing the meaning, he also introduced certain concepts and ideas that were not present in the original. Some could have even been considered heretical or, at the very least, not orthodox. At the same time, Vetancurt was the most well-known and trusted scholar of Nahuatl writing in the late seventeenth century. He frequently read texts in Nahuatl for the archbishop and inquisitors to assure them that the Nahuatl writing was orthodox. Studying the Nahuatl text and looking at it in the context of the period within which it was written, we gain added insights into both the language and the religion and religious practices of the period. It is a unique glimpse into the sentiments and faith of the late seventeenth century.

The words of the text clearly represent the era in which they were written. The use of superlatives, the repetition of ideas and concepts in slightly altered form, the passionate exhortation, and the extremely detailed descriptions all indicate the literary style of the baroque in Spanish. Interestingly enough, these same rhetorical techniques were common in classical Nahuatl and continued to be further developed after the Spanish invasion. The Spanish style found a close analogue in Nahuatl rhetoric. This undoubtedly assisted Vetancurt as he labored to translate the text into Nahuatl. Nahuatl had been going through its own development since contact. We also see this in the inclusion of Spanish words into the Nahuatl text but in forms that were altered in accordance with Nahuatl rules. Thus, in so many ways, the translation of the Stations of the Cross into Nahuatl is a prime example of the baroque style in colonial New Spain.

Chapter Five
Illustrating the Stations of the Cross

While the Stations of the Cross is a devotion that consists of meditations and prayers meant to allow the believer to spiritually share in Christ's Passion, in modern parlance the phrase also refers to the assembly of decorations that provide a focus for participants' thoughts and prayers. As was noted earlier, in the late Middle Ages and the start of the early modern era—the fourteenth and fifteenth centuries—some pilgrims returning from the Holy Land had replicas of the holy places made in order to use them as memory aids in their worship. Modern scholars sometimes refer to these replicas and assemblages as "virtual pilgrimages" since they allowed the place-bound person of faith the opportunity to make a pilgrimage that was otherwise impossible.[1] These assemblages became the beginning elements of the formal Stations of the Cross. At the same time, many aspects of what would become the Stations were already being depicted in works of art. Certainly, the Middle Ages were filled with paintings illustrating every scene of the Stations, from Christ's sentencing by Pilate to his entombment. It is the production of all these as an assemblage that marks them as part of a set—the Stations of the Cross.[2]

Perhaps the most unique feature of Vetancurt's *Via crucis en mexicano* manuscript is that it is illustrated with sketch-like line drawings. They are one of the most distinctive parts of the manuscript. The illustrations in the manuscript do not have the control and clarity of line that one would expect from a trained artist. They clearly came from the same hand that copied the text, meaning an artist was not commissioned to provide illustrations. In this, the manuscript represents a trend that began shortly after the Spanish invasion. In pre-Hispanic times, Native scribes were fluent in the pictographic idiom of record keeping. With the Spanish invasion, the tradition of Native scribes continued, but now with the added need to manage new alphabetic writing in addition to pictograms. Thus, alphabetic writing was augmented by pictographic representation.[3] While the drawings are from the hand of the copyist,

1. Rudy, *Virtual Pilgrimages*, 19–38.
2. Robin, "Vía crucis," 130–45.
3. Mundy, "The Emergence of Alphabetic Writing," 388.

they convey a great deal of information beyond what is found in the text and also manifest a fairly high degree of iconographical sophistication. Only eight of the fourteen Stations of the Cross are illustrated, and all but one of these appear in the latter half of the devotion. The illustrations also convey the sense that this is a popularized version of Vetancurt's work, illustrated to local tastes rather than with the high baroque style of the European engravings and woodcuts normally found in this type of work. This chapter will look at the development of artistic depictions of the Passion in New Spain from the time of the conquest up to the late seventeenth century. It will also analyze the depictions of the Stations of the Cross that were roughly contemporary with the Vetancurt *Via sacra*. Lastly, there will be an analysis of the pictures in the manuscript held by the Academy of American Franciscan History, comparing them to other works from this same period. All of this will also assist in seeing whether there was a model or other set of images that the copyist, Matheo de San Juan Chicahuastla, used in creating his drawings.

History of the Representation of the Stations

As noted earlier, the devotion of the Stations of the Cross exists both as a set of words and as images, all linked by a performance aspect. As Derek Burdette explains in his discussion of the image that accompanies another devotion, the Most Holy Christ of Atonement (also known as the Holy Christ of Redress, see chapter 3), "Visual, textual, and embodied evocations of Christ's pain and suffering were mutually interdependent in the eighteenth century."[4] The words of the Stations of the Cross continue to be somewhat flexible even to the present day, although by the late seventeenth-century there were standard texts. A person of faith can recite the prayers and meditation alone, contemplating the moments of Christ's Passion, but from earliest times, the performance aspect has been important. The practitioner would walk from one spot to another and there engage in spiritual acts. Indeed, the handbooks studied here provide the number of steps between each of the stations. But from the earliest examples of the devotion, an essential element of each station was an artistic expression of one sort or another: something that could transport the faithful into Jesus's experience. Some of the earliest examples in Europe consisted of small chapels or even replicas of buildings found in cloisters in order to spiritually transport the penitent to Jerusalem and the site of the Passion. Soon churches themselves featured a focal point in the form of a bas-relief depicting the events of the station. In other churches, sculptures helped to represent the specific moments in the Passion. But far more common were paintings or prints of the events described at each station.

4. Burdette, "Reparations for Christ Our Lord," 360.

Each of these parts of the devotion (words, art, actions) then provides a text to explore, allowing for a more complete view of the devotion's essence. By combining the elements of prayer and meditation, movement, speech, and the contemplation of symbols of the Passion, the Stations of the Cross came to exemplify the baroque and its emphasis on engaging the viewer or participant on multiple levels using many of the senses.

The use of illustrations is in many ways emblematic of the historical development of the devotion that was outlined in chapter 2. The Stations of the Cross is rooted in an imagined physical reality of the route from Pilate's praetorium that Jesus took while carrying his cross to Golgotha, leading to his crucifixion and entombment. Two traditions emerged in the late Middle Ages. One was based on Scripture and the actual physical arrangement of holy sites in Jerusalem. The other was based on the imagined geography of those holy sites derived from the mental images of European Christians, which were embellished with legends, some dating from the early days of Christianity. The final form that the Stations has taken seems to have attempted to rationalize the actual with the imaginary.[5]

The devotion of the Stations of the Cross began as a private, spiritual devotion of contemplation on the Passion of Christ. The late Middle Ages brought a radical change in devotional life, making interior things exterior, and so the precursor devotions began to be commemorated with physical actions. Thus, various convents, monasteries, and churches added decorations to assist the faithful in their execution of various prayers and meditations by providing illustrative scenes from Christ's Passion. At roughly the same time, there were several places in Europe that built and made models and replicas of the holy places, which also served as mental triggers to aid in contemplating Christ's life.

The specific events in Jesus's Passion, certainly the crucifixion, deposition, pietà, and entombment, were widely depicted in paintings, sculptures, and other media. Other moments were less frequently portrayed. The Stations of the Cross stimulated the creation of a set of similar images in a variety of media, all generally linked by a common style, representing the fourteen stations. The same is true for the other stational devotions such as the Seven Falls or the Seven Sorrows of Mary.[6] As the prayerful devotion contemplating Christ's suffering gave way to the more movement-oriented stational devotion wherein the faithful walked from place to place images were developed to identify each station and provide both prompts for contemplation as well as pictures to contemplate.

---

5. Lenzi, *The Stations of the Cross*, 197–210; Rudy, *Virtual Pilgrimages*, 119–20.

6. Rudy provides European examples for these devotions, Rudy, *Virtual Pilgrimages*, 218, 243.

In the late fourteenth and early fifteenth centuries, European churches began to build what were thought to be replicas of holy sites, such as the Church of the Holy Sepulchre. In other places, the faithful would merely build elevated places with crosses atop to represent Golgotha. In Córdoba, a Dominican friar named Álvarez, upon returning from the Holy Land, built a set of chapels that depicted some of the scenes from Christ's Passion. Other convents and monasteries also followed this new trend.[7] At the same time, the devotions of the Seven Falls, the Seven Sorrows, and others gained adherents. Some convents and monasteries commissioned works of art to illustrate the various stations associated with different devotions. The Lowlands, what are now Belgium and the Netherlands, saw a proliferation of such devotional elements.[8]

One important early set of works dedicated to the Passion of Christ, which was seen by some as a point of departure for the development of the Stations of the Cross, was a set of eight bas-relief stations in a monastery in Louvain, in modern-day Belgium. Upon his return from the Holy Land in about 1506, a pilgrim had undertaken the project. In setting up the stations, while working from memory, he had attempted to respect the distances between the original sites in Jerusalem.[9]

As was noted in chapter 1, two related traditions emerged in Spain. One was the construction of replicas of Golgotha at the edges of towns and cities. These were *humilladeros*, often also known as *Calvarios* (Calvaries), that marked the end of a town's authority and the beginning of the countryside. One example is the Cuatro Postes of Ávila. Legend has it that King Sancho built the site during the Reconquest after having regained the city from traitors. It is located outside the city walls, on the other side of the Adaja River, and is accessible by an ancient Roman bridge. The site also figures as a destination in pilgrimages of Saint Teresa of Ávila. The essential feature of *humilladeros* is that they were used in processions and served as representations of Calvary. Throughout Latin America, many town and citie edges were marked by *humilladeros*. A few of these have survived. Some notable examples are located in Cuernavaca and Pátzcuaro, although the latter was later walled up to become a roadside chapel.[10]

Paintings and Chapels in Early Colonial Mexico

In the early days of the evangelization of the Natives in what is now Mexico, the missionary friars used a variety of tools to help convey their les-

7. Storme, *The Way of the Cross*, 110.
8. Kirkland-Ives, "Alternate Routes," 259–66.
9. Storme, *The Way of the Cross*, 118–19.

sons. Obviously, there was a significant language barrier, but as has been noted, the missionaries quickly learned to communicate in the principal Native languages. At the same time, a few Natives learned Spanish, especially children of the elites who were chosen to be trained by the missionaries. Nonetheless, oral communication was greatly assisted by pictures that helped to convey the message of Christianity.

The early missionaries understood the difficulty of explaining Christian concepts to the Natives when they themselves lacked a solid grounding in the Native languages. Early in the evangelization, the first friars were believed to have used sketches as a visual aid to outline the important features of Christianity. These pictorial aids came to be known as Testerian catechisms, named after one of the early friars, Fr. Jacobo de Testera. The images that we have of friars actually using drawings to instruct the Natives all feature one of Testera's companions, Fr. Pedro de Gante (Peter of Ghent). Somewhat later, Fr. Diego de Valadés produced two images in this teaching style. In his book, Valadés describes the first missionaries using pictures to explain the Passion. In the accompanying engravings, there are two images. One shows the church courtyard, where a variety of activities are taking place. In the upper-left section of the courtyard, a friar identified as Pedro de Gante instructs using a set of pictures or logograms on a large board or poster. The legend under the scene reads *Discunt omnia*, "discusses all things" (see fig. 5.1). In another engraving from Valadés, the teaching friar points to seven images of the Passion, which are hanging at the tops of the church columns. The images include Jesus praying in the garden, the scourging at the column, the ecce homo, Jesus carrying the cross, the crucifixion, the interment, and the resurrection (see fig. 5.2).[11] Clearly this is not a set of images for the Stations of the Cross. Two of the seven fall outside the devotion: praying in the garden and the resurrection. Of the remaining five, the ecce homo, as noted, was only sometimes part of the collection, serving as it did in some instances for the judgment of Pilate. Nonetheless, the engraving provided by Valadés does demonstrate that from the very earliest moments of the evangelization, missionary friars used Christian iconographical content as a method for teaching the basics of the new faith and that scenes from the Passion played a very important role in evangelization.

The genre of Testerian catechisms is notable as a part of the evangelization of the New World. Yet recent scholarship has indicated that nearly all the examples available today date not from the sixteenth century but rather from the mid- to late seventeenth century.[12] This places the time of the extant Testerians' production to coincide with the growth in popularity and expansion

10. McAndrew, *The Open-Air Churches*, 281, 445–46.
11. Valadés, *Rhetorica Cristiana*, folios 211–12.
12. Burkhart, "The 'Little Doctrine,'" 199–200.

FIGURE 5.1. Fr. Pedro de Gante Teaching in the Atrium, Valadés, *Rhetorica Cristiana*, John Carter Brown Library.

of the Stations of the Cross. It also suggests that the scribe who copied the Vetancurt *Via crucis* might also have been familiar with the contemporary Testerian production of evangelical materials. Indeed, in looking at the little figures that made up the Testerian catechisms, there is a similarity in their economy of line. The images merely suggest features rather than fully develop them. A few of the images in the iconographic repertoire of the Testerian catechisms refer to the Passion, such as Christ crucified. Yet in one of the best-known works, the crucifixion appears only as a stick figure on the cross with blood flowing from his wounds.[13] Other vignettes from the Passion appear in the Nicene Creed: God the father, Christ's torture, the crucifixion, and his burial (see fig. 5.3).[14] Yet none of these is similar to the figures found in the *Via crucis* manuscript.

The important distinction that we can draw between the images in a Testerian catechism and the images from the *Via crucis* manuscript is that they were used for two rather different purposes. The images in the Testerian catechisms function as pictograms: the picture represents a word or phrase. Thus,

13. Boone, Burkhart, and Tavarez, *Painted Words*, p. 170, image 53.

14. Boone, Burkhart, and Tavarez, *Painted Words*, p. 176, images 154, 156, 157; pp. 186–87, images 321, 322, 325, 329. León Portilla, *Un catecismo en Nahuatl*, 19

FIGURE 5.2. Fr. Pedro de Gante preaching with images, Valadés, *Rhetorica Cristiana*, John Carter Brown Library.

in the Testerian catechisms the basic prayers of Christianity are depicted in a series of pictures to represent the ideas and words of the prayer. This is described as a "pictographic vocabulary." Each image carries with it a set of meanings in the context of the prayer to be remembered.[15] The drawings function almost like mnemonic devices to recall the content of the prayer. The illustrations found in the Vetancurt *Via Crucis* are more simply illustrations of the event described in the station. They are not pictographic in that they do not necessarily carry any meaning beyond what they represent.

In addition to his role in the use of images to teach the natives about Christianity, Fr. Pedro de Gante also produced the first published booklet to teach reading in the New World in 1569. The small work (eight leaves long) introduces the letters and syllables used in Spanish. The book also includes the basic prayers written in Latin, Spanish, and Nahuatl. Several small prints illustrate the book. Two of them feature events that can be associated with the Stations of the Cross. The image introducing the Our Father in Spanish is of Saint Veronica holding up her cloth with the face of Jesus imprinted on

15. Boone and Burkhart, "The Pictographic Vocabulary," 53–54.

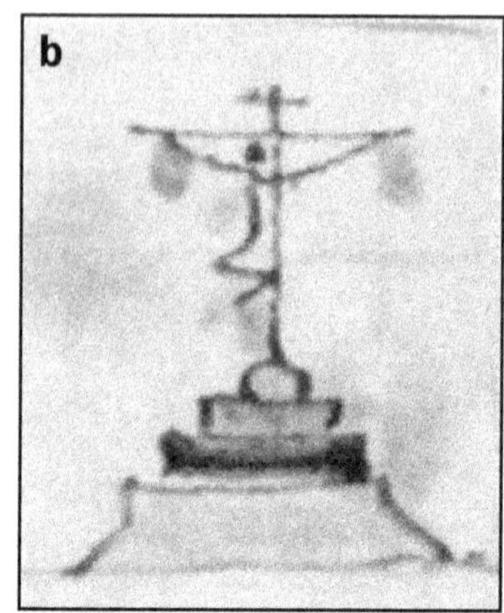

FIGURE 5.3. (a) God the Father, image 248. Atzaqualco catechism. (b) Crucifixion, image 295. Atzaqualco catechism. (c) Was buried, image 328. Atzaqualco catechism. (d) Totecuiyo Jesucristo. Catecismo Nahuatl. Bibliotheque Nationale de France.

it. Although it is very difficult to ascertain definitively, the image at the start of the Creed in Nahuatl seems to be Jesus before Pilate (see fig. 5.4).[16]

In the first century following the conquest in Latin America, many different artists painted scenes from the Passion of Christ. In early colonial Mexico, perhaps the best-known examples of works of art depicting the Passion are wall paintings found in the cloisters of churches. Perhaps the most famous of these is the church of San Andrés Apóstol at Epazoyucan. The church at Epazoyucan was probably founded by Franciscans, but as early as the 1540s the Augustinians took over administration of the church.[17] The paintings include scenes found in special framing arches (*testerae*) at the ends of the cloister walls: the ecce homo, Jesus carrying the cross, the crucifixion, and the descent from the cross, all of which are images from the Stations. Their placement at the side of the cloister allows for their contemplation while engaged in prayerful walking, such as in the devotion of the Stations of the

16. Valton, *El primer libro de alfabetización*, folios 1v, 3v.
17. Kubler, *Mexican Architecture*, 2:509–10.

FIGURE 5.4. (a) Veronica. Gante, *Cartilla*. (b) Christ before Pilate[?]. Gante, *Cartilla*. John Carter Brown Library.

Cross. In addition to these, a scene of the Dormition of the Virgin can be found over a doorway in the cloister walk.[18] Yet the central issue is whether these murals constitute part of an assemblage for the Stations of the Cross.[19] While the paintings were executed by a Native artist, a *tlacuilo*, research has shown that the designs were based on or taken from European models, in particular from engravings that were quite popular in the period. The Epazoyucan murals were based on several disparate European engravings that were widely available in sixteenth-century Mexico.[20]

In her work on the Stations of the Cross in Latin America, Alena Robin established norms to see whether depictions were a part of a series or were self-contained works. Because by nature depictions of the Stations of the Cross implicitly invite the observer to accompany Christ in the Passion, they seldom depict Christ looking directly at the viewer, separating the devout person from the action. Similarly, if they are part of a collection for the Stations, all the images should be oriented in a manner to project movement in a single direc-

18. The Virgin was believed to have died without pain and suffering. In recognition of this state of peace the term "dormition" was applied, signifying an eternal rest with God. In the Roman Catholic Church, Mary is believed to have been wholly assumed into heaven at her death. "Pope John Paul II, General Audience, Wednesday, 25 June 1997," Vatican, http://w2.vatican.va/content/john-paul-ii/en/audiences/1997/documents/hf_jp-ii_aud_25061997.html.

19. For a general overview of the frescos at Epazoyucan, see Moyssen, "Las pinturas murales," 20–27. See also Peterson, *The Paradise Garden Murals*, 63–65.

20. Moyssen, "Las pinturas murales en Epazoyucan," 20–21; Kubler, *Mexican Architecture*, 2:373–74.

tion, right to left or left to right, and thus be placed in a series. The next characteristics are fairly obvious. Each image may have any of these elements: a gloss giving the number of the station, a statement of the indulgences, a portion of the meditation or prayer associated with the station, or the number of steps from the previous station. All these additions to a painting are indicators of a piece pertaining to a collection. Any one of them can strongly argue in favor of the image being part of a set.[21]

Using these criteria in attempting to understand the murals from Epazoyucan, it seems unlikely that the paintings were part of a via crucis. They have none of the characteristics outlined by Robin and thus seem to be simply a collection of wall paintings representing themes of the Passion. Moreover, Robin notes that the Stations usually begin with the condemnation by Pilate. It would seem reasonable to represent this station with images prior to the appearance before Pilate, such as of the discussion in the garden or the ecce homo. Yet these are relatively infrequently used in depicting the Stations of the Cross in spite of their high emotional content. By far the most common image used for the first station is the flagellation at the column.[22] This again would call into doubt the use of the Epazoyucan images as part of a formal Stations of the Cross, since there is no representation of any event from early in the Passion story. In addition, none of the paintings at Epazoyucan have numbers associating them with specific stations. Since there is only one painting of Jesus carrying the cross, and no other painting shows movement from side to side, one cannot determine whether all the paintings might be oriented in the same direction.

While there are few other examples of early colonial wall paintings that feature images associated with the Passion, another important theme in wall decoration is that of the Holy Week processions that occur throughout the Hispanic world. These processions are clearly closely associated with the Stations of the Cross since they commemorate many of the same events. But unlike performances of the Stations of the Cross, wherein the faithful process from one station to another, reciting prayers along with way, with fixed prayers and meditations for each stop, Holy Week processions are not tied to specific prayers, although they frequently make stops along a determined route. Holy Week processions normally went from one neighborhood church or chapel along a route to the local cathedral (or main church) and then back to the home church. Not all processions took the same route aside from specific legs approaching and leaving the cathedral, based on the example of Seville. The Holy Week procession itself is thus both a type of walking prayer and an act that allows the penitent to spiritually engage in Christ's Passion.

21. Robin, "Via crucis," 134.
22. Robin, "Via crucis," 134–35.

The most famous set of paintings depicting Holy Week processions appears on the walls of San Miguel in Huejotzingo. As has been noted earlier, processions and religious dramas were important tools for evangelization. They provided both entertainment and a didactic experience for those who witnessed or participated in them. The missionaries used plays and processions to mark the important festivals of the Christian calendar: Christmas, Holy Week, Easter, Pentecost, and Corpus Christi, to name but a few. In the same manner, the friars urged the creation of sodalities or confraternities among the Natives to provide yet another means of expressing spirituality in a small group. By the latter part of the sixteenth century confraternities had become very important institutions in Native communities. Indeed, Natives increasingly took control of the sodalities and began to use them as part of their internal social and political hierarchy.

In Huejotzingo, the current church and convent, which were under the administration of Franciscans, were completed in the early 1570s.[23] There, the Confraternity of the True Cross (La Vera Cruz) was featured in a series of murals painted on the walls of the church of San Miguel, depicting their processions and several images of the Passion. Because the confraternity had a central focus on the veneration of the cross, the group's ritual activities came to a peak during Holy Week, culminating on Good Friday and the commemoration of the crucifixion. Consequently, many of the images are also linked to the Stations of the Cross. The painting also illustrates the santo entierro (holy burial) on Good Friday, which was also featured in the Stations of the Cross as the entombment.[24] The Huejotzingo paintings date to the last quarter of the sixteenth century. These paintings can be seen as an example of early colonial devotion to the Passion. Many of the same impulses that stimulated people to join confraternities and to participate in Holy Week processions were also at work encouraging the faithful to perform the Stations of the Cross, either individually or collectively.

As was noted in chapter 2, in the late sixteenth and early seventeenth centuries, a series of chapels was constructed in Mexico City along the Alameda, stretching west from the Church of San Francisco. These chapels were, perhaps, the ultimate expression of the enthusiastic support for the devotion of the Stations of the Cross. They also constitute some of the oldest documented works of art dedicated specifically to the devotion, as opposed to Passion-centered art of earlier periods. New Spain, in general, saw a rapid increase in the

---

23. Kubler, *Mexican Architecture*, 2:459–60.

24. Webster, "Art, Ritual, and Confraternities," 22–26. See also Estrada de Gerlero, "El programa pasionario." Estrada de Gerlero suggests that the sodality in Huejotzingo was that of the Holy Burial, which was associated with the Dominicans. Huejotzingo was a Franciscan dependency in the early colonial period.

number of works of art generated for the devotion of the Stations toward the end of the sixteenth century.[25] In addition to Mexico City, both Puebla and what is now Antigua, Guatemala, boasted of having their own sets of chapels for the Stations.[26]

Seventy years after their initial construction, the original chapels had fallen into disrepair. At that point, in 1684, as part of a major period of ecclesiastical construction in Mexico City, the Franciscans petitioned for permission to build a new set of chapels explicitly dedicated to the Stations of the Cross. The First Order friars collaborated with the Third Order in this major construction project in both the design and fundraising. This effort occupied the Franciscans for the rest of the seventeenth century. This second construction project, or reconstruction, occurred just as support was building for papal recognition of the devotion of the Stations of the Cross with indulgences. As we have seen, it was also the period in which various authors were busily producing devotional handbooks.[27]

A possible precursor to the chapels dedicated to the Stations of the Cross might have been the *posas* that were constructed inside the atria of early colonial churches. As was noted in chapter 2, the *posas* provided stopping points where prayers and other devotions could be performed within the confines of a consecrated space. There is ample evidence that, during Holy Week, processions occurred, although no specific evidence points to the celebration of the Stations of the Cross. Nonetheless, just as the Stations of the Cross came to rely on paintings and sculptures as points of reflection in the execution of the performance, the *posas* were also frequently decorated to also assist in the execution of prayers and devotions.

One of the most complete assemblages of *posas* is found at Calpan, in the state of Puebla. This Franciscan church as well as its cloister and *posas* were probably built at roughly the same time and were completed by 1548. Each of the four *posas* is slightly different, and each is devoted to a different theme. The first is dedicated to the Virgin Mary, the second to Saint Francis, and the third to Saint Michael. The last *posa* seems incomplete because it lacks sculpture or even clear themes. Vetancurt indicated in 1697 that the chapels were dedicated to Saint Michael, Saint John the Evangelist, the Assumption of the

---

25. Iguiniz, *Breve historia*, 89–90.

26. Iguiniz, *Breve historia*, 94–97; Robin, *Las capillas*, 33, 55.

27. Robin, *Las capillas*, 57–86. Comparing maps and paintings of the city from the seventeenth century, it seems that the chapels were also moved from a location near the great Franciscan church located just east of what is now the Latin American Tower, along Avenida Juárez roughly in front of what is now the Palace of Fine Arts. The new location was farther to the west, just beyond the western edge of what is now the Alameda.

28. Kubler, *Mexican Architecture*, 453; Vetancurt, *Teatro mexicano*, 3, 235, Vetancurt, "Chronica de la provincia del Santo Evangelio de méxico," Tratado Segundo, para. 247.

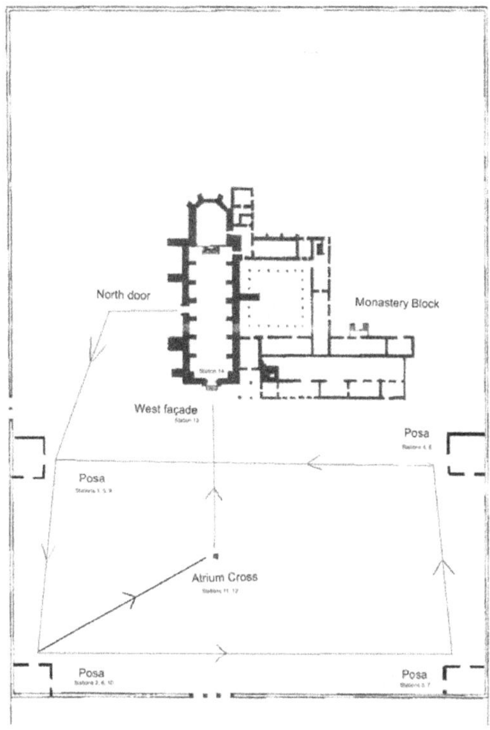

FIGURE 5.5. Processional route in an atrium, drawing by the Author.

Virgin, and Saint Francis.[28] This would indicate that the fourth *posa* was that to Saint John the Evangelist. The bas-relief decorations on the *posas* are taken from fairly well-known engravings available in New Spain in the mid-sixteenth century. These include one of Our Lady of Sorrows (Nuestra Señora de los Dolores), Saint Francis receiving the stigmata, and a scene of God overseeing the resurrection of the dead.[29] While the decoration on the Calpan *posas* does not immediately relate to Christ's Passion, they might well have still been used as stops for the celebration of the Stations of the Cross. The procession could have begun in the church, made two circuits of the *posas*, included a stop at an atrium cross for the crucifixion, and then ended in the church for the burial (see fig. 5.5).[30]

A pilgrimage site related to the Stations of the Cross was developed near the city of Amecameca. Although it has its roots in the colonial period, the

29. McAndrew, *The Open-Air Churches*, 324–32; Kubler, *Mexican Architecture*, 2:392–93.

30. McAndrew, *The Open-Air Churches*, 281.

Stations of the Cross there date from the nineteenth century. Amecameca lies in the southeastern corner of the Central Basin of Mexico, at the foot of the Popocatepetl volcano. What makes the story of this site so rich is that a series of historians of the Franciscan Order wrote about the site as did the Nahua intellectual and historian of the region Chimalpahin. The Franciscan authors include several of the chroniclers of the Province of the Holy Gospel including Motolinia, Jerónimo de Mendieta, Pedro Oroz, Juan de Torquemada, and Vetancurt himself. The different friars presented the same general story. At some point in the sixteenth century, a chapel to the Holy Sepulchre (El Santo Entierro) of Christ, was built partway up the side of the volcano, overlooking the Central Basin. At the end of the sixteenth century there was a well-established chapel that was dedicated to the holy burial. The Franciscan chronicles attributed its founding to the first leader of the province, Fr. Martín de Valencia. The chapel began as a small cave in the hillside, which Valencia used as a hermitage for periods of reflection. Valencia had to trek there from the Franciscan convent in Tlalmanalco, some ten kilometers distant. Upon Valencia's death, local Natives carefully guarded some of his clothing as relics. Even in the late sixteenth century, the hermitage was dedicated to Christ's Passion and death.[31]

In the 1580s, the town of Amecameca passed to Dominican administration. The order also took control of the relics and hermitage of Fray Martín. Eventually the relics were returned to the cave, and the Dominicans created a true chapel there in about 1584. The central sculpture in the chapel was a statue of a reclining Christ associated with the holy burial. The Franciscans reported that, especially on Fridays, special processions were made to the chapel in honor of Christ's Passion. Perhaps even more important, a whole series of special devotions occurred during Holy Week. One should also note that although the site seems isolated and remote, perched on the side of a volcano, in reality it was not that remote. One of the major roads from the coast entered the Central Basin of Mexico by way of the same pass and went near the chapel.[32]

The cave chapel dedicated to the holy burial bearing a lifelike image of Christ came to serve as a representation of the holy sepulchre. Since the chapel cave was located on an impressive hillside, the place became known as the Sacromonte (Sacred Mountain). Between the sixteenth and eighteenth cen-

---

31. One should note that these relics of Valencia became important because at some point his body, which had been buried in Tlalmanalco, was lost. Motolinia, *Memoriales*, 185; Mendieta, *Historia eclesiastica Indiana*, 4:38–41 (book 5, part 1, chap. 13); Oroz, *The Oroz Codex*, 193–97; Torquemada, *Monarquía Indiana*, 6:164–70; Vetancurt, *Teatro mexicano*, 4:251–52.

32. Mendieta, *Historia eclesiastica indiana*, 4:46–50 (book 5, part 1, chap. 16); Oroz, *Oroz Codex*, 201–5.

turies the shrine developed as an important pilgrimage site, with the faithful coming from as far as a hundred kilometers. It was reported in the sixteenth century that in the ensuing decades the most popular time to worship was during Holy Week, recognizing Jesus's Passion.[33]

Native sources also describe the development of the cave chapel but assert greater Native agency, rather than simply a reaction to the missionary friars' actions. In particular, the annalist Chimalpahin tells a tale that differs from the friars' accounts in many details, even including miraculous events, but it describes them in a down-to-earth manner. In particular, Chimalpahin credits the Dominican friar Juan Páez with bringing and installing the Christ figure of the holy burial in the cave chapel.

According to Chimalpahin, on June 20, 1583, the chapel of the Holy Sepulchre (Santo Sepulcro) was constructed in a miraculous manner. The original name of the cave was Chalchiuhmomoztli Amaqueme (Turquoise Altar of Amecameca), although Chimalpahin wondered who might have given it that name. It was in this cave that had been converted to a chapel that the sculptural image of Christ lying in his tomb was installed. Chimalpahin asserts that the cave was the same one that had been used as a hermitage or retreat by Fr. Martín de Valencia some fifty years earlier. The Nahua chronicler notes that participating in the dedication of the new chapel were the vicar, Fr. Juan Páez, and Native leaders including don Felipe Páez de Mendoza the elder, Juan de la Cruz, and don Bartolomé de Santiago. The Native leaders were responsible for the arranging the chapel and for its upkeep. After mentioning a statue of Christ crucified and its installation in a local church, Chimalpahin notes that in the same year of 1583 the Dominican friars and local Spaniards processed on Good Friday, celebrating the Passion and burial of Christ in a manner that had not yet been done.[34] Given the acquisition of a new statue of Christ buried and another of Christ crucified, it seems likely that the procession traveled from the one church to the new chapel of the holy burial and that the group celebrated the Stations of the Cross along the route.

Several important features emerge in Chimalpahin's account as written in Nahuatl. First, he uses the word *ixiptlatzin* (*ixiptla* plus the honorific -*tzin*) to describe the image of the Santo Entierro (Holy Burial). This term had a very particular meaning in the precontact period. While it is frequently translated as an image, it actually referred to a person or object that served as a local embodiment of a deity. In the precontact period, both sculptures of the Native deities and individuals who donned the regalia and pretended to be the deities were considered *ixiptla*. In this instance, Chimalpahin also added the suffix of

33. Osowski, "Passion Miracles," 607–12.
34. Chimalpahin, *Las ocho relaciones*, 2:254–57.

-tzin to indicate divinity, or something to be honored. By the end of the sixteenth and early seventeenth centuries, this word had come to mean a statue of a sacred image, such as of a saint.[35] In all likelihood, it still retained some of its earlier connotations of being a local embodiment of a deity.

A second feature of interest was the Nahuatl name of the place, Chalchiuhmomoztli. To heighten the curiosity, Chimalpahin even questioned the origin. On the surface it can be translated as "a turquoise (or jade) altar." Turquoise was one of several materials that were held by the Nahua as extremely precious, along with quetzal feathers. Consequently, whenever a word was modified by "turquoise" or "quetzal" it could also carry the connotation of "precious." This then would render the name of the place as "precious altar." A *momoztli* was a small raised platform that would hold a sacred object. Frequently they were miniature temples. As was noted earlier, crosses in the atria of churches were placed on small platforms in the manner of *momoztli*. Consequently, an analysis of the names for the object and of the place itself indicate that for the Nahua this was a place of great spiritual importance.[36]

In further discussing the special things that occurred at this site, Chimalpahin refers to it as a *tlamahuizolli* (a miraculous or astounding event). In particular the Nahua chronicler describes it as happening "by miraculous deeds."[37] The Nahuatl word was *tlamahuiçoltlachihualiztica*. The root of the word was *tlamahuizol(li)*, which was then combined with *tlachihualiz(tli)*, something that was made, with the ending *-tica*, which creates both a noun and then an adverbial meaning "by means of." An alternate translation might be "by means of a wonderous thing that was made." The root word of *tlamahuizolli* occurs in other works from roughly the same period as Chimalpahin's, most specifically in the descriptions of the miraculous events associated with the apparition of the Virgin of Guadalupe. One of the most famous Nahuatl accounts of the appearances is called the *Huei tlamahuizoltica*, (By a great miracle).[38] Through his word choice, Chimalpahin clearly establishes that the creation of the devotional site was of great religious significance. One might note that he was writing two decades before the Guadalupe accounts. This might be why the Guadalupe descriptions called it *Huei*, "Great," in

35. Louise Burkhart, personal communication, February 3, 2020. For *ixiptla*, see Bassett, *The Fate of Earthly Things*, 132–35.

36. Osowski, "Passion Miracles," 620–21. Tena, in his translation of the Nahuatl opted not to translate the Nahuatl place-name. Some scholars have wrongly believed that Chalchiuhmomoztli somehow referred to the cave, since the Nahuatl word for cave is *oztotl*. Chimalpahin Quauhtelhanitzin, *Ocho relaciones*, 2, 254–57.

37. Osowski, *Indigenous Miracles*, 37. By comparison, Tena translates the word as "se hizo con magificencia," (done with magnificence).

38. Sousa, Poole, and Lockhart, *The Story of Guadalupe*, 48–49.

order to distinguish it as more important than other earlier occurrences. But at the same time, the Nahuatl term that describes the creation of the chapel of the holy burial signifies that it was built or created through a miraculous event. Clearly, this was a very special place.[39]

A closer look at the development of the cult of the Sacromonte also demonstrates that the Natives were not just passive observers of actions by Franciscan and Dominican friars but took active control of many aspects of the devotion. Native leadership sought and received title to the grasslands near the sanctuary, along with other pieces of property on the flanks of Popocatepetl near the royal road. They also became direct patrons of the sanctuary, providing it with money and sustaining its development. In many ways, the Native leaders were responsible for converting a hermitage of Fr. Martín de Valencia, into a chapel dedicated to the buried Jesus, El Santo Entierro. In colonial times, the law required that in order to show ownership, a person needed to go to a piece of land, pull weeds, cuts trees and move rocks. In a similar way, the Natives of Amecameca took the responsibility to clean and maintain the sanctuary.[40]

As was noted in both the Spanish and Nahuatl versions of the chapel's foundation story, the sanctuary of El Santo Entierro of Sacromonte, Amecameca, became a destination for religious processions, particularly on Fridays, and especially on Good Friday. In the ensuing years, perhaps as late as the early nineteenth century, a series of chapels was built on the road from Amecameca up to the sanctuary. The pilgrimage route began with the parish church in Amecameca, Nuestra Señora de la Anunciación, and then wound up the mountainside. Along the way there were fourteen chapels leading ultimately to the holy burial in the cave chapel founded by Valencia. This is a strong indication that a tradition of using the route as a pathway to celebrate the Stations of the Cross had developed in the colonial period, which is confirmed by constructions in the nineteenth century.

From an artistic point of view, the chapel is important because it is an early documented image of the holy burial, which appears in many other colonial churches in Mexico. The sculptural image is of Christ, who has died and been placed in his tomb. Frequently, the sculpture is encased in a glass or crystal coffin decorated with gold and velvet. Many other churches have these images. There are annual processions with such an image in San Miguel de Allende. In Huauchinango and Tzintzuntzan there are also famous images of the buried Christ. Unlike many of the others, the image of the buried Christ in Ame-

39. Osowski, "Passion Miracles," 620–21; Osowski, *Indigenous Miracles*, 37–41.

40. Osowski, "Passion Miracles," 621–25; Osowski, *Indigenous Miracles*, 41. For an alternative interpretation regarding Saint Thomas as the first Christian saint associated with the site, see Ragon, "La colonización de lo sagrado," 281–300.

cameca is placed in a deep niche above and behind the altar, and not in a free-standing coffin or glass case. The niche has a glass front facing the congregation and a very elaborate red-and-gilt frame surrounding it. The statue is covered with a burial cloth so that only the bruised head of Jesus can be seen.

In addition to sculptures associated with the Passion, artists in the early colonial period also produced paintings and other, smaller objects to aid the faithful in their contemplation of Christ's suffering and death. The most common forms of devotional objects were paintings. Alena Robin has studied twenty-six examples, largely from the eighteenth century. She found that while there was some variation, the theme for each station became fixed quite rapidly. Nevertheless, in some instances only twelve paintings might be included in a set. As has been noted, in some of the printed devotional guides, there were either too few stations or extraneous stations in addition to the fourteen that became canonical. In paintings, there were also some variations. Moreover, for a given station, different artists might choose to emphasize one theme over another.[41] Thus, the illustrations manifest the same kind of variation that occurs in printed material. The number of stations eventually consolidated around the fourteen accepted stations outlined by the pope in 1731.

In the seventeenth and eighteenth centuries, scores of paintings dealt with the themes of the Passion. Looking at the inventories of the holdings of the National Institute of Anthropology and History, there were several sets of paintings specifically dedicated to the Stations of the Cross.[42] These manifest one or more of the indicators outlined by Robin: they are numbered, the movement depicted is in a single direction, there is a notation about how far each station is from the previous one, or there is a meditation or prayer appropriate to the station. While not every set has every one of these indicators, they normally comply with at least two. The most common combination is that they are numbered and that the direction of movement is consistent.

In looking at the corpus of paintings from the Stations of the Cross in colonial Mexico, the great majority are tentatively dated to the eighteenth century, with a few coming earlier. In addition to being numbered and depicting actions going in a single direction, some of the images are nearly identical. There seem to have been two or three standard models, and these were repeated time after time in different sets. Moreover, many of the individual paintings are essentially duplicates of others. For instance, there are only very slight differences among the paintings for each of the three falls in several of the series. In these same series the image for Simon the Cyrene assisting Jesus looks generally like one of the falls, with the addition of a man helping to carry the cross. In nearly every instance, while Jesus is the focal point of the

41. Robin, "Via crucis," 135–40.
42. Mexicana, https://mexicana.cultura.gob.mx/.

painting, there are numerous other figures surrounding him. Frequently these are the guards who accompanied him. Other instances include the women of Jerusalem, his mother, Simon of Cyrene, and often just bystanders. Only in the images of the crucifixion and the burial will Jesus be represented alone, and even in the crucifixion there are generally the two thieves, and frequently Mary and Saint John are present. Lastly, in these most common sets, the direction of movement is always from right to left. In general, it is not a difficult matter to detect which paintings formed part of a series and which merely depicted a scene from the Stations of the Cross. The iconography and depictions did not differ wildly from series to series, painting to painting.

Engravings and Presses

In the seventeenth century, not unlike the present, one of the largest expenses involved in publishing a book had to do with the cost of the illustrations. Printers would acquire a selection of engraved plates or woodcuts and use them in all their books. Consequently, in order to determine whether the illustrations of the *Via crucis en mexicano* as found in the manuscript copy were present in the original printed volume, it is necessary to survey the other works published by the press of Francisco Rodríguez Lupercio. According to textual evidence and testimony from Vetancurt himself, Rodríguez Lupercio originally published the book. A survey of other books from that publishing house can determine if the press had an appropriate set of prints that the printer could use to illustrate the Stations of the Cross.

The John Carter Brown Library holds one of the largest collections of early colonial imprints from Mexico. The catalog lists a total of seventy-nine books from Rodríguez Lupercio in its collection from 1661 until the end of the century, comprising a significant percentage of the total output of the press. Rodríguez Lupercio ran the press until his death in 1673. His widow then took over the leadership, as happened to many print shops. The widow managed the shop until 1694 and her own death. The press was abandoned for a while, only to be revived by the couple's heirs in 1698, who then continued operations for nearly forty years.[43] This study focuses primarily on books published by Rodríguez Lupercio and his widow, since after the original publication of the *Via crucis*, the press might well have acquired a whole new set of engravings and woodcuts. Consequently, only works published before the death of Vetancurt could reasonably be expected to have engravings that would have also been used in his book.

Assuming that the collection of the John Carter Brown Library is a general cross section of all the imprints from the press, which it seems to be, if

---

43. Medina, *La imprenta en México*, 1:157–58, 160–61.

engravings of the Stations of the Cross existed, they would probably appear in some of the volumes held there. Unfortunately, no such illustrations exist. The collections of illustrations used by the firm of Rodríguez Lupercio fall into several categories.[44] The press used about eight sets of illustrated capitals, that is capital letters surrounded by various designs, and these sets fall into two groups. One set of four appears in early imprints and is characterized by a filigree type of line, usually of a floral decoration. The other set of four depicts the capital letter superimposed over a basket or vase of flowers. There were capitals that take up three, four, five, and even six lines of text: small, normal, large, and very large. The press also had several types of floral typographical ornamentations that could occupy up to half of a page. These changed slowly over time, with older versions disappearing when new styles were added. The press had several different coats of arms, largely of political and ecclesiastical figures (for viceroys, archbishops, patrons of convents, etc.) and of the male religious orders (Franciscans, Dominicans, Augustinians, and Jesuits). There were fewer portraits or depictions of individuals. These include various saints (Saint Ignatius Loyola, Saint Anthony the Abbot, Saint Joseph, etc.) and various advocations of the Virgin (del Pilar, Assumption, Guadalupe, etc.). Of all these illustrations, there is only one that resembles any of the images in the *Via crucis* manuscript: a drawing of a monstrance that appears as part of a crest for the Confraternity of the Blessed Sacrament (Cofradía del Santíssimo Sacramento). This closely resembles the cup and consecrated host that appear on the title page of the manuscript (see fig. 5.6).

The illustrations found in the manuscript copy of the *Via crucis* do not appear to have been present in the original printed version of the book, quite simply because the publisher, Rodríguez Lupercio, did not have these images as part of his stock.[45] At the same time, there are some features of the manuscript that are consistent not just with imprints from Rodríguez Lupercio but also with those of all other printers as well. There are simple floral elements as section dividers along with stars and crosses to set off various words to imitate typographical ornamentation. Unfortunately, these are all found in nearly every printed work of the period and cannot link the manuscript to any specific printer of the era.

There is one more argument against the original imprint from which the manuscript was copied having had some sort of illustration: the physical size

44. See Garone Gavier, *La historia de la imprenta*. Although Rodríguez Lupercio was based in Mexico City, all printers had access to the same relatively limited supply of illustrations.

45. The John Carter Brown Library holds seventy-nine works printed by the firm of Rodriguez Lupercio in the latter part of the seventeenth century. None of these imprints has any illustrations of any type that might be seen as an influence on the drawings in the manuscript.

FIGURE 5.6. Santíssimo Sacramento. Rodriguez Lupercio Press, John Carter Brown Library.

of the imprint was simply too small. Most of these devotional books were pocket sized, approximately three inches tall by two wide (75 cm by 50 cm). In objects this small, it would have been hard to have illustrations and still allow for legible text. Of the several score devotional works examined in the John Carter Brown Library collection, only a few were even as large as six inches by four inches (150 cm by 100 cm). Thus, for reasons of size alone, one must conclude that in all likelihood the original imprint was not illustrated.

Illustrations of the *Via crucis en mexicano*

The illustrations in the manuscript must be considered as part of the overall vision of the copyist, Matheo de San Juan Chicahuastla. Because the images depart significantly from known European engravings and woodcuts used in other works, they must have been designed as well as executed by him. Nothing is known about the life of Matheo de San Juan Chicahuastla. From his name we can conclude that he was an Indigenous person from the village of San Juan Chicahuastla. Given that he served as both copyist and artist for the work, he must have fulfilled the role of the Indigenous *escribano*. As Barbara Mundy has observed, *escribanos* bridged the precontact and Hispanic periods of New Spain. While in precontact times, Native communities relied on the *tlacuiloh*. But with the arrival of the Spanish and their system of using notaries and archiving written documents, this ancient group of skilled artisans came to occupy a new niche, that of Native *escribano*. Mundy describes the *escribano* as "someone well versed in Spanish scribal protocols, capable of writing fluently in Nahuatl, and having mastery of the calligraphic codes found in both manuscripts and the typefaces of printed works."[46] Uniquely, this group of professionals operated both within the universe of the written word but also within that of the pictorial and pictographic. While Native communities moved rather quickly to alphabetic record keeping, they did not entirely abandon the older pictographic system. This is precisely what we see in the case of Matheo de San Juan Chicahuastla. Since he does not seem to have based his work on other paintings or woodcuts, he was clearly aware of the styles and iconography of the times. This is a popular version of Vetancurt's work, illustrated by an *escribano*. Importantly, while his handwriting is not the elegant hand of the metropolis, it is clear and conventional, in much the same way that hundreds of provincial *escribanos* of his time period were writing. Additionally, building on Mundy's definition, in the manuscript one can see the *escribano*'s attempt to create floral elements to divide different sections and typographical ornamentation such as one would find in a printed book. He has a fully illustrated frontispiece and what was supposed to be a colophon at the end.

The illustrations in the manuscript fall into two broad categories: major illustrations and designs used as chapter heads or textual separators. There are ten major illustrations, two of which are not part of the Stations of the Cross: the title page and a flowered cross near the end (see fig. 5.7). The other eight depict specific stations in the devotion: Christ carrying the cross to Calvary (station 1), Christ fallen with the cross (7), a second Christ carrying the cross (8), a second Christ fallen (9), Christ stripped of his garments prior to the crucifixion (10), then Christ laid on the cross (11), the pietà with the symbols of the Passion (13), and the interment (14).

Nearly all of the major illustrations depict events in the second half of the devotion. Ironically, the one event that serves as the culmination and focal point of the devotion in general is absent: namely, the crucifixion itself. Some of the other famous moments of the Passion, such as Veronica wiping Christ's face, the meeting with the Blessed Virgin, and the moment when Simon the Cyrene takes up the cross, are likewise absent. Yet a less picturesque moment, the second fall, is depicted. In the drawing for station 8, when Christ meets the women of Jerusalem, only Christ is depicted, not the group of women.

The illustrations are unique on several levels. Unlike most images associated with the Stations of the Cross, they lack any context. One does not see crowds, architecture, or even other participants, other than the Virgin in station 13. They focus only on Jesus, the cross, and the instruments of the Pas-

46. Mundy, "The Emergence of Alphabetic Writing," 388.

FIGURE 5.7. (a) Vetancurt, *Via crucis.* Frontispiece. (b) Vetancurt, *Via crucis.* Flowered cross.

sion. Even the sparest sets of engravings and paintings for the Stations of the Cross will depict the street along which Jesus walked or soldiers accompanying him or participating in the act of crucifying him. As noted above, for station 8, there are no women. Were it not for the fact that the image was clearly placed as part of station 8, it would be impossible to determine that it deals with the theme of Jesus meeting the women. The figures lack rounding and do not occupy space. The stances are awkward and stiff. Jesus wears a robe, a rope around his neck, a rope belt, a crown of thorns, and a halo, as will be explained below. All of the images focus on Jesus and only Jesus, except the pietà, when Mary holds her dead son.

In all scenes prior to the crucifixion, Christ has a rope around his neck, the crown of thorns, and a rope belt, and he carries the cross. The manner in which these elements are depicted does not vary considerably from one image to another. The ropes and the cross are decorated with dots along their surface or edges. In the case of the rope, these dots almost lead one to believe that Christ is carrying a rosary rather than the rope of the Passion. The dots in this context give texture to the surface, although they are actually represented to one side. In the case of the cross, the dots are less representational and more decorative. In some of the illustrations the dots become lines, conveying the feeling of the texture or grain of the wood. The two ropes represent two very different things. The guards used a rope around Christ's neck to pull him along. Fulfilling a completely different function, the rope around his waist is a belt or girdle. These details usually are depicted in the sets of paintings for the Stations of the Cross, but they are also present in many sculptures of Christ, such as those used during Holy Week.

The Christ figure also bears the crown of thorns, one of the most important signs of the Passion. If we look closely, we can see that the crown of thorns also has starburst figures at three points: on the forehead and over each temple. Pál Keleman has identified this decoration as the *tres potencias* (three powers).[47] These are rays of light or tongues of flame added to the nimbus or halo. These are frequently seen on baroque statues of Christ, especially those used in Holy Week processions, such as in Seville (see fig. 5.9).Originally these symbolized the cross within the halo, but by the baroque period the cruciform had been lost and only the three front-most parts remained, since the lower section of the halo cross would have appeared behind Christ's head. Among the Spanish mystics of the early modern period, the *potencias* became associated with the three faculties of the soul: memory, understanding, and will.[48]

The illustrations for stations 11 and 13 are important in that they depict the collection of the symbols of the Passion. These include nails, hammer, lance, sponge, tongs, ladder, winding cloth and/or robe, crown of thorns, dice, and rooster among other items. In the illustration of Christ laid on the cross (station 11), the implements are used—the hammer, nails, tongs, and rope (from the earlier station)—all lying to one side of Jesus. In the deposition (station 13), also known as the pietà, a somewhat larger repertoire of symbols is present since the lance is also depicted. The relevance of most of these to the Passion should be clear. The tongs, among the less obvious implements, were used to hold the nails while they were hammered, securing Jesus to the cross. The lance was used to pierce his side; the sponge, not depicted in the manuscript, but often seen on the end of a reed or lance, was used to offer him bitter wine. The dice and rooster, also not depicted in this manuscript, are taken from the Gospel accounts. The soldiers used the dice as they cast lots for Jesus's robe, while the rooster or cock symbolizes Peter's threefold denial of Christ. All these symbols were frequently used in other popular representations of the Passion, especially on atrium crosses from the sixteenth century (see fig. 5.10).[49]

At the base of the cross in stations 13 and 14, one sees a face or skull and crossbones. This symbol frequently appears in other paintings and engravings in conjunction with the crucifixion. The names Golgotha and Calvary, mean

47. Keleman, *Baroque and Rococo*, 1:50–51; Lara, *Christian Texts*, 216–16.

48. Some cities have religious brotherhoods dedicated to the veneration of Jesus Nazareno de las Tres Potencias that participate in Good Friday processions.

49. McAndrew, *The Open-Air Churches*, 249–52.

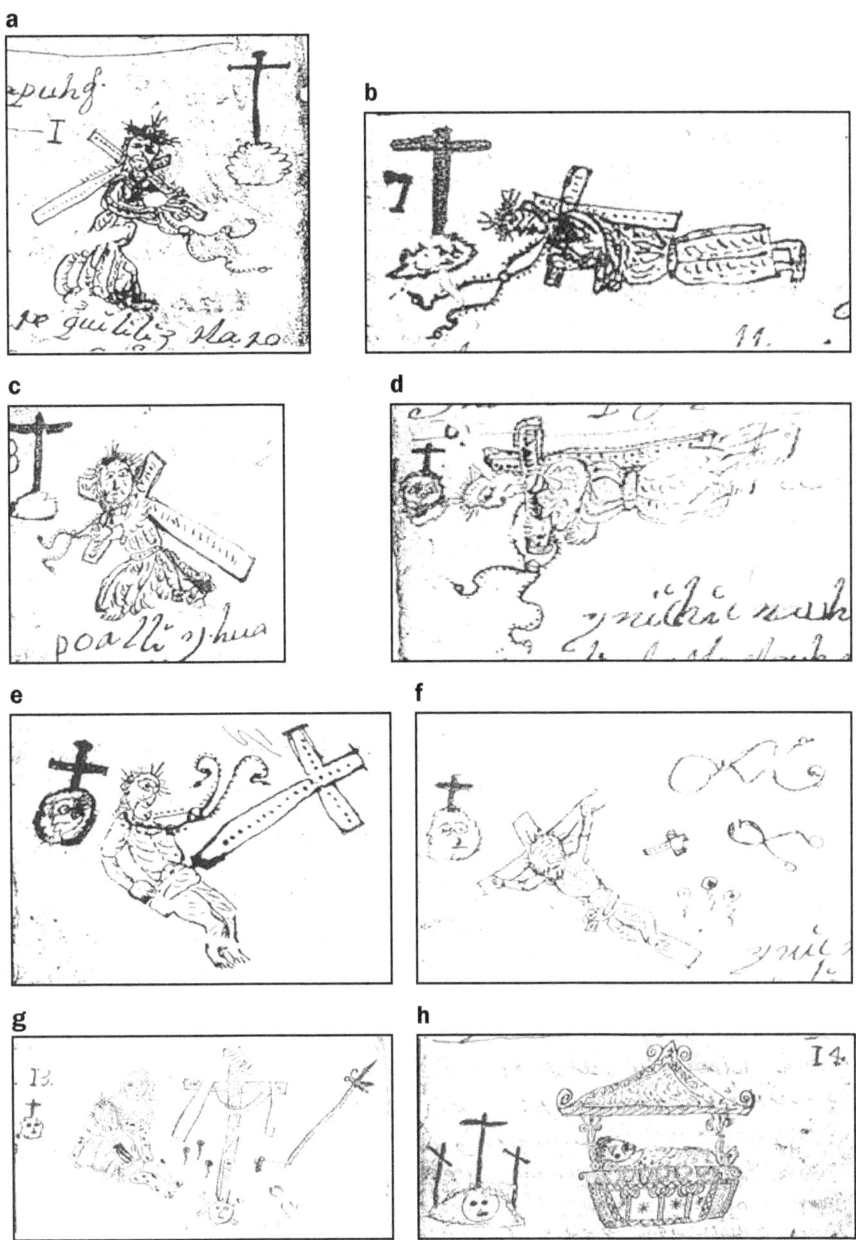

FIGURE 5.8. (a) Vetancurt, *Via crucis.* Station 1, p. 13. (b) Vetancurt, *Via crucis.* Station 7, p. 24. (c) Vetancurt, *Via crucis.* Station 8, p. 25. (d) Vetancurt, *Via crucis.* Station 9, p. 28. (e) Vetancurt, *Via crucis.* Station 10, p. 30. (f) Vetancurt, *Via crucis.* Station 11, p. 33. (g) Vetancurt, *Via crucis.* Station 13, p. 37. (h) Vetancurt, *Via crucis.* Station 14, p. 39.

FIGURE 5.9. Tres potencias. San Jerónimo Tlacochoaya, Oax, photograph by the Author.

"Place of the Skull." According to a pious legend, the place-name refers particularly to the skull of Adam. Supposedly, Adam, the first man, was buried on that site. Thus, many medieval illustrations of the crucifixion, and of the cross itself, also include a small skull and crossbones underneath. The symbolism is that Christ was the new Adam. One should also notice that at the beginning of all of the stations there is a small cross coming out of a circle, not unlike an orb. In many of these, one can see the face of the skull under the cross. Perhaps the most interesting of these faces is the one found in station 10, which seems extremely similar to a Maya glyph.[50] The skull and cross for station 14 differ from all the others in that the hill of Calvary with three crosses on top of it are depicted. Thus, these little markers for each station are undoubtedly miniature depictions of the cross on Calvary.

The two most complex illustrations are the title page and the interment. The title page shows two angelic figures holding either end of a stone arch, upon which rest the three crosses of Calvary. All three crosses have the X (or chi) figure through them. The cross of Christ is further decorated with five flowers, one on the cross's left, and four on the lower portion of the main member. Contrast this to the flowered cross seen in the depiction of the holy cross, where there are flowers at each hand, one at the head and one at the feet. Christ bore five wounds that are frequently represented as flowers, per-

50. Eric and Thompson, *Maya Hieroglyphic Writing*.

FIGURE 5.10. Atrium Cross. Huichapan, Hgo, photograph by the Author.

haps from the Spanish expression *flor de la sangre* meaning "wound." The traditional five wounds correspond to the two hands and two feet, as well as the side where Christ was pierced during the crucifixion to determine if he still lived. These became part of the coat of arms of the Holy Gospel Province of the Franciscans in Mexico, to which Vetancurt pertained (see fig. 2.1). As noted earlier, at least one of the devotions that appeared in the early modern period was one to the Five Wounds of Christ. In the early modern period and especially in New Spain, the flowered cross was associated with the resurrection. Thus, it appears as an illustration toward the end of the devotion. In Latin America, in particular, May 3 is celebrated as the Day of the Holy Cross, known as the *cruz de mayo*. The tradition is to completely cover a cross with as many flowers as possible to symbolize Christ's return to life from death.[51]

On the title page, under the arch, there is an image of the chalice and consecrated host on a shield surrounded by a halo or nimbus. The juxtaposition of the Passion with the Eucharist is a relatively common feature of baroque art. This can be seen in the atrium cross from Huichapan, where at the base of the decorated cross there is a chalice and host (see fig. 5.11). The arch itself is very similar to several others in central Mexico, especially some used in open chapels, such as Tlahuelilpa and Epazoyucan, or over north doors in places like

51. Lara, *Christian Texts*, 227.

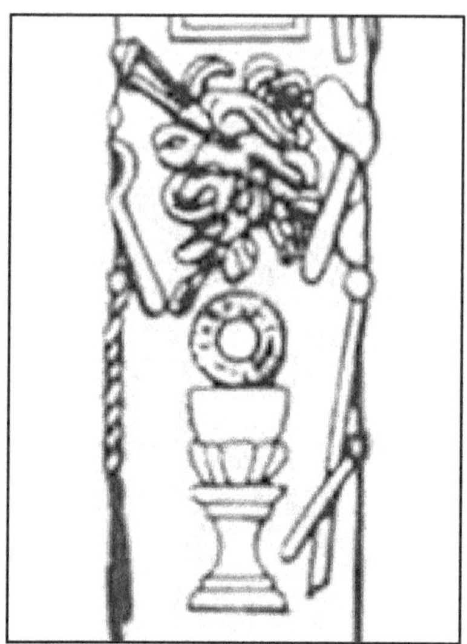

FIGURE 5.11. Chalice and Host. Huichapan Atrium Cross. Drawing by the Author.

Huejotzingo (see fig. 5.12).[52] The one engraving from the repertoire of Rodríguez Lupercio features the consecrated host superimposed over the chalice, which is very similar to what is seen in this drawing (see fig. 5.13).

The illustration of the burial or interment of Christ is unique. Rather than the cave burial that is described in the Bible, Matheo de San Juan Chicahuastla has represented Christ in an ornate coffin. These coffins, often with glass or crystal sides, are found throughout central Mexico and usually contain sculptures of the buried Christ, although saints are also frequently depicted. In this drawing in the manuscript, bruises are seen on Christ's cheek, and the wounds on the feet are also visible. It is unclear whether or not Christ still wears the crown of thorns in this drawing. The coffin is ornately decorated with stars and other symbols and is topped with a canopy. This is all associated with the Santo Entierro (Holy Burial), which was an important devotion in colonial Latin America and still is today. For example, the Cofradia de la Vera Cruz, Huejotzingo, or Santo Entierro, made the buried Christ a central figure in its devotion, as did the Santo Entierro of Amecameca.

The illustrations of the Vetancurt *Via crucis* manuscript housed by the Academy of American Franciscan History supply a great deal of information to the viewer that goes well beyond the material provided by the text alone. On the one hand the images firmly place the work in the baroque period, yet they still manifest some medieval symbols. The illustrations demonstrate a

52. Kubler, *Mexican Architecture*, 2:401.

FIGURE 5.12. Open Chapel Arch. Tlahuelilpa, Hgo. Drawing by Kendra Farstad.

fairly high level of sophistication when it comes to the realm of symbolism and iconography in general. While they may merely have been images copied from paintings and sculptures known to Matheo de San Juan Chicahuastla, they are accurate and effective in conveying a significant level of meaning beyond the text. We know from Vetancurt's *Teatro mexicano* that confraternities in San Josef de los Naturales had full figures that they would parade in procession during Holy Week. The drawings seem to be images taken from those *pasos* more than copies of engravings.

These images can be seen as falling between the *tequitqui* art of the sixteenth century and what would become known as naïve art (*art naïf* in French).[53] The images lack many of the hallmarks of a more traditional European artist. The sketches seem to have been done quickly. They include only the central figure, and the figures that are present are flat. Images are placed in a context to assist in interpretation: the symbols of the Passion are depicted arranged alongside Christ as he is laid on the cross. In most instances, although Christ's body is twisted and tormented, he faces the viewer fully, front-on.

It is difficult to imagine what Matheo de San Juan Chicahuastla used as a model for his work, but through the process of elimination, we can reach some preliminary conclusions. As has been shown above, images like these are not found in contemporary engravings. While there are numerous engravings of scenes from the Passion in general and the Stations of the Cross in

53. Webster, "Art, Ritual, and Confraternities."

FIGURE 5.13. Chalice. Frontispiece. *Via crucis en mexicano.*

particular, none conform to the images Matheo de San Juan Chicahuastla used in the Vetancurt manuscript. In addition, no complete set of engravings from New Spain representing the Stations of the Cross has emerged. Paintings are also unlikely exemplars for these images. Paintings tend to be more complex, featuring landscapes, cityscapes, and scenes populated by other actors in the drama. Except for a few instances of Christ at the column, Christ is usually shown surrounded by others: guards, the people of Jerusalem, the women of Jerusalem, or specific actors such as Simon of Cyrene or Veronica. The one genre in which the Christ figure appears to the exclusion of most other figures in the Passion drama is the sculptures of Christ used in Holy Week celebrations. These sculptures are frequently held in churches during the year and are accessible to the faithful. When used in processions, the figures can appear alone or in groups; individual statues can be placed alongside one another to create tableaux. Additionally, by the seventeenth century articulated figures, especially of Christ, were constructed in New Spain. Called "puppets" by Jaime Lara, these figures could be posed in a wide range of positions. They had their roots in the sixteenth century and in the practices of various confraternities dedicated to the celebration of the events of Good Friday and the *santo entierro* (holy burial). Articulated figures also have roots in preconquest times, when figures of deities were made from amaranth paste and then used in rituals and celebrations.[54] These statues, either articulated or rigid, were

54. Lara, *Christian Texts*, 219.

undeniably commonplace in seventeenth-century churches. Similarly, they were used in Holy Week processions, as was and still is the custom in Spain. Thus, in the absence of other possible sources, and with such a strong similarity to a contemporary practice, it seems reasonable that the sketches that accompanied the manuscript copy of Vetancurt's *Via crucis* have their roots and inspiration in the baroque figures of Christ found in many parish churches that were frequently used in Holy Week processions. The Stations of the Cross is a quintessentially baroque devotion. It extolls extremes of passion. It combines prayer and meditation with movement, as the penitent retraces Christ's last steps. In addition, it is a multimedia experience, tying the written and spoken word to movement and to illustrations in two or three dimensions. If one adds the songs that are frequently also sung during processions, then it includes even more types of artistic expression. In adding incense to the procession, the devotion involves nearly all the senses. Consequently, one can see how the devotion to the Stations of the Cross achieved such a widespread following in the late seventeenth and early eighteenth centuries, just as the baroque style, with all its excesses and appeals to the senses, was dominating European culture, in the Old World and the New.

Chapter 6
Conclusions: A Colony Embraces a Devotion

The devotion of the Stations of the Cross creates a spiritual place that links participants across time and space with Jesus Christ in his last hours. Because it focuses on Jesus's walk from the seat of the Roman government in Jerusalem to his crucifixion and entombment, practitioners feel that the practice must be an ancient remnant of the early Church. Indeed, the first serious scholarship on the devotion looked to the Holy Land for the roots of the practice. And, certainly, Christian pilgrims to Jerusalem across the ages have been attracted to the sites associated with Jesus's ministry on earth. But the best evidence that has been uncovered points to the devotion having a European origin. Rather than being as ancient as Christianity itself, the preponderance of evidence points to the devotion beginning to take its present form in the fourteenth or fifteenth century. Moreover, the Stations of the Cross as a devotion is merely one of many different devotions that emerged in the period, as sensibilities regarding prayer and secular participation in spiritual acts became more inclusive. Even with a burgeoning interest in participatory and stational devotions, it still took until the early eighteenth century for the Stations of the Cross to receive papal sanction and endorsement.

It is a surprise, then, that the devotion already had multitudes of adherents in sixteenth-century Mexico. The celebration expanded beyond a few churches or convents as it flowed out to the streets and roads of the city. In addition, permanent chapels were erected to link the church of San Francisco with the *humilladero* on the edge of town. Stranger still, the devotion attracted so many adherents, particularly in the Franciscan Order, that it was seen as a tool for the further evangelization of the Natives, and a small handbook to the devotion, written in Nahuatl for that Native market, was printed toward the end of the seventeenth century, a full fifty years before the pope recognized the devotion.

The popularity of the Stations of the Cross emerged as a result of several trends in Western Christianity. Central was the fascination with the holy places of Jerusalem. On top of that was the medieval Church's focus on the suffering of Jesus during his final hours. Those two trends intermingled with innovations in spiritual disciplines of the *devotio moderna*, whose practices included silent prayer and the contemplation of religious themes, such as the lives of the saints and Christ's Passion. By the fourteenth century, some Christians who wanted to immerse themselves even more in the life of Christ found that images from the events of the Passion assisted them in their contemplation. Others imagined walking alongside Jesus as he moved toward his crucifixion. These trends, then, linked to create the devotion that we now know as the Stations of the Cross.

Similarly, the Spanish took the devotion and used it to build upon trends that were already present in the Iberian Peninsula. In medieval times, roadside crosses were erected to denote the edges of cities. These came to be representative of Golgotha, the site of Jesus's crucifixion. People also built churches, chapels, and palaces in imitation of the holy sites in Jerusalem. With the importation of the devotion of the Stations of the Cross from the Lowlands, these structures easily became stand-ins for the actual biblical sites. Spanish Christians could then use the chapels, crosses, and palaces as focal points for their celebration of the Stations, moving through the streets as they prayed and sang. At this time, other traditions involving religious processions in towns and cities marked the important events of the Church year. Weekly or monthly processions for the Stations, usually on Fridays, fit easily into the ritual calendar.

Christian worship in Spain became the model for worship in newly settled areas. As the Spanish brought Christianity to the New World, it was perfectly natural for them to bring with it all the trappings that had developed on the Iberian Peninsula. Processions and stational devotions, including the Stations of the Cross, were part of the Spanish liturgical and devotional repertoire. In Mexico, in particular, the Spanish encountered a Native religion that also valued public displays in processions and stational devotions. Thus, these practices provided the missionaries with a means of introducing the new religion to the Natives. But clearly, large numbers of Spaniards were already practicing the devotion of the Stations of the Cross, since chapels dedicated to that devotion were erected within a few decades of the Spanish invasion.

The seventeenth century witnessed the full flowering of the Stations of the Cross as a popular and widely practiced devotion. This period when the Catholic Church came to grips with reforms that had been proposed by various critics inside and outside the Church is called the Catholic Reformation. The period also coincided with a movement in the arts that came to be known as the baroque. In the baroque, artistic sensibilities appreciated complexity over simplicity, the hidden over the obvious. Opera, for instance, is a baroque art form in that it includes many layers of artistic performance that come together to create a complex and multifaceted work. It requires a suspension of disbelief in that the actors address one another not in conversation but in song. The action is punctuated by dance sequences. The sets and costumes are lavish and frequently stand as works of art in their own right. In very much the same way, the devotion of the Stations of the Cross is a baroque devotion. It is not merely a set of prayers. There are actions that accompany the prayers. The practitioner is required to walk from station to station, frequently engaged in prayer or song. Each station is also multilayered in that a bas-relief, painting, or sculpture illustrates the essential features of that station. Thus, the devotion exists as prayers, actions, works of art, and frequently songs all at once. And while millions of adherents still practice it today, in the eighteenth century any particular celebration of the devotion might have involved hundreds of participants. In its complexity, the Stations of the Cross is a supremely baroque practice.

The pinnacle of the Catholic Reformation roughly coincided with the baroque period in art. Thus, the two terms are frequently used to describe the seventeenth and early eighteenth centuries. The Stations of the Cross is also a supreme example of the Catholic Reformation. If the Protestant Reformation tended to make spirituality more internal and personal, devotions like the Stations of the Cross reflect the external and collective. While the devotion can certainly be followed in private and in silence, it became an important tool the Catholic Church could use to organize popular celebrations not only in churches and convents but also through the streets.

In colonial Mexico, the Stations of the Cross and other devotions were important tools in the spread of Christianity. They allowed the faithful to participate as individuals in a mass of others. As a missionary tool, it must have provided a comfortable way in which to become familiar with Christianity. The Mexica, prior to the arrival of the Spanish, also used processions and stational devotions to create a sense of collective identity in the worship of the divinities. While the missionaries attempted to avoid confusion of Christianity with precontact religions, the use of certain practices from the old faith allowed for an easier transition into the new faith. Clearly processions and devotions like the Stations of the Cross were important pieces in this process.

The Catholic Reformation and the baroque were both ways that Europeans influenced the populations of colonial Mexico. What is most remarkable about the Vetancurt translation of the *Via crucis* is that it bridges European and Native cultures. While on the one hand, as a Christian devotion, the book was clearly of European origin. But at the same time, it was popular enough in colonial Mexico to warrant two editions. It stands as a unique example of a work written with Native readers in mind. Many manuals and handbooks that allowed parish priests to operate in a Nahuatl-speaking parish were bilingual, offering prayers and responses in both Spanish and Nahuatl. This work, however, was written completely in Nahuatl. It did not have the Nahuatl and Spanish versions in a single volume. In this regard, it fits into a thread of works that had disappeared more than thirty years earlier: recreational works written with a Nahuatl readership. In the circle of Horacio Carochi, an important Jesuit linguist and scholar of Nahuatl, several works appeared in Nahuatl that were not purely destined for the evangelization. The *Via crucis* can be seen as a continuation of that brief tradition. Indeed, the Vetancurt *Via crucis* is actually precocious in that the Nahuatl version of that devotion appeared well before the devotion itself gained widespread support in the larger population. Clearly, there were adherents in the cities, as is evidenced by the construction of chapels in Mexico City and Puebla, but it was not until the early eighteenth century that the pope authorized and regularized the devotion.

The specific manuscript, held by the Academy of American Franciscan History, is remarkable itself. No original printed versions of the work are known to exist. The one copy that we have was copied by hand in the early eighteenth century by Matheo de San Juan Chicahuastla. Everything indicates that Matheo was himself a Native. Where he lived is subject to some speculation. His name suggests that he was from a village called Chicahuastla. Currently in Mexico, the only village named something like Chicahuastla (in reality the phonetically similar Chicahuaxtla) is located in the modern state of Oaxaca, San Andres Chicahuastla (or Chicahuaztla, or Chicahuaxtla). It was not known as a Nahuatl-speaking region. Currently, residents speak Trique. By contrast, within the historical record, there is evidence for a village named San Juan Chicahuastla located in the Huauchinango region of what was Tlaxcala, now the state of Puebla.[1] While several languages are spoken in that region, Nahuatl was and continues to be important. It is located in a larger region known as the Huasteca, where Nahuatl is still spoken by a large number of people. It is mostly likely that the sole existing copy of the Vetancurt *Via crucis* was copied in the Huauchinango village of Chicahuastla.

Matheo de San Juan Chicahuastla accomplished a remarkable feat. Unfortunately, we know nothing at all about him except what we can infer from the pages of the text that he copied. Because his work includes both the alphabetic text and illustrations, he fits into the category of Native *escribano*, as explored by Barbara Mundy. In all likelihood, Matheo worked with the Native leadership of his community in various writing projects. These might include petitions to government officials in the region or even the Kingdom of New Spain. He undoubtedly also served in the parish by assisting the priest, possibly by keeping parish records in Nahuatl. It is assumed that he just copied the

1. AGN, Indios, vol. 70, exp. 238, folios 264–264v. "Para que el subdelegado de Huauchinango informe sobre los particulares a que se contrae el escrito inserto de los indios del pueblo de San Juan Chicahuaxtla. 1803." See also AGN Tierras, 2684, exp. 14, 1786–89; AGN Tierras, 1417, exp. 9, 1786–1819; AGN, Indios, 38, exp. 24, 1712. Thanks to Dr. Jamie Forde for his suggestion to look through the AGN catalogs.

text of the Vetancurt *Via sacra* with added material. Thus, the words of the text were the fruit of the labors of Vetancurt and his assistants.

Looking at the illustrations provided by Matheo de San Juan, we see that they provide a great deal of content beyond the text itself. This is most clearly seen in the illustrations that include the implements of the passion. Other than nails and the cross itself, the devotion does not discuss the implements. Nonetheless, the lance, for example, appears in the illustrations. Perhaps the most curious aspect of the illustrations is the absence of any figures other than Christ, with the exception of Mary. Matheo de San Juan placed his full attention on Christ. This is in accord with the focus of the devotion, which is of Christ's suffering along the path to his crucifixion. Yet many other collections of images, including prints and paintings, depict other individuals as well, especially others involved in the story, such as the guards, Simon of Cyrene, and Veronica. Thus, in all likelihood, prints and paintings were not the source of the images in Matheo de San Juan's sketches. Because of his drawings' similarity to sculptures of Christ seen in Passion floats popular in Spain and her colonies, it seems more reasonable to assume that Matheo de San Juan drew on those images for his illustrations.

For his part, Vetancurt provided the translation. Clearly, he had a command of the Nahuatl neologisms having to do with the Christian faith. While we have seen that he uses words for "prayer," "cross," and "mantle or cloth" that appear in other devotional works of the period, he had to develop new words for the specific issues presented by the devotion of the Stations of the Cross. Central to this was the word for "station," which had not yet appeared in the literature. At the same time, he uses at least one word, *xipehualiztli*, in a unique manner. In all likelihood the word he needed was the phonetically similar *chipeuiliztli*. He also continued to use some Spanish words, such as *cruz* but managed to use them in accordance with the rules of Nahuatl grammar. These examples demonstrate the evolution of Nahuatl in the colonial period, as charted by Frances Karttunen and James Lockhart.

As a product of both the baroque and the Catholic Reformation, the copy of Vetancurt's *Via crucis* that we have represents even more layers of complexity. In addition to being a late-medieval devotion based on events from the Bible, interpreted by Europeans (largely in the Lowlands), and translated into the Mediterranean culture of Spain, this work was based on a Spanish version. It was translated into Nahuatl by a well-known Franciscan expert in the languages, and, in turn, copied and embellished by a Native of central Mexico. Each layer of the work's creation adds its own flavor and complexity. The result is that the work manifests an eighteenth-century Nahuatl speaker copying a work translated by a seventeenth-century creole Mexican Franciscan from an original written by a seventeenth-century Spanish Franciscan from the port city of Cadiz.

From such a small work, a whole world can be glimpsed. Nahuatl imprints were relatively uncommon in the late seventeenth century. The fact that this work went through multiple editions demonstrates both the market for the text and the popularity of the devotion. Indeed, other scholars have written about the spread of the devotion of the Stations of the Cross in Mexico, but the relationship of the Natives with the devotion has been ignored. Clearly, as evidenced by this work, the devotion was being offered to the Natives at the same time as, or prior to, its full embrace in Europe. The devotion built on a tradition of religious processions that began before the Spanish invasion, was used by the earliest missionaries, and then continued into the seventeenth and eighteenth centuries. It also drew from decorative and artistic developments in the larger colonial society as artists and architects continued illustrating images of and erecting buildings for the Stations of the Cross. In this little book, we see so many of the trends that were present in late seventeenth-century Mexican society. The implications of this work not only affect our understanding of Native communities but reflect important trends in the larger colonial society. It is indeed a microcosm for understanding Mexico at the turn of the eighteenth century.

Appendix 1
English Translation[1]

In order to know how to walk the stations of the via sacra and the indulgences that are gained visiting them. Translated into the Mexican language by the Reverend Father fray Augustín de Vetancurt, ex–reader of theology, retired general preacher, apostolic chronicler and vicar <2> of the chapel of Saint Joseph of the Natives of this city of Mexico of this year of 1680. <3>

Shining examples, mirrors of advice that speak about the beloved ones of our Savior Jesus Christ, those who acknowledge His death, how they will be able to determine to live upon the road called the via sacra, meaning, the road of divine suffering. But as to how they persecuted the Savior when they took Him out of Pilate's royal place of judgment: they make Him carry crossed sticks, the holy cross, on His shoulders until He reached Skull Mountain Place, Calvary, where He suffered and died on the cross in order to save us sinners. But it also says and is so arranged so that many perfectly spiritual favors are received, <4> the loosening of sins, what are called indulgences; they will earn and enjoy them, obtain them through divine commands, pondering the divine suffering over there with which all go to Calvary. The humble son of fray Francis [i.e., Saint Francis of Assisi], fray Augustin de Vetancurt, [of the Chapel of] Saint Joseph [of the Natives of] Mexico [City], wrote and translated it into the Nahuatl language.

This road is called the via sacra, [which] in the Nahuatl language [means] the road of divine suffering. It is what is now being recounted. Thus they made a determination about our beloved Savior: they took Him out of Pilate's royal home of judgment there until He reached Skull Mountain Place, Calvary, where He died. He suffered on the cross and died. His weeping mother, the queen of heaven Saint Mary, initiated it. Let it not just be from heaven. <5> Our Savior lay dawn in the place of the golden cave, especially the short time while He still lived on earth. His beloved mother still lived sixteen years, always sadly remembering His death and His various torments. Not a little she pondered His tormented death and where her beloved child used to live, for He greatly pleased and gave joy to His beloved Father, God.

1. Because of Nahuatl syntax, the page breaks marked in this translation <p> are only approximate.

And so that we completely understand in a very illuminated place the various surpassingly [great] sufferings, in remembrance of our Savior above all other diverse honors paid to Him with which His servants honor Him, it is because of them that they honor His suffering. Through recollections they exert all their efforts from this time forward to do what <6> they would do when and if their beloved Savior would have suffered in their presence. There He comes setting down on His road of torment all His anguished distress, His flaying and His skinning, His nakedness and His shame, and the other many pains that happened to Him. It makes them cry and pains them, it especially makes them angry because there they see how much their Savior suffered on their account and they recognize it, their sins make them cry and hurt their hearts. There they firmly proposed to jointly burn it; they will eternally thank our Lord Jesus Christ for His task of salvation. And it is this that gives our Savior joy and happiness in all good and proper lives. As He said to the completely <7> penitent priest, talking and saying to him: Come hither, press close to Me; you will help Me. We will both carry my cross, the holy cross. And the penitent answered Him, saying: O beloved Savior, how shall I do it so that I will help You? For I am powerless, I am a great sinner, four hundred [i.e., many times] [over]. Our beloved Savior said to him: It is just by My will that you will help Me. With all your inner self, remember and ponder My death and all My torments, for I pay the penalty on your account and on account of the people of the earth, [all of you being] sinners. Never forget it! Afterward you will pray with your offering. Honor Me, for you will greatly enrich Me, give me joy. He saw another frightening sign and example. A just man of saintly life <8> at the time of his death heard a big metal bell ringing. On account of this the devils gathered together. But when they had gathered together their ruler said to them: O my friends, you already know concerning what our God made the people of the earth. It is because of it that he was crucified and died. Now no longer get tired concerning confusion because then they will remember on account of how much He suffered. Then he quickly came to when he heard the statement of the ruler of the devils. Then a great old devil stands up before them. He said: O lord! O ruler! Your words are very true. Thus I myself say that the believers, the Christians, will confuse themselves and commit errors. Let us repeatedly provoke them about a life of joyful sin [such as] over-eating and over-drinking. And they will forget this business of the bloody torment of our Ruler. The leader answered them: Let it be so ordered. Perhaps with that they will fling themselves into sin. It is with great clarity we see and recognize what is the will of our Lord God. He is necessary for those who acknowledge <9> His death so that He will pardon us our sins and He will give His goodness to our souls so that we will save ourselves. Because it is this we will forever go about sadly remembering His suffering there on His road of torment with which ail go to Skull Mountain

Place, Calvary. And the sign of the road, the example they will take so that they will arrange it is called the via crucis. With it they will properly lay it down. And when they are all gathered together it is this suffering that is the beginning. All will kneel, bow low and makes the sign of the cross. <10> He who reads books will read it. Here are the prayers along with their responses; prayers of offering and offerings [follow].

+

O God, completely honorable and divine ruler! With deep bowing I place it entirely in Your hands. Through all His suffering here on Your road of torment I will perform my recollections and kneeling, my weeping and sadness. But if you provide a dwelling for it, receive it on our account and on account of the people who went along setting down on the road of suffering a great many acts of obtaining blessings, [what are called] indulgences. Thus may You receive it because of the pardon of our sins and because of the souls who are waiting to be assisted in the place of purifying by fire, [what is called] purgatory. <11> Then he who reads books will explain to people [the following.]

—1 Here begins a kneeling prayer called a station. It is the royal home of judgment of Pilate in the place called Praetorium. It is where and when the six soldiers beat Him to earth with lashes, thorns and chains. [However,] just four of them repeatedly pushed Him, kicked Him and angrily whipped our beloved Savior. They repeatedly tore apart His precious body with a whip. Then Pilate sentenced Him to death, standing Him up before those who hated Him, the Jews. Very quickly they entwined a knotted whip around His neck, with which they will drag Him and with which they hurried Him along.

Prayer <12>

Alas, O completely sweet one, Jesus! You wanted them to tie you up in the fashion of one of the thieves [or] like a slave is tied up, and they sentenced You to death. May it be Your precious will, on account of Your humble patient suffering, that with Your help I govern my heart and pride. Let me free myself from my sins so that I will live happily and peacefully and so that I will enjoy pardon of sin, and afterward in Your land of heavenly joy. So be it, Jesus.

Then a kiss is laid down [on the dirt] and [the following] will be said:

O our Lord, O God, I have greatly sinned; pardon me. <13> We have greatly sinned; pardon us. For I very much regretted [the sins I/we committed?] in Your presence.

Again let a kiss be laid down [on the dirt] and [the following] will be said:

Perfectly praise the suffering and precious death of our beloved honored Savior Jesus Christ and His pure birth from the royal virgin Saint Mary whom original sin never reached. So be it, Jesus.

—2 The second place of kneeling prayers called a station. Our beloved Savior was walking about; it was 21 steps. Here is where they put on the neck of our beloved Savior Jesus Christ the very heavy crossed sticks, the cross. In order to properly set it on Him they first put on Him a garment, then they adjusted it on Him. <14> They put the red worn out blanket on Him when He was being made sport of Finally they again put His garment on Him and again on top of His head they laid sticks and thorns, a round crown of thorns. These thorns painfully and repeatedly entered in many places, causing His blood to flow forth.

Prayer

Alas, O only God, O Master of Heaven, O precious ruler Jesus! You wanted to cast Yourself into the hatred of the scoundrel-like Jews who took You into custody and loaded onto Your shoulders the crossed sticks of wood, the very heavy cross. I implore You: Help me so that I will bring to a [successful] conclusion and will patiently receive penance so that I will take on the burden of the proper life <15> of heaven as You wish. And with You, afterward, You will give me heavenly joy. So be it, Jesus. O our Lord God. [The following] will be said: Perfectly . . . [Refrain as above]

—3 The third place of kneeling prayers [called] a station. Our God was walking around; it was 80 steps. Here is where with weeping and sighs our Savior bears the cross on His shoulders. He could absolutely no longer raise it so that He completely fainted, for those who hated Him drove Him on until He fell to the earth at the foot of the cross. He firmly fell to earth, His flayed [skin] opened, and His precious blood repeatedly poured out.

Prayer <16>

Alas, perfectly lovable Jesus! So that we would recognize the heaviness of our sins (for the very heavy cross You bore on Your shoulders because of us is just a stand-in for them) You fell because of Your weariness at the foot of the holy cross. I implore You: with the help of Your precious firm will, Your grace, may I quickly rise so that Your divine will shall be realized. Here I will live in the penance You want until I enjoy the final fruits of the holy cross You revealed to me, [i.e.,] heavenly joy, glory. Perfectly [praise?] [etc.] O Our Lord, O God. [The following] will be said: Perfectly . . . [Refrain as above] <17>

—4 Here is the fourth place of kneeling [prayers called] a station. Our beloved Savior was walking around; it was seventy steps. There is where His weeping mother Saint Mary and her afflicted beloved son recognized themselves on the road and met face to face. How they mutually loved each other!

Darkness broke, like a big thorn that quickly pierced through her heart; it was a great affliction of the heart. Even though she did not wipe His face she follows Him with weeping until He reaches the top of the mountain, Calvary.

Prayer

Alas, O merciful precious honored mother, O poor Saint Mary! You surpassed absolutely all women in weeping and heartfelt bitterness when you saw your youngest child, your only child, darkness on Him, His honored face blackened, His fresh body ripped to shreds, <18> thorns piercing His head and His bones going numb with the great weight of the holy cross! And when the Jews dishonored Him, the people of the earth idly laughed. He became our God. O my beloved mother, since I have pained you with my sins may it be your precious will (because of what you suffered) that as your sadness pained you may likewise my sins worry me so that I will merit and enjoy confession and pardon of sin; thus I will be purified here on earth and afterward over there in heaven, the place of eternal riches, glory. So be it. O our Lord, O God.

[The following] will be said: Perfectly praise the precious honored suffering and the precious honored death [Refrain as above] <19>

—5 The fifth place of kneeling [prayers called] a station. Our beloved Savior was walking about; it was seventy-one steps. Here is where they lifted the body of Simon Sixineo [Simon the Cyrene] so that He will help our Savior. He is the first. They were not compassionate; the laborer did it just because of his fear that He would not suffer from faintness on the road. Because He showed the heaviness of the cross to others it is as though He was about to suffer. His face greatly swells up with His tears and His blood, His eyes completely blind. [?] and they came to severely judge Him; the two thieves next to Him will be judged [too]. O our Lord, O God.

Prayer

Alas, O You completely loving one, Jesus! It is just because of Your loving charity that You wanted to go carrying on Your shoulders <20> Your entirely heavy crossed sticks of wood, this holy cross which made Your precious shoulders black-and-blue and inflicted burning pain on them. And You wanted with the image of Simon Sixineo that we will help You so that we will merit and enjoy what You revealed to me here, the very high value of the cross. O my God, let it be Your precious will. I will enter from below into penance and despise the evil life. Let me just occupy myself in following after You here on earth so that I will merit and enjoy heavenly joy. So be it.

O our Lord, O God. Perfectly [Refrain as above]

—6 The sixth place of kneeling [prayers called] a station. It was ninety-one steps; our God was walking about. Here <21> is where the honored person named Veronica encountered our Savior on the road. When she saw Him His precious face was greatly swelled up, very blackened and bruised. What a state His eyes were in! Then she quickly pulled out for Him a thin white honored cloth with which she wiped His tormented face. A very great miracle occurred, so that in three places where the cloth was covering [Him], the precious face of our Savior was copied in [those] three places.

Prayer

Alas, O perfectly beautiful one, Jesus! How Your precious face suffered, how they struck you in the face! They dirtied You when they spat in Your face. You received the help of the lady Veronica when she wiped Your precious face with a soft cloth. May it be your precious will that through Your help, <22> Your precious face is copied onto my spirit so that there I will eternally honor You and so that I will obtain and enjoy heavenly joy. O our Lord, O God. Perfectly praise [Refrain as above]

—7 The seventh place of kneeling prayer [called] a station. Our beloved Savior was walking about; it was 336 steps with which He arrived [here?]. Here is where He was taken out from a house. It was the entrance of the palace [where] He fell to earth for the first time and there [where] His strength was completely spent with the weight of the holy cross. <23> How He fainted with a great flaying. The precious shoulder of our beloved Savior Jesus Christ greatly swelled up and ached.

Prayer

Alas, O completely honorable Jesus! You wanted this. With dishonor they accompanied You. Those scoundrels greatly worked at Your death so that with fainting and numbness Your precious body, You, fell to the ground. Help me so that I will relieve the heaviness of my sins, so that I will no longer bear on my shoulders the burden of my sins. Give me my strength [back?] so that [?] in the place where He was condemned. Especially let the service concerning Your work touch me in passing. So be it, Jesus.

O our Lord, O God. Perfectly praise the precious death of our beloved Savior. [Refrain as above] <24>

—8 The eighth place of kneeling prayers [called] a station. It was 308 steps; our God was walking around. Here is where the compassionate women of Jerusalem were when they saw sinless Jesus in the place of crucifixion not long [after] the city [*altepetl*] had honored Him because of all the miracles He had wrought; <25> everyone had wept for Him. But our Savior gazed at the women, saying to them: You are the children of Jerusalem. Do not weep for My death. Cry more especially for yourselves and weep because of your children.

Prayer

Alas, O heavenly teacher! Even though You follow with torment Your road of suffering You did not abandon Your task of teaching with which You revealed to me how [one's] sins will make [one] cry. Also show and teach me how with weeping, tears, and sadness, all my sins with which I blackened and dirtied my soul made me cry; <26> let me wash and purify it with my tears. Let me occupy myself in loving You so that I will earn and enjoy Your instrument of sadness, [i.e., Your] grace. So be it. O our Lord, O God. Completely praise [Refrain as above]

—9 The ninth place of kneeling prayers [called] a station. It was [300?] steps; our God was walking around. Here is the third time our Savior fell to the ground. <27> Moreover His precious blood was very much spilling [out] so that His strength was entirely spent, because when He would have gotten up He was no longer able to do it, He again fell to the ground and His elbows and His face and His hands and His feet vehemently hit the ground. [He/His body?] was hurt in many places because [He was?] badly [beaten?] on the road.

Prayer

Alas, O perfectly compassionate Jesus! You [suffered/paid the price to?] the enraged workers of death; they flayed You so that You fell to the ground [a third time]. May it be Your precious will that with Your help I will conquer those who hate me, in this fashion doing penance to You. Afterward I will earn and enjoy happiness, [i.e.,] glory. So be it. <28>

—10 The tenth place of kneeling prayer [called] a station. It was eighteen steps; our Savior was walking around. Here is where he reached Skull Rack Mountain Place, Calvary. There they disrobed Him; there they laid on all the lashes until they [removed?] His garment from Him. Again with torment the spilling of His blood was renewed and [with] all His flaying <29> and because of His bloody fainting He asked them for a small bit of water. Likewise they angrily gave him a bitter potion [as] a drink; with it He just fainted. It is very necessary for us to go about sadly remembering when our beloved Savior thus [went]. He was naked in public—How ashamed He was! For truly His precious body was shamefully naked before all kinds of people.

Prayer

Alas, O perfectly and completely peaceful Jesus! You patiently suffered Your shameful nakedness before the perverse Jews. They undressed You so that the spilling of Your blood <30> was renewed. May it be Your precious will because of all Your burning aching blood, all Your painful exhausted blood. For truly it is on our account that with Your joyful mouth You drank the first bitter liquid. But as for me: Your precious will be done that I will no longer drink or take for myself something which perverts people, the various earthly things which are the hateful instruments of my perverted enemies. Let me not [erase?], let me not [soil?] so that I will leave myself entirely in Your hands, the reason being because You remained naked and died on the cross. So be it. O our Lord, O God. Completely [Refrain as above] <31>

—11 The eleventh [place] of kneeling [prayers called] a station. It was twelve steps with which our Savior arrived. Here is where on the crossed sticks, the cross, they laid down Jesus, our beloved God [and where?] His precious hands were nailed down. They repeatedly crossed Your precious feet over one another, [hammering them down] with metal nails. And when Your beloved mother heard then right away on His account [?] she weepingly fainted. The workers of death <32> were not sad in the least, but again laid on top of His head the round thing of thorns. They were unable to see where His eyes ended, right where the thorns ended. His eyes and His mouth were very [?].

Prayer

Alas, O compassionate Jesus! You dearly wanted through Your loving charity to suffer on the cross. They crucified You, piercing each of Your precious hands and feet with metal darts. O my Lord: I pray and implore You, just because of Your perfectly great loving charity do not [?] my hands and feet <33> so that I will sin. May I not take [not even] a handful for myself of the evil life. Let me, through my compassionate offerings and with Your help, [i.e.] grace, bring my life of penance close to me. O our Lord, O God. Perfectly praise [Refrain as above]

—12 The twelfth [place] of kneeling prayers [called] a station. It was fourteen steps with which our Savior arrived. They quickly raised Him up there [in the place full of people's bodies?] They angrily abandoned Him; they despisingly rejected Him. His body relapsed into sickness with His fall to the earth; again His precious earthly body suffered with what was another [?]. And His beloved sorrowful <34> mother Saint Mary was [in?] such [a state?] when she saw her beloved son! Right then her precious heart was anguished [to the point of?] fainting.

Prayer

Alas, divine being, Jesus! On the cross in the middle of the two thieves, You wanted various torments so that You would die in public. I pray and implore You: Cure me of the sinful sickness of my spirit so that right at my feet I will cast earthly confusions. And as for my eyes and heart, my sight and my will: may I alone want for them the things of heaven. So be it, Jesus. O our Lord, O God. Perfectly praise [Refrain as above] <35>

—13 The thirteenth [place] of kneeling prayers [called] a station. Here is where they lowered our Savior into the lapfolds of [and], laid Him down for, His weeping mother Saint Mary. We will go about remembering with sad weeping her anguish, for she was very hurt in her heart when she saw her only child. Her heart and honor blackened and numbed, she cried right out [because?] His precious body no longer appeared human. And <36> He also was very anxious: How sad my mother is! For He was given to her so that He was left locked up in His sepulchre.

Prayer

Alas, O our beloved honored mother, O perfectly merciful one, beloved honored mother of my beloved Savior Jesus Christ! It was just on account of His very anguished death that Your precious heart suffered burning pain when you saw that they laid Him down in the tomb. Let me be helped with your strength. I will place and copy the torment of my beloved Savior on my heart. Let me regard His torment as a medicinal plant. Let His flaying be my food, <37> my proper deportment will be His precious blood. Let His precious death become my life. Let His cross be my vow so that I will eternally serve Him until I go to see Him in heaven. So be it. O our Lord, O God. [Refrain as above]

—14 The fourteenth place of kneeling prayers [called] a station. Here is what is called His stone burial house, the grave of our beloved Savior. With loving charity He was [covered] with flower water that was like [the extract of a] medicinal plant. [?] <38> His precious dead body was dressed in a new, white, soft covering. Then they laid Him in a tomb. They covered up the entrance of the cave with a big stone. But when His beloved mother saw Him she wiped the face of her beloved child and youngest child. She suffered beyond all [others] when they spread out a big covering stone on Him. Then a great affliction [darkened] [her face] Let us piteously call to [Him?/her?] Let all of us pray to [Him?/her?]

Prayer

Alas, O Deity Who is perfectly worthy of love, O God! You thus suffered all the unspeakable, immeasurable and diverse pains, <39> torments, dishonors and sufferings! But afterward You wanted Your dead body to be buried with honor, also in a new grave. I pray and implore You: just because of Your tormented passion may You purify my spirit. Renew me so that I will receive Your precious esteemed body, the Most Holy Sacrament [in which?] You are seated until the world will come to an end, with purity of heart. So be it, Jesus.

Let us perfectly praise Him with all our heart [and will?] Such are You, God of Love! He wanted through His loving charity to save us, so that on our account He suffered everything. But if truly we will thank Him, let our sins make us cry, let us vow before Him, [let?] us say <40> our words of heart-felt affliction, let us cry before Him.

Act of Contrition + Heartfelt pain

O my God, O God, my Savior! I have very greatly sinned; pardon me. It greatly worries me that I have doubly offended You. I am a sinner 400 [i.e., many times] [over]. In what I did and in what I cast myself. I did not defend it [i.e., You/Your honor?] O my Lord, have pity on me. Let Your precious blood not have been wasted in vain. Did You not save me? Do You want my soul to be cast down into hell? O my Savior, mercy! Let Your good heart receive [my prayers?], for I make a vow that I will cast down and despise absolutely all the iniquities of life. I will turn toward You, for I have taken and will embrace it [as] my work. <41> I cast myself at Your feet. In the moment of my confession. I will say absolutely all my sins. And so that I will merit and enjoy Your health, [i.e.,] grace, I pray and implore our intercessor, your beloved mother Saint Mary: May she take away[?] Your anger, may she soften Your good heart. O my Deity, O God! Let me obtain and enjoy the pardon of sin for I have greatly sinned; may You have pity on me. I will not sin again. I will never again offend you. O my God, let that be all, for my sins and my defects will make me very sad and regretful. Receive my heart-felt pain and sadness, my heart-felt offerings, so that I will obtain and enjoy pardon of sin and help, [i.e.,] grace. Afterward I will see You in Your royal home in heaven. So be it, Jesus. <42>

Thus comes to an end the pondering of this suffering. And so that the doubts will be satisfied of those who did it [i.e., walked the stations of the cross], each and every one of them will have obtained 370 pardons of sin, [i.e.,] plenary indulgences, what are remissions of sin, and they [will] have helped by means of penance 24 souls [by] getting them out of the place of purifying by fire, [i.e.,] purgatory, and the "Perfectly praise the dear honored [etc.]" will be said. So that we will completely understand how much our Savior suffered in His [time?/place?] of suffering, here is a separate section [where all?] will be put in order and in some particular places [the details of His passion?] will be declared. Seven times they hurled Him down to earth. When they took Him to the home of Ananias it was 144 kicks <43> with which they kicked Him. 120 times they stoned Him. It was 102 slaps in the face with which they slapped His face. 28 times they struck His chest with stones. 80 [times] they mistreated Him on His shoulders. 77 times they [laid] the whip on His neck. 350 times they [beat] Him [at the] stone base. 70 times they [whipped] Him on the stone column, beating Him with a whip. It surpassed 5,200 and [x times?] [that] they tore up His precious body with a whip. Three times He fainted dead away when they beat Him with a whip. It was 1,000 thorns with which they made holes in His precious head. <44> Three times He fell to earth with the heaviness of the holy cross. It was 73 sorrows with which [His] precious heart was made to feel anguish. It was 62 [times] that they spit on His precious face. It was 26 times that they beat on Him with metal nails when they made holes in each of His precious hands. It was 35 times when they pierced His precious honored feet with a metal instrument. It was 109 times He sighed in His [place] of suffering. It was 5,475 flayings with which they hated His precious, honored, fresh earthly body. It will be 384,<45> 060 [i.e., 384,060] drops of His blood [that] they make. It was 230 [times] that He paid for us so that on our account He spilled His precious esteemed blood. It was 16,200 of His dripping tears that [He] cried for us because of our sins. And then will be said [etc.] Perfectly praise how He is. The completely esteemed God of love and charity suffered all on our account, He suffered in order to save us now and forever eternally. So be it, Jesus. The[?] [will be said?]. <46>

The Station of the Holy Cross

O you who are the precious esteemed crossed sticks of wood, the cross! O you who are a mountain, perfectly precious! O you who are the honored stone foundation of my Savior! O you who are hurt, you who are the torment of my God. O you who are the burning pain of repeated flaying! O you who are the suffering of anguished affliction! O you who are the spilling of the blood of my God! <47> O you who are the precious death of my God. O you who are His completely honorable kingdom! O my Lord, help me at the moment of my death so that I will deserve and enjoy eternal living life. So be it, Jesus.

The high pontiff Pius V [1566–72] favored those who will say these prayers before the holy cross with many favors [called] indulgences, [which] are [as] many [as] the stars and also [as many as] the grains of sand that lie scattered on the shore of the sea. [By?] my hand and pen, Mateo de San Juan Chicahuastla, [done in] the year of 1738.

Appendix 2
Original Nahuatl[1]

<1> Para saber Andar las Estacion de la via sacra y las ynDulgēCias Que se ganan Vitando la traducido en legua mexicano por el R P. fra[y] Aug[usti]n de Vetacur[t] Ex lector de teologia predicandor [predicador] gen[e]ral Jubilado chornista [chronista] Apostolico y Vicaro <2> de la Capilla de San Juseph de los naturales desta Ciudad de mexico deSte Año de 1680 <3>

tlanexmachiotl tenonotzalistescatli ytechpa quitosque yn itlasohuan yn imiquisnecuiticatzitzinhuan y totlasotemaquixticatzin JeSu ChrSto y quename yc huelitisque ContlayeyeCalhuisque ynic ypa nemisque yn otli motenehua Via SaCra yn quitosnequi teotlayohuiliztli Auh Ca yehuatli yniquimotoquilitiasqui yn temaquixtiani yn iquac quimoquixitilique yn itetlatzontequilistlatoCayeyan Pilato omoquimoquechpanoltitia yn [?] quautlanepanoli Santa Cruz yn ixquichca omaxilitito yn quaxiCaltzontepec CalVaro ynnoca omoCiauhCopinaltizino Cruztitech omomiquilitzino ynic otechmomaquixtilitzino yn titlatlacoanime Auh Ca no mitoa motecpana yniC yn senquisca miec teoyotica tlacnopilhuilistli <4> tlatlacolcaxahuanlistli yn itoCa yndulgenCias yn quimomasehuisque quicnopilihuisque tlateonahuistilistiCa quinemilisque yn teotlayohuilistli ynnopa yc huiloa yn CalVaro Oquimotlilanili y nahuatlatolCopa oquimocuepilitzino yn fray franc[iscan]o ycnopiltzin fra[y] Augs[ti]n de Uetacut [Vetancurt] Sn Juseph mexico

ynin otli motenhua Via sacra nahuatlatolcopa teotlayohuisotli ca yehuatl ynnaxcan yc omopouhtia yc quitlayeyeCalhuisque yni ychuipatzinco yn totlasotemaquixitiCatzin yni oquimoquixitilique ynnocan ytetlatzōtequililistlatoCachan yn pilatos yn ixquichCa OmaXilitito yn quaxicaltepec yn calVaro yn ocan omomiquil Cruztitech omoCiauhcopinaltintzino omomiquilitzino Auh ca yehuatzin oquimopehualtili yn ilhuicac tlatocaCihuaPili ychoquiznantzin Santa maria Auh aCamo san iquac ye ilhuicacpa <5> omonoltiticatCa yn teocuitlatepetlaoztoc yn totemaquixiticatzin yn ilhuiÇe oc yxquichi cahuitli yn oc omonemiliti y tlalticpac Caxtolose xihuitli oc omonemilti yn

1. The beginning of a page is marked by <p>.

itlasonātzin Semicac oquimotlaocolylnamiquiliyaya yn imiquilitzin yhuan yn inepapatlayohuilitzin Ca ahachiCa oquimonemililiyaya yn itlayohuilismiquilispātzinco yn Capa omonemilitiaya yn itlasoconetzin Ca senCa oquimohuellamachtili oquimopaquilismaquili yn itlasotatzin Dios

Auh ynic huel tlanesyan ticaSicamatisque yn catlehuatli y nepapan tlapanahuia yn tlayohuilistli yn ilnamicoCatzin yn totemaquixtiCatzin yn ipan yn ixiquich oc sequi nepapa ynmahuistililocatzin yc quimomahuismaquiliyaya itetlayecolticatzitzinhuan Ca yehuatli Ca ynpapa ynic quimahuistilia quitlasomati yn itlayohuilitzin yn ixiquich ytlapal quichihuan ytlalnamiquilistica axCanpan <6> quichihuaSque yn tien oquichihuasquia yn iquac yntla mixpan omotlayohuilitiani yn itlasotemaquixiticatzin Ca oCan quitlalitihuitz ytlayohuilisOhuipantzinco yn ixiquich yn iolpatzimiquilitzin yn ixixipehualistzin yn ixoxolehuanlitzin yn ipetlahualistzin yn ipinahuistzin yhuan oc sequi miec tecoco ypantzico omochihui Çenca quichoctia quiyoltonehua yequeni quiyolquixitia ynic onCan quita yn quexquich ynpapa oquimiyohuiliti yn itemaquixiticazin yhuan quiximati quichoctia quiyoltequipachoan yn itlatlacol onca tlaÇemitoayaya oquisepatlatlacaz Semicac quitlasoCamatisque yn itemaquixitilistequitzin y t[o]t[ecuiy]o Jesu Chr[i]sto Auh ca yehuatli yn cenCa quimotlamachtilia quimopapaquilitilia yn totemaquixitiCatzin yn ipa yxiquich quali yectli nemilistli yn iuh yehuatzin oquimolhuili Çen <7> tlamaseuhcateopixCatzintli oquimonotzaltitzino oquimolhuili xihualasi notlan xihualmopacho tinechpalehuis tonehuan tichuiCasque yn noquauhnepanol santa Cruz Auh yn tlamaseuiCatzintli oquimonaquilili oquimoohuili o tlasotemaquixitiCatzin queninichuas ynic nimitzinopalehuilis Ca atle nochicahualis yn nihueysentziontlatlacoani oquihualmitahui y totlasotemaquixticatzin Ca san motlanequilistiCa ynic tinechpalehuis senca moch ica yn mix yn moyolo xiquilnamiqui ypa ximoyolononotza y nomiquilitzin yhuan y ixiquich notlayohuilitzin ca mopapatica yhuan ynpapa y tlaticpac tlaca tlatlacoanime onictzacuitia ynnayc tiquilCahuas Auh satepan mohuentica timotlatlauhtis xinechmahuistili Ca senCa yc tinechtlamachtis papaquilistli tinelmacas oc sentetl machiotli octaCatli temamauhti yn oquiotili Se yecnemilisseCatzintli ynmiquilistenpatzinco quiCaC Se huey <8> teposcoyoli capana tlamatzinlitica Auh yehuatli yc omonenechicoque y tlatlacatecolo Auh yn iquac yn omosentlalique ye quimilihui yn itlatoCauh nocnihuitzitzihuane Ca ye aquimati yn tle ytechcacopa yn tlalticpac tlaca ynnoquimochihuili yn toteotzi yn ipapatiCa Omamasohualtiloc Omomiquili Auh yn axca acmo XimoCiahuiltican ytechcopa yn netetlapolotilitli yeiCa Ca yn iquac quilnamiquisque yn quexiquichi ynpapa oquimiyohuiliti Niman omocuitihuetzin yn iquac Oquicac yn itlatol y tlaCatecolotlahtohuani Auh niman no moquetztehue se huey huehue tlaCatecolotli ynmixpa Otlato oquito tlaCatle tlahtohuanie huel melahuac ynnamotlatoltzin ye ic niquitohua yn nehuatli ynic motlapolotisque ynteotlaneltoCanime ChrCtianome [cristianome] ma tiquincuicuitlahuilitica ynpapa paquislistlatlacolinemilistli tequitlaquallistli tequiatlilistli Auh ca yehuatli miquilCahuasque <9> yn imiquilitzin yestonehuilitzin yn totlatoCatzin otlanaquili teyaCana ma yuh tlanahuatilio aso tel yCa ynontzin motepexihuisque tlatlacozque ÇenCa ye ic tlanesyan tiquita tiquiximati y catlehuatli yntlanequilitzin yn t[o]t[ecuiy]o Dios ytech monequilitilia yn itimiquisnecuitiCatzizinhuan ynic huel techmopopolhuililis yn totlatlacol yhuan techmomaquilis yn iqualltilis yn toanima ynic titomaquixtisque Ca noso yehuantli yn CemiCac tictlaocolylnamictinemisque yn itlayiohuilitznNilhuiSe oncan ytlayiohuilisOhuipantzinco yc huilaayn quaxiCaltzinOtepec CalVaro Auh yn imachio otli octaCatli quiCuisque ynic quiyecchihuasque yn motenehuan Via Cruzes Ca yehuatl ynic quiyectecasque Auh yn itla ye onesentlaliloc o Ca pehuanS yni tlayiohuilistli Netlaquaquetzalos Nepechtecoz Nemachiotilos <10> Auh ynnamapuhqui quipuas yn isCatqui yn tlatlauhtilistli yhuan tlannaquilitiasque Nehuentilistlatlauhtilistli OfreCimiēto

+

Cenquizcamahuistililoni teotlatohuani Diose NepechtequilistiCa moCenmactzinco yn nocōtlallia yn ixquich yn iCa yn itlayiohuilitzin yn nican motlayiohuilisOhuipantzinco nicchhuas yn notlalnamiquilis Nonetlanquaquetzalis yn nochoquiz yn notlaocoyaliz Auh yntla ticmocalitiliz ma XicmoCelilitzino topāpa yhuan ynpapatzinco yn tlatocateopixCatzitzintin yn CenCa miec tlacnopilhuiliztli [in]dulgenCias ypan oquimotlalilitiaque yn tlayiohuilizOtli yn iuh ma xicmolselili ypampa yn ipopolhuiloCa yn totlatlacol yhuan ynpampa yn Animas tlechipahualoyan purgatorio <11> q[ue]mochialitiCate ynpalehuiloCatzin Nima quiteCaquiztilis Amapuhq[ue]

—1 Nicā pehua yn Centetli tlatlauhtiliztli netlanquaquetzalistli yn itoca EstaCion yn itetlatzontequililiztlatoCachan yn pilatos yntoCayoCan Pretoria yn canin yn iquac yn ie ihui chiquaSeme yaoquizque meCatiCa huitzitiCa teluzmeCatica tlali yc oquimohuitequilique San nahui oquimototopehuilique Oquimotetelicxilique Oquimotlahuelhuitequilique yn totlasotemaquixiticatzin OquimomeCatzazayanililique yntlasonaCayotz[in] niman oquimomiquiztlatziotequilili yn Pilatos ynmixpan oquinhualmoquechilili yntecocolicahuan yn Judiosme huel yCihui ca yquechtlantzinco OquilCatzioque yn tetetzilimeCatli yquimohuilanilizque y quimiCihuitilique tlatlauhtiliztli <12>

yio CenquizCatzopeliCatzintle Jesus Ca ticmonequiliti yn iuh Seme ychteque omitzimomayilpilique yn quename tlahcohtli mayilipilos yhuan omitzmomiquiztlatzōtequililique Auh ma xicmotlasonequiltitzino ynpāpatzincao yn mocnotlapaCayiohuilitzin ynic motepalehuiliztiCatzinco nicpachoS yn noyolo yn nonepoalis ma yitechcopa ninotoma yn notlatlacolo ynic paca yocoxca ninemiz ynic nicnomasehuiz yn tetlapopolhuilistli Satepan yn motlaltzinco yn ilhuiCac papaquilistli ma yhui mochihuan Jesus

Niman otennamiquiztlali yhuan mitoz

toteCuioe Diose Ca CenCa huel onihueytlatlaco ma xinechmotlapopolhuili<13>tzino Ca CeCa huel otitlatlacoque ma xitechmotlapopolhuili Ca CenCa huel oninoyolotequipacho mixpantzinco

OCCepa ma tenamiq[ui]tlalli mitos

ma CenquisCayectenehualo yn itlayiohuilitzin yhuan yntlasomiquilitzin yn totlasomahuiztemaquixitiCatzin JesuChr[is]to yhuan ychipahuaCatlaCatililoCatzin yn tlatoCaychpochhtli Santa maria ynnayc ytetzinco oaCic yn tlatlacolpeuhCayotli Ma yuh mochihua Jesus

—2 ynic OC Can tlatlatlauhtiliznetlaquaquetzaliztli yn itoca estaCion Cenpoalli yhuan Se y tlacxineanaliztli Ca monenemilititia yn totlasotemaquixitiCatzin niCan Cani yn oquimoquechpanolltilique yn totlasotemaquixtiCatzin Jesu Chr[i]sto yn CenCa yetecCatzintli Cuauhnepanoli Cruz Auh ynic quiyectlalilizque achtopa oquimoquitililique yn tlaquentzin ye niman oCaquilitique <14> yn chichilitic tilimasoli oquimoquentilique yn iquac yhCatzinco omahuilitequi Auh yequene oc Cepa oquimoquentilique yn itlaquentzin yhuan oc Cepa ycpactzinCo oquimomanilique yn tlacotli yn huitzintli yn tepeyotli yn xocohuitzyahuali cexna huel tecocoCayotiCa miecca oCaCallactia yni huitzintli ynic omeyancuinli yn iEsnoquihuilitzin

tlatlatlauhtiliztli

iyo ySeltzin teotzintle ylhuicacqueCatzintle tlasotlatohuane JeSuS yn oticmonequilitin yn ipan timomayahuitzinoz yn iteCayecocoli yn tlahueliloque Judiosme yn omitzmomaylPilique yhuan Omitzmamaltilique yn quauhnepanoli CenCa yetecatzintli Cruz ni~~ich~~mitznotlatlauhlitla ma xinechmopalehuilitzino ynic nictzioquixitiz nicpaCaseliz yn tlamaCehuiliztl ynic nicnoma<15>maltis ylhuicac yecnemiliztli yn iuh ticmonequilitia Auh satepan motlaqmrtzinco tinechmomaquiliz yn ilhuicac papaquiliztli ma y mochihua JeSuS t[o]te[Cuioe] D[io]se mitos Cenq[ui]zC

—3 ynic yexCa netlaquaquetzialistli tlatlatlauhtiliztli EstaCion yn ohualmonenemilititia yn toteotzin Nauhpohuali ychixineanaliztli niCa Cani choquiztiCa elCiCihuiliztica quimimamalia yn Cruz yn totemaquixiticatzin Auh Ca huel ÇenCa acmo quimehuilia ynic CenCa ye omosotlahualtitzino ynic quimototoquiliaya yntecocoliCahuan asta tlalpa omohuetzitin ytzintlan yn + Cruz huel chiCahuac Omotlahuitectzino yc Çenohuian omoya[Catia?] omotlatlapo yn ixipehualitzin huel CenCa yc ohualnonoquiuhtia yn itlasoyesiotzin

tlatlatlauhtiliztli <16>

yio CenquizCatlasotlani Jesus moCiahuizticCatzinco ytzintlan otimohuetziti yn santa Cruz ynic tiquiximatizque yn ietiliz yn totlatlacoll Ca san quixiptlayotia yn CenCa yeteCatzintli Cruz yn topampatica oticmomamaltitzinno nimitzinotlatlauhtilia ma ytepalehuiliztica yn motlasochiCaliztlanequilitzin~~tli~~ yn moGraCiatzin ma yhuan ninehuantiquetzi ynic neltiz yn moteotlanequilitzin niCa ye ipan ninemiz yn ticmonequilitia yn tlamaCehualiztli ynic ixquichiCa nicnomasehuiz yn itzōpeuCa yn itlaquilotzi yn santa Cruz ynnotinechmonextilili yn ilhuiCac papaquiliztli yn la gloria māchā ma CenquizCa t[o]te[Cuioe] Diose mitoz <17>

—4 Ca ye niCan ynic nauhCan netlaquaquetzaliztli EstanCion ohualmonenemilititia yn totlasotemaquixtiCatzin yepohuali yhuan matlactli tlacxineanaliztli ōCan Cani omiximatque OtlicCa omixinamictzinoque yn ichoquiznatzin santa maria yhuan yn itonehuiliztlasoconetzin Auh yn queni Omonepantlasotlatzinohuaya ytlapantzinco otlayohuac yn iuhqui Cenhueyhuitztli Onalquiztiquiz yn iolotzin yn huey yolopatzimiquilitzin Auh yn maCihui ynnamo oquimixipolihui Ca choquiztica oquimotepotzitolitia yn no quixquichCa maxilititiuh yn tepeticpac y CallVaro

tlatlatlauhtiliztli

iyo ycnohuatlasomahuizchoquiznatzine Santa mariatzine chOquiztzicA yolchichiCaliztica ynnotiquinmopanahuili yn Cenmixiquichitin yn Cihuan yn iquac oticmotili yn moxocoyotzin yn moCenteconetzin ynpantzinco otexyoatiquiz ynic otlitli~~ehi~~leuehtia yn imahuizxayaCatzin Otziatzayantia <18> ynCeliCatlanaCayotzin onanalquiztia y huiztli yn itech ytzinotecontzin oÇeÇepoCatia yn iomiotzin yn iCa yn huey yetiliz yn sa[n]ta Cruz Auh ynic oquimahuizpoloque yn Jodiosme yn mahttizhuilihuetziquiz yn tlaticpac tlaca Omochihuitzino yn toteotzin ô notlasonantzine Canel Ca nehuatli yn notlatlacolltiCa ônimitzinoyoltonehuili ma xicmotlasonequiliti ypāpatzinco ynnoticmiohuilititzino yn queni omitzymoyoltonehuili yn moyoltequipacholiztzin ma Sa no yuhqui nechtequipacho yn notlatlacoll ynic nicnomaÇehuiz yn neyolcuitiliztli tetlapopolhuiliztiCa ynic niChipahualoz y niCan tlalticpac Auh satepan yn onpalhuicac neÇetlamachtoloyan yn gloria ma yUh mochihua—totecuioe D[io]se

mitoz ma ÇequizCayectenehualo yn tlasomahuiztlayiohuilitzin yhuan tlaçomahuizmiq[ui]litzin <19>

—5 ynic maCuilCan netlaquaquetzaliztli EstaCiOn ohualmonenemilititia yn totlasotemaquixiticatzin yepoali yhuan matlatli oCen—tlacxineanaliztli niCan cani oquitlaquehueuhque yn Simon Cixineo ynic quimopalehuiliz yn totemaquixiticatzin ynic Çe amo teyxnoytaliztli ynnoquichiuhque San imauhCaCopa yn milichiuhqui ynnotetlaCamac ypāpan Amo otlica mosotlauhCamiquiliz yeiCa quimotililiaya yn ietiliz yn santa Cruz ynuhquima ye moÇiauhcopanaltiznequi ye huel opoposahua yn ixayaCatzin yxayotica yhuan yestica yn ixitelolotzin huel ye mioCahualtitihui ye mohuihui Oquilitinelan yhuan yn mohuicatihuitzie quimotequitziotoquilitihuitzie Omentin yn ichteque ynahuactzinco tlatziôntequililozque—totecu[i]oe Diose

tlatlatlauhtiliztli

iyo in tiÇequizcatlasotlallonitzontle JeSuS san ipampatzio yn motetlasotlalitzi oticmonequilititzinno y topapatica yn <20> yn ticmoquechnoltitias yn CenquizCayetec yn moquauhnepanoltzin ynyn santa Cruz yn oquixoxohuili ynnoquitotoneuh yn motlasoacollotzi yhuan oticmonequilititzino yxipitlayotica yn Simon Sixineo ynic timitztopalehuilizque ynic tictomasehuizque yn nican otitechmonextilili yn CenCa tlasotli ypatiuhtzin yn Cruz ma xicmotlasonequilititzino noteotzine yny no ytlanpa niCalaquiz yn tlamasehualiztli yhuan nictelchihua yn aqualli nemiliztli ma Sa niq[ui]xCahuiz y nimitzomotepotziotoquiliz y nican tlalticpac yn inic nicmasehuiz yn ilhuicac papaquiliztli ma iu mochihuan

totecuioe Diose—ma CenquizCa

—6 ynic chiquaSeCa netlaquaquetzaliztli EstaÇiÔn Nauhpohualli ~~tla~~ yhuan matlactli OCe ycxineanaliztli omonenemilititia yn toteotzin niCan Cani OtliCa oquimonamiquilico <21> yn totemaquixticatzin yn mahuiztlaCatzintli ytocatzin Veronica yn quac oquimotili huel Çenca Opoposaa~~hauh~~ huel otlitlileuh oxoxohuixi yn itlasoxayaCatzin ôyeyez tien yn ixtelolotzxin nimân ôquimoquixitilitihuetzi yn iztaCanahuac yn tilmatzintli yniquimixpopohuiliz yntonehuilizxayaCAtzin AUh CenCa huey tlamahuisoltican omochiuh ynic yexCanpa cuell pachiuhtiCa yn tilmatli OmoyexCâCopintzino yn yn itlasoxayaCatzin yn totemaquixtiCatzin

tlatlatlauhtiliztli

iyo CenquizCaquallnesCatzintle Jesus Ca yniquixototoneuhticatCa yni motlasoxayatzin ynic Omitzinmixitlatlatzinilique omitzmocatzahuilique yruc mixtzinco ochichaque oticmoÇelili yn itepalehuiliz yn Cihuatzintli VeroniCa yn yamanqui tilmatican ynnoquimopopohuili yn motlasoxayacatzin ma no xicmotlasonequilititzino yn iCa yn motepalehuitzin <22> yn motlasoGraCiatzin ma ytech noyolia mocopintzino yn motlasoxacatzin ynic onCa ÇenmiCac nimitznomahuiztililiz ynic nicnomasehuiS yn ilhuiCac papaquiliztli—totecuioe Diose—ma ÇenquizCayectene

—7 ynic chicōCa netlaquaquetzialliztli tlatlauhtiliztli EstaCion yni Omonenemilititia y totlasotemaquixitiCatzin Caxtoli oÇe pohualli yhuan Caxtoli oÇe ycxinmamaltzin ynic Omaxillitico ~~ynic ma xilli~~ yn totemaquixiticatzin ye niCan yn Cani ynic Callpan omoquixititzino tlahtoCaCallquiyahuac[t]enco yc cepa tlalpan omotlahuitectzino yhuan CenCa ônCan nepoliuhCa yn ichiCahualliztzin yCa yn ietiliz y Santa Cruz <23> ynic huel omosotlahualtitzino ycCa Çe huey xixipehualiztli CenCa opoposahuac ototoneuh yn itlasoacolltzin yn yny totlasotemaquixitiCatzin Jesu Chr[i]sto

tlatlatlauhtiliztli

iyo CenquizCamahuiztililoni Jesus ynin oticmonequilititzino yn temahuizpoliztiCa yn mitzinmohuiquilizque ynic Çenca omitzmomiquiztequipannilihuiquetiaque yn tlahueliloque ynic sotlahualiztica osesepocatia yn motlasonaCayotzin ynic opa tlalipa otimohuetziti otimotlahuitectzino ma xinechmopalehuitzino ynic niquixitiz ynietiliz yn notlatlacoll ynicCacmo nicnomamaltiz yn itlatlacoll ma xinechmomaquili y[?] notechiCahualitzin inicamo [?]tiliztzaz imiquiztetlatziontequililoyan ylhuiSe ma notech quisan yn tetlayecolltiliztli ytechpa yn motequipanollCatzi—ma yuh mochihua Jesus

totecuioeDioe

ma Cenquiz Cayecteneahualo yntlasomiquilitzin yn totlasotemaq[ui]xiticatzin <24>

—8 ymc chiCuexCan netlaquaquetzaliz tlatlatlauhtiliztli estaÇiÔ Caxtolli poalli yhuan ChiCuey ycxineanalliztli ynnomonenemilititia yn toteotzin niCan Cani yc no aCaCi Cihuatzintzintin Jerosale yn iuhCatzintli ynnoquimotilique ynnamo tlatlacolleCatzintli Jesus mamasohualtiloyan quimohuiquilia CenCa temauhCatzitzinti ynic motonehualtitiuh ynnayamo huehCahuis yn quimomahuisoltiliyaia ynnah ynnaltepetli ypampa yn ixichi yn itlamahuisolotlachihualtzin oquimochihuilitzinno <25> yn ixiquich tlaCatli yCatzinco omochoquillique Auh yn totemaquixitiCatzin ynhuiccopa omotlachialti yn Cihuatzintzintin oquinmolhuilin ynnamopilhuan Jerosalen maCamo Ximochoquilican NomiquiliztiCa ylhuise Sannapampa xichoCaCan yhuan ynpampa ynnamopilhuan XimochoquiliCan

tlatlatlauhtiliztli

Iyo ylhuiCaC temachitiCatzintle maCihuin tonehuiliztiCa yn no ticmotoquilitia yn motlayohuilizohuitzin Ca amo oticmoCahuili yn motemachtiltequitzin ymc otiquinmonextilili yniquename quichoquiltiz quenyn itlatlacollo Auh mano nehuatli Xinechmonextilili Xinechmomachtili yn quenin choquiztiCa yxayotica yolotequipacholiztica nechoctiz yn ixquichi yn notlatlacoll yni onictlilehui onicCatziahui yn noanima ma yc nic <26> pahca yc nicchipahua yn nixayo ma niquixCahui ynic nimitznotlasotlitiliz ynic nicnomaSehuiz yn motequalltiayatzin yn GraCia ma yuh mochi—totecuioe ~~Diose~~ Diose—ma CenquizCayectehuallo—

—9 ynic chicnauhCan netlaquaquetzaliz tlatlatlauhtiliztli estaCiô ~~Ca~~xtilco poalli~~anpa~~ omomopohuilli ycxineanaliztli omonenemilltitia yn toteotzin yn niCan Ca yc yexpa omohuetzinti yn totemaquixitiCatzin yCa yCamachlltzin yc Omotlahuitectzinno <27> Auh yequeni huel CenCa ononoquiuhtia yntlasoyesyotzin ynic huellopolihuiCa yn iChiCahualitzin yehiCa yn iquac omoeUatzinnozquiaya ayocmo omohuelitilitzinno San no Sepa Omotlallhuitectzinno yhuan tlalliitech Omotzotzonate ynnimolictzin yhuan yxayaCatzin yhuan ymatzitzin yhuan ycxixitzitzin miyeCannomococotzinno Ca nozo huel CenCa tetetlan ynnotliCa

tlatlatlauhtiliztli

Iyo CenquizCa tetlaocoliayanie Jesus ynin ticmopayohuititzino yn tlahuelmiquiztequipanoque omitzmoxixipehuilique ynic yexpa Otimotlahuitectzinno ma san xicmotlasonequiltitzino ynic motepalehuiliztiCatzinCo ynic nicpahuiz yn notecocoliCauh yn iuh mohuictzinco nitlamahSehuaz Auh satepan nicnomasehuiz yn papaq[qu]liztli yn Gloria—ma y mochihuan <28>

—10 ynic mahtlaCan Netlaquaquetzializtlatlatlauhtiliztli estaCiOn CaXtoli Omey ~~poalli~~ yicxineanaliztli omonenemilititia yn totemaq[ui]xitiCatzin y niCan Cani Omaxilitico yn tziõpantepec CalVaro Auh Ca onCan oquimopetlahuilique enCan yXiquichi asote oquimotlalilique asta oquimotlahuelquitililique~~tzin~~ yn tlaquentzinn oc Cepa tonehuiliztiCa OmoyaCuilitia yn iesnoquihuilitzin yhuan yn ixiquichi yxixipehualitzin <29> yiesSotlahualiztiCatzinco Oquimitlaniliaya tepitzon atzintli San no quimotlahuelmaquilique ChiChic patli atli Sa yc OhualmoSotlahualtitzino Auh Ca huel toteChi monequi tictlaocollylnamictinemizque yn iquac yuhCatzintli Omotatzinno yn totlasotemaquixitiCatzin teyxipan OmopetlahuititiCatca quexquichi yPinahuiztzin Ca ye neli pinahuiliztica OpetlauhtimoCauh yn itlasonaCayotzin yn mixipan yn nepampa tlaca

tlatlatlauhtiliztli

Iyo CenquizCa tlapaCayeliz ehCatzītle JeSuS ynnoticmopaCayohuilititzinno yn mopetlahualitzin pinahuiliztica ynmixipan yn tlahueliloque JuDiosme omitzinmopetlahuilique ynic OmoyanCuiltia yn moyesnōq[ue]<30>huilitzin ma xicmotlasonequiliti ypapatzinco yn ixiquichi moyestonehuilitzin yn ixiquich moyeschichinaquilitzin Ca neli yc CamonepapaquiltizCamactzin ynic ~~C~~a topāpatica yc ce ticmititzinno yn chichiC atli Auh ne yn nehuatli ma san xicmotlasonequilititzino maCacmo niquiz maCacmo nicnomaCaS ynta yhuin yn teyolmalaCacho yn nepapan tlalticpac tlaelhuiloni ynitetlapololtiliz ynoteyauohu yn tlahueliloc ma yc niquixipehui ma yc niCatzelhui ynic mosemactzinco ninoCahuas ynic ypampatiCa petlauhCatzītli otimoCauhtzino Cruztitech Otimomiquilitzino ma uh mochihua toteCuie Diose—ma Cen[quiz] <31>

—11 ynic matlactli oCe Netlaquaquetzaliztli estaCiOn y matlactli om~~ey~~me ycxineanaliztli ynic omaxilitico yn totemaquixitiCatzin y niCan Cani ypan quauhnepannoli Cruztzin no quimotequilique yn totlasoteotzin JeSuS oncan ohualteposquauhmiminaloc yn itlasomatzin tepostlaxichtiCa ynnoquihualmonenepanilihuique yn motlasoyecycxitzin Auh yn iquac OquimoCaquin ynimotlasonātzin yn tepostehuilonitzitzinCatiCa Ca Sa niman ypāpatzinco otlaoana [?] ynic Omochoquizsotlahuiltitzino Auh yni miquiztequipanoque <32> niman amo omotlaocoyalitique Sannoc Cepa ycpactzinco Oquimomanilique yn tetepeyotli y tlacotli yn xocohuitziyahualli ynnahuelloquitilique yn campa tlami yn ixitelolotzin huellopā otlatlamito yn huitzitli huel CenCa yc Ohualyeyesten yn ixitelolotzin yhuan yCamachtzin

tlatlatlauhtiliztli

Iyo ycnohuaCatzintle JeSus yn San motetlasotlaliztiCatzinco ynnoticmotlasonequilititzinno yn Cruztitech timoCiauhCopinalititias omitzmomamasohualtilique tepozmimitica omitzimococoyonilique yn motlasomatzin yn mocxitzin nimitznotlatlauhtilia NoteCuiotzine ma San ipampatzinco yn CenquizCahuey motetlasotlalitzin maCamo nimaloa [?] yn noma yn nocxih <33> ynic nitlatlacoz maCamo nicCuic nicnomatziolololotiz ynnaqualli nemiliztli ma San nicnoyolmanaliztiCa notech nicpachoz yn notlamaCenhualiz nemiliztli yn iCa yn motepalehuilitzin yn GraCia—t[o]t[ecui]oe D[io]se Ma Cenq[ui]z Cayectenehuallo

—12 ynic matlatli omome Netlaquaquetzaliztlatlatlauhtiliztli eSTaCiOn matlatli onnahui ycxineanaliztli ynic omaxilitico yn totemaquixiticatzin Auh

Ca ye onCa ôquimehuatiquechilique tetlaCayoCo OquimotlahuelmaCahuilique Oquimotlalhuitequilique AUh Ca yCa yn itlalhuitequilitzin omoCaxanitzinno yn inaCayotzin oc Cepa yc oce Cepo Catca omoCiauhcopinni yn itlasotlaltzin Auh yn itlasochoquis <34> nantzin Santa maria yn iuhcatzintli yn oquimotili yn itlasoConetzin Auh San niman omosotlauhpātzimiquititia yn itlasoyolotzin

tlatlatlauhtliliztli

Iyo teoyelizCatzintli JeSuS quauhnepanolititechi yn nepantla Omentin ychteque otiquinmonequilititzino NepapatlayohuiliztiCa ynic teyhixpan timomiquilitzinnoz nimitznotlatlauhtilia ma Xinechmopatilili yn notlatlacolcocoliz yni noyolia ynic huel nocxitlan nictlaSas yn tlalticpac tetlapol占olotin Auh yn nixi yn noyolo yn notlachializ yhuan yn notlanequiliz ma san noCellquinequiliz yn ilhuiCacCayotli Ma y mochihuan Jesus—t[o]te[cuioe] D[io]se ma Cenq[ui]zCayectenehualo <35>

—13 ynic matlactli omey netlaquaquetzaliztlatlauhtiliztli eStaCioñ Ca ye niCa yn Canin oquimotemohuilique yn totemaquixitiCatzin yCuixantzinco Oquimotequililique ynchoquiznantzin Santa maria tlaocollchoquiliztiCa ticlnami~~quiz~~tinemizque yn inetequipacholtzin Ca CeCa omoyolotoneuhtzino yn iquac oquimotili ynCenteconetzin Otlitlileuh oCeCepoliuhtia yn yolotzin yn imahuizyotzin huellotzatzantia yntlasonaCayotzin ayocmo motlaCaneXititzinoa Auh Ca Oc no <36> CenCa no huel omotequipachotzinoaya ynic notlaocollnantzin Ca oquimotemaquili ynic quimoCalltzaCuilitihue ynin imiquiztepetlaCaltzinco

tlatlatlauhtiztli

Iyo totlasomahuiznatzine CequizCatetlaocolltiCatzintle ynnitlasomahuiznatzin yn notlasotemaquixiquetiCatzin JeSuChr[i]Sto nimitzinnotlatlauhtilia ma San papatzīco y moYolopatzinmiquilitzin ynic Otoneuh yn motlasoyolotzin yn iquac oticmottili yn motlasonConetzin ynic quimotequilitihueh ynnoztoc tepetlaaCallco ma moChiCahualiztiCatzinco nipalehuilo ~~yeh~~ ytechi nictlaliz ytech niccopinaz y noyolo yn itonehuitzin yn notlasotemaquixitiCatzin ma yehuatzin yn ipan nicmatiz yn teuhuitzitzilipātli yntlayohuilitzin ma notlaquall yes yn ixixipehualitzin <37> y nonemachis yes yn itlasoyesyotz ma noyoliliz mochihuas yn itlasomiq[ui]litzin ma nonecuillnetoll yes yn iquauhnepanolltzin ynic ma semiCaC ninotlayecolltiz yn ixiq[ui]chiCah nicnotiliztiuh yn ilhuiCatl itehc ma yuh mochihuan—t[o]t[ecuio]e Diose—ma[cenquiz]

—14 ynic tla matlatli onnauhCa netlaquaquetzaliztlatlauhtiliztli estaCion Auh Ca ye niCan yn motenehuan yn inetoquiliztepetlaCalltzinco yn

SepullCrO yn totlaSotemaquixitiCatzin yn Cani yeh iuh tetlasotlaliztiCa huitzitzilipatli yuhqui quename xochiatli yc o[?]ui ma matelloquen Yc oquimomeCatla tlapachilihuique Çe yztac yanCuiC <38> yamāqui tlachpachiuhcayotli yc oq[ui]miloloc yn itlasomiquiliztlactzin niman oquimotequilique yn miCaoztoctecochoCon Çe huey ixitlapalli tetl yC oquixitlahpachoque ynnoztoCalltentli Auh yn iquac Oquimotili yn itlasonantzin ye q[ui].mixipolluia yn itlasoConetzin yn ixocoyotzin oquiCenpanahui yn ixq[ui]chi ynnoquimiyohuilititzino yn ipatzinco oquiteCaque yn huey yn tlapalltetli Auh niman ypantzinco otlxyoatia ynnica yolopatzimiquilitzin ma no tictotlaoCollnochilliCa ma timochintin tictotlatlauhtiliCan

tlatlatlauhtiliztli

Iyo Çenquizcatlasotlaloni yCeltzin teotli Diose yn ye uh oticmonequilyohuilititzino yn ixquich amoyhtolon ynnamo tamachiuhqui ypapan tecoco <39> tetoneuh emahuizpolo tlayohuiliztli Auh satepan oticmonequilititzino mahuizyotiCa motoCatzinoz yn momiquiliztlactzin yn no çan yāCuiC tecochco nimitzinotlatlauhtilia ma san ipapantzinco yn motlayohuilizpanSSiontzin ma xinechmochipahuilili yn noyolia ma xinechimoyanCuilili ynic noneyollchipahualiztica nicnoCeliliz yn motlasomahuiznaCayotzin y SantiSSimo SaCramento yn timehuilititiCa yn ixquichca tzonquizaz yn Çemanahuactli ma yuh mochihua Jesus

AUh ma tictoÇenquizCayectenehuiliCa moch iCa yn toyolo ynCiahuiliz yn iuhCatzintli y yn titlaÇotlalizteotli yCa ytetlaSotlalitzin Oquimonequilititzino yn techmomaquixitilitzinnoz ynic topapatiCa yn ixiquichi oquimiyohuilititzino Auh yntlanell tictlasoCamatizque ma ma [te]chocti yn totlatlaColl ma yxpantzinco titonenetolotiCa ya tiquitoCan <40> yn toyolochichinaCaliztlahtolitzin ma yhxipantzinco timochoquiliCan

acto de ContriCion + Nenyoltequipacholiztli

Noteotzinne Diose notemaquixitiCatzin CenCa huel onitlatlaco ma xinechmotlapopollohuilitzino Ca Çenca nechtequipachoa ynic OnimitzinnoyolitlaCalhui huel mixitzinco mocpactzinco onine ônoÇentziontlahuellilitic Ca amo onicmalhui yn tlen onicchuh yn tlennipan oninomayahui noteCuiotzinne ma xinechmocnoyhtilitzino maCamo nenpolihuiz yn motlasoyezyotzin Cuix amo tehuatzin ynnotinechmomaquixitilitzino Cuix ticmonequilitia mictlan tlaSaloz yn noanimatzin miSSericordia NotemaquitiCatzine ma xxicmoSehuilitzino yn moyecyolotzin Ca ye ninonehtoltia ynic nictlaSas nictelchihuas yn Cemixiquichi tlahueliloCayotli nemiliztli mohuictzinco ninoCuepas Ca ye nicCuih ye nicmallcochoa yn notequipanollCatzin <41> mocxitlantzinco ninomayahuiz neyollocuitilizpan nictoz yn

Çenmixiquichi Notlatlacoll Auh ynic nicnomaCehhuiz yn motechiCahualitzin yn GraCian nicnotlatlauhtilia yn totepantlatlauhtiCatzin yn totlasomahuinatzin in Santa maria ma yehuatzin quimoSehuiliz yn moqualllantzin ma quimoyamanili yn moyecyolotzin ô noteotzinne Diose ma nicnomaSehui yn tetlapopollhuiliztli Ca CenCa huel nitlatlaco ma xinechmocnoyhtilitzino Ca ayocmo oc Çepa nitlatlacoz ayoquic nimitzinoyolitlaCallhuiz ma ye ixquichi noteotzine Ca Çenca nechyollotequipachoz yn notlatlaColl yn nopilichihuall ma xicmoCelili yn noneyollotequipacholiz yn noneyolomanaliz ynic nicnomaSehuiz y tetlapopolhuiliztli yhuan yn tepalehuiliztli GraCia Auh Satepan nimitzinotiliz yn motlahtoCachantzinco yn ilhuiCaC ma y mochihuan JeSuS— <42>

yhu tlami yn inemililocan yni tlayyiohuilitzintli Auh ynic yiolpachihuilozque ynnaquique oquichiuhque Ca huel mochitin ÇeÇe tlaCatli ÇeÇenyaCa Oquicnopilhuique Caxtolli omomey poalli yhuan mahtlactli tlatlaCollpolihuiliztli dullgenCias Pllenaria yn ithoCa tlatlacollpolihuiliztli yhuan Cenpohuanlli yhuan nahui Animas oquinpalehuique oquinhualmoquixtilique ynnopa tlechipahualoya Porgatorio otlamahseuhticatCa yhuan mitoz ma CenquizCayectehualo yn tlasomahuiz Auh ynic ticCencaCicamatizque yni quexquichi yn itlayiohuilizpantzinco Oquimihiohuilititzinno yn totemaquixitiCatzin NiCan nonoqua motecpanas CeCeCni motenehuas

Chicopa tlalpan ôquimomayahuilique * yn iqua ychan Anas oquimohuiquilique * chiConpohualli yhuan nahui * tlatelicxiliztli * yc <43> oquimotetelicxilique * ChiquaCenpoalli ypan oquimotehuilique ynmatiCa * maCuillpoalli yhuannome yxtetlatzinniliztli yC oquimixtetlatlatzinnilique * Cenpoalli yhuan ChiCueXPa yhielpantzinco oquimotehuililique * nauhpoalli yn iaCollpantzinCo oquimococollhuilique * yhepoalli yhuan CaXtoli omexpan oquitititzique yquechtlantzinco yn meCatli * Caxtoli omey poalli yhuan mahtlacpan Oquihuihuichilique [erasure] *yn itentziontzin * yhepoalli yhuan mahtlacpa oquitititzique yn itetziontzin yn temimiloli ytech oquimomeCahuitequillique * mahtlatli omeytziontli yhuan oquiPanahui yn meCatli yc oquimomeCatziatziayanililique yn itlasonayotzin yexpa omosotlauhCamiquilizquiyaia yn iquac OquimomeCahuitequilique * ontziotli yhuan mahtlacPoalli yn ihuitzitli yc oquimococoyolilique yn itlasotziontecontzin * <44> yhexpa tlalpan OmohuetzitiCa * yhcan yn iyetiliz yn sāta Cruz * yhepoalli yhuan mahtlatli omey tlaocoyaliztli yc opatzimictiloc yntlasoyiolotzin * yhepoalli yhuan onpa oquichichaque yn itlasoxayaCatzin * Cenpoalli yhuan ChiquaCehpan Oquitehuilique yn tepoztlaxichitli ClaVoz yn iquac oquimococoyonilique yn itlasomatzin * Cenpoalli yhuan Caxtoli ypan yn iquac oquitepozmimique yn itlasomahuizyhcxitzin * macuillipoali yhuan Chicnauhpan omelCiCihuititzinno yn itlayiohuilizpantzinco matlactli omeytziontli yhuan mahtlatli omey poalli yhuan Caxtolli xixipehualiztli * yc cequi moCoColiliquen yn itlasomahuizCeliCatlalnaCayotzin * Ompoalli yhuan maCuilli xiquiPili <45> yhuan yhiepoallitziontli yhuan yhepoalli yhieztlaChipinalliztzin * quiChihuan matlactli oCe poalli yhuan matlactli milli * ynic oteChmopatiotilli * ynic topampantiCa oquimonoquilli yn itlasomahuizyezhiotzin * Omtziontli yhuan matlacpoalli milli yn ixayotlaChipinalliztzin * ynic topampatiCa Oquimochoquilili yn totlatlacoll

yhuan niman—mitoz

ma CenquizCayectenehuallo yn iuhCatzintli ynin oquimihiohuilititzino yn CenquizCahuiztic tetlasotlallizteotli yn ixiquichi topapa oquimihioHehhuilititzino ynic otechmomaquixitilitzino ynnaxaCan yhuan moChipa Cemicac ma yuh moChihuan Jesus x[i]toz factuSte [?]<46>

la etacion de la Santa Cruz

o yn titlasomahuizquauhnepanoli Cruz o yn titepetli o yn tisenquizCatlasotli yh timahuiztetziotzin yn notemaquixititiCatzin o yn tiChiChinaquiliztli o yn titonilitzin yn noteotzin o yn titoneuhCaxixipehuiliztli ~~otito~~ o yn tiyhoiopatzinmiquiliztli o yn tiyeznoquihuilitzin yn noteotzin <47> o yn titlasomiquilitzin y noteotzin o yn titlatocayotzin yn senquizCamahuiztililoni ma nonemiquiliztepayh ic xinnechmopalehuilitzino Notecuiotzine ynic nicmasehuiz yn senmicac yoliliztli nemiliztli ma y mochihua Jesus

yni huey teopixcatztli Pio. V. oquinmotlauhttili ynnaquique quitozque yni tlatlauhtiliztli yxipantzinco yn santa Cruz miec tlacnopilihuiliztli dullgenCias Ca no yxiquichi CiCitlatlaltin yhuan Ca no yxiquichi yn xali huey apante[n]co toxauhtoc Ve mi mano y ploma Matheo de sa Jua Chicahuatla a0 s de 1738

Bibliography

Aguilar-Moreno, Manuel. "Transculturation in Art: Sculpture in the Posa Chapels at the Monastery of Calpan, Mexico." *Colonial Latin American Review* 22 (2013): 39–66.

Alva, Bartolomé de. *A Guide to Confession Large and Small in the Mexican Language, 1634.* Edited by Barry Sell and John F. Schwaller. Norman: University of Oklahoma Press, 1999.

Álvarez, Victor. *Diccionario de conquistadores.* 2 vols. Mexico: Instituto Nacional de Antropología e Historia, 1975.

Antigua, Sor María de la. *Cadena de oro evangelica red, arrojada a la diestra de los electos, y escogidos,: que muestra el mas cierto, seguro, y breve camino para la salvacion eterna[.] Las estaciones de la dolorosa passion, y muerte de Nuestro amantissimo redemptor Jesus.* Mexico: Viuda de Joseph Bernardo de Hogal, 1745. (Among many others.)

———. *Via dolorosa o estaciones de la sagrada passion y muerte de nuestro redemptor y amante Jesus.* Mexico: Francisco de Rivera Calderon, 1722.

Anunciación, Antonio de la. *Luz para saber andar la Via sacra.* Bound with, Francisco Soria, *Manual de exercicios para los desagravios de Christo nuestro señor.* Mexico: Herederos del Lic. D. Joseph de Jauregui, 1778.

Bacci, Michele. "Materiality and Liminality: Nonmimetic Evocations of Jerusalem along the Venetian Sea Routes to the Holy Land." In *Natural Materials of the Holy Land and the Visual Translation of Place, 500–1500*, edited by Renana Bartal, Neta Bodner, and Bianca Kuhnel. London, Routledge, 2017.

Bassett, Molly H. *The Fate of Earthly Things: Aztec Gods and God-Bodies.* Austin: University of Texas Press, 2014.

Battle, Michael. *Blessed Are the Peacemakers: A Christian Spirituality of Nonviolence.* Macon, GA: Mercer University Press, 2004.

Bazarte Martínez, Alicia. *Las cofradías de españoles en la ciudad de México (1526–1860).* Mexico: Universidad Autónoma Metropolitana, 1989.

Belanger, Brian C. "Between the Cloister and the World: The Franciscan Third Order of Colonial Querétaro," *The Americas*, 49 (1992): 157–77.

Beristain de Souza, José Mariano. *Biblioteca Hispano-americana septentrional.* 5 vols. México: Editorial Fuente Cultural, 1947.

Bleichmar, Daniela. "Science." In *Lexikon of the Hispanic Baroque*, edited by Evonne Levy and Kenneth Mills, 298–303. Austin: University of Texas Press, 2013.

Boone, Elizabeth Hill, and Louise M. Burkhart. "The Pictographic Vocabulary: Ideography, Phonography, and Syntax." In *Painted Words*, edited by Boone, Elizabeth Hill, Louise M. Burkhart, and David Tavarez, 43–66.

Boone, Elizabeth Hill, Louise M. Burkhart, and David Tavarez. *Painted Words: Nahua Catholicism, Politics, and Memory in the Atzaqualco Pictorial Catechism*. Washington, DC: Dumbarton Oaks, 2017.

Borah, Woodrow W. *New Spain's Century of Depression*. Berkeley: University of California Press, 1951.

Boyd-Bowman, Peter. *Indice geobiográfico de cuarenta mil pobaldores españoles de América en el siglo XVI*. 2 vols. Bogotá: Instituto Caro y Cuervo, 1964.

Brading, D[avid] A. *The First America: The Spanish Monarchy, Creole Patriots, and the Liberal State 1492–1867*. Cambridge: Cambridge University Press, 1991.

Burdette, Derek Scott. "Reparations for Christ Our Lord: Devotional Literature, Penitential Rituals, and Sacred Imagery in Colonial Mexico City," in *Sensuous Suffering: Pain in the Early Modern Visual Art of Europe and the Americas*, edited by Lauren Kilroy-Ewbank and Heather Graham. Leiden: Brill, 2018.

Burkhart, Louise M. *Holy Wednesday: A Nahua Drama from Early Colonial Mexico*. Philadelphia: University of Pennsylvania Press, 1996.

———. "The 'Little Doctrine' and Indigenous Catechesis in New Spain." *Hispanic American Historical Review* 94 (2014): 167–206.

———. "Pageantry, Passion, and Punishment: Eighteenth Century Nahuatl Community Theater." In *Nahua Christianity in Performance*. Vol. 4 of *Nahuatl Theater*, edited by Barry D. Sell and Louise M. Burkhart. Norman: University of Oklahoma Press, 2009.

———. *The Slippery Earth: Nahua-Christian Moral Dialogue in Sixteenth-Century Mexico*. Tucson: University of Arizona Press, 1989.

Carrasco, David, ed. *To Change Place: Aztec Ceremonial Landscapes*. Niwot: University Press of Colorado, 1991.

Cervantes de Salazar, Francisco. *México en 1554 y Túmulo imperial*. Mexico: Editorial Porrúa, 1963.

Chimalpahin Cuauhtlehuanitzin, Domingo Francisco de San Antón Muñón. *Annals of his time: don Domingo de San Antón Muñón Chimalpahin Quauhtlehuanitzin*. Translated and edited by James Lockhart, Susan Schroeder, and Doris Namala. Stanford, CA: Stanford University Press, 2006.

———. *Las ocho relaciones y el memorial de Colhuacan*. Translated and edited by Rafael Tena. 2 vols. Mexico City: Consejo Nacional para la Cultura y las Artes, 2003.

Códice franciscano. Siglo XVI. Mexico: Salvador Chávez Hayhoe, 1941.

Concilio III Provincial Mexicano. Mariano Galvan Rivera, ed. Mexico: Eugenio Maillefert y Compañía, 1859.

Cope, R. Douglas. *The Limits of Racial Domination: Plebian Society in Colonial Mexico City, 1660–1720.* Madison: University of Wisconsin Press, 1994.

Curcio-Nagy, Linda Ann. *The Great Festivals of Colonial Mexico City: Performing Power and Identity.* Albuquerque: University of New Mexico Press, 2004.

Dávila Padilla, Juan de. *Historia de la fundación y discurso de la Provincia de Santiago de Mexico de la Orden de Predicadores.* Brussels: Ivan de Meerbecque, 1625.

Dibble, Charles. "The Xalaquia Ceremony." *Estudios de Cultura Nahuatl* 14 (1980): 198–202.

Directory for Confessors 1585: Implementing the Catholic Reformation in New Spain. Translated and edited by Stafford Poole. Norman: University of Oklahoma Press, 2018.

Durán, Diego de. *Book of the Gods and Rites of the Ancient Calendar.* Translated and edited by Fernando Horcasitas and Doris Heyden. Norman: University of Oklahoma Press, 1971.

Elizondo, Virgil, ed. *Way of the Cross: The Passion of Christ in the Americas.* Maryknoll, NY: Orbis, 1992.

Eric, J., and S. Thompson. *Maya Hieroglyphic Writing.* Norman: University of Oklahoma Press, 1971.

Espíndola, Nicolás. *Desagravios de Jesus nuestro bien; y tiernas meditaciones, para meditar y contemplar lo que padeció en la noche del jueves en el asqueroso e indecente aposentillo.* Mexico: Viuda de Miguel de Ribera Calderon. [1707–14].

———. *Exercicios de desagravios de Christo nuestro señor en la cruz.* Mexico: Viuda de Miguel de Ribera, 1725. https://archive.org/details/exerciciosdedesa00espn.

———. *Via dolorosa.* Mexico: Francisco de Ribera Calderon, 1761.

Espinosa, Isidro Felix de. *Crónica de los colegios de Propagnda Fide de la Nueva España.* Edited by Lino Gómez Canedo. Washington, DC: Academy of American Franciscan History, 1964.

Estrada de Gerlero, Elena. "El programa pasionario en el convent franciscano de Huejotzingo." *Jahrbuch fur Geschichte Lateinamerika* 20 (1983): 642–62.

Flynn, Maureen. *Sacred Charity: Confraternities and Social Welfare in Spain, 1400–1700.* Ithaca, NY: Cornell University Press, 1989.

Gage, Thomas. *Thomas Gage's Travels in the New World.* Edited by J. Eric S. Thompson. Norman: University of Oklahoma Press, 1958.

Gante, Pedro de. *Cartilla para enseñar a leer.* Mexico City: Academia Mexicana de la Educación, 1959.

Garibay K., Angel María. *Historia de la literatura Nahuatl.* 2 vols. Mexico City: Editorial Porrúa, 1953–54.

Garone Gavier, Marina. *La historia de la imprenta y la tipografía colonial en Puebla de los Angeles (1642–1821).* Mexico City: Universidad Nacional Autónoma de México, 2018.

Gerhard, Peter. *Guide to the Historical Geography of New Spain.* Cambridge: Cambridge University Press, 1972.

Gibson, Charles. *The Aztecs under Spanish Rule: A History of the Indians of the Valley of Mexico 1519–1810.* Stanford, CA: Stanford University Press, 2002.

Gil Atrio, Cesáreo. "Cuestionario histórico: ¿España, cuna del viacrucis?." *Archivo Iberoamericano* 11 (1951): 63–92.

Handbook of Middle American Indians. Austin: University of Texas Press, 1969–2015.

Iguiniz, Juan B. *Breve historia de la tercera orden Franciscana en la Provincia del Santo Evangelio de Mexico desde sus orígenes hasta nuestros dias.* Mexico City: Ed. Patria, 1951.

Karttunen, Frances. *An Analytical Dictionary of Classical Nahuatl.* Revised ed. Norman: University of Oklahoma Press, 1992.

Karttunen, Frances, and James Lockhart. *Nahuatl in the Middle Years: Language Contact Phenomena in Texts of the Colonia Period.* Los Angeles: University of California Press, 1976.

Keleman, Pál. *Baroque and Rococo in Latin America.* 2nd ed. 2 vols. New York: Dover, 1967.

Kirkland-Ives, Mitzi. "Alternate Routes: Variation in Early Modern Stational Devotions." *Viator* 40 (2009): 249–70.

Kubler, George. *Mexican Architecture of the Sixteenth Century.* 2 vols. New Haven, CT: Yale University Press, 1948.

Kuryluk, Ewa. *Veronica and Her Cloth: History Symbolism, and Structure of a "True" Image.* Cambridge, MA: Basil Blackwell, 1991.

Landa Abrego, Maria Elena. "Presencia de simbología indigena en una capilla posa del siglo XVI." *Jahrbuch fur Geschichte Lateinamerika.* 20 (1983): 637–42.

Lara, Jaime. *Christian Texts for Aztecs: Art and Liturgy in Colonial Mexico.* Notre Dame, IN: University of Notre Dame Press, 2008.

———. *City, Temple, Stage: Eschatological Architecture and Liturgical Theatrics in New Spain.* Notre Dame, IN: University of Notre Dame Press, 2004.

Larkin, Brian R. *The Very Nature of God: Baroque Catholocism and Religious Reform in Bourbon Mexico City.* Albuquerque: University of New Mexico Press, 2010.

Lavrin, Asunción. "Convent." In *Lexikon of the Hispanic Baroque*, edited by Evonne Levy and Kenneth Mills, 95–101. Austin: University of Texas Press, 2013.

Lenzi, Sarah. *The Stations of the Cross: The Placelessness of Medieval Christian Piety.* Turnhout, Belgium: Brepols, 2016.

Leonard, Irving. *Baroque Times in Old Mexico; Seventeenth-Century Persons, Places, and Practices.* Ann Arbor: University of Michigan Press, 1971.

———. *Don Carlos de Sigüenza y Góngora: Mexican Savant of the Seventeenth Century.* Berkeley: University of California Press, 1929.

León, Nicholás. *Bibliografía mexicana del siglo XVIII.* Mexico: Díaz de León, 1906.

León Portilla, Miguel. *Un catecismo en Nahuatl en imágenes.* Mexico: Cartón y Papel de México, [1979].

Levy, Evonne, and Kenneth Mills, eds. *Lexikon of the Hispanic Baroque.* Austin: University of Texas Press, 2013.

Llewellyn, Nigel. "The Stations of the Cross and Popular Piety." In *Baroque*, edited by Michael Snodin and Nigel Llewellyn, 216–17.

Lockhart, James. *The Nahuas after the Conquest.* Stanford, CA: Stanford University Press, 1992.

Martindale, C. C. "Father Herbert Thurston, S. J. 1856–1939." *Studies: An Irish Quarterly Review* 28, no. 112 (1939): 662–66.

Maza, Francisco de la. "Fray Pedro de Gante y la capilla abierta de San José de los Naturales." *Artes de Mexico.* No. 150 (1972): 33–38.

McAndrew, John. *The Open-Air Churches of Sixteenth-Century Mexico.* Cambridge, MA: Harvard University Press, 1965.

McCarty, Kiernan. "Apostolic Colleges of the Propagation of the Faith: Old and New World Background." *The Americas* 19 (1962): 50–58.

McCloskey, Michael B. *The Formative Years of the Missionary College of Santa Cruz Querétaro, 1683–1733.* Washington, DC: Academy of American Franciscan History, 1955.

Medina, José Toribio. *La imprenta en México.* 5 vols. Santiago de Chile: Imprenta Medina, 1906–12.

Melvin, Karen. *Building Colonial Cities of God: Mendicant Orders and Urban Culture in New Spain.* Stanford, CA: Stanford University Press, 2012.

———. "Clergy." In *Lexikon of the Hispanic Baroque*, edited by Evonne Levy and Kenneth Mills, 73–79. Austin: University of Texas Press, 2013.

Mendieta, Jerónimo de. *Historia ecclesiastica Indiana.* 4 vols. Mexico City: Chávez Hayhoe, 1945.

Merrim, Stephanie. *The Spectacular City: Mexico, and Colonial Hispanic Literary Culture.* Austin: University of Texas Press, 2010.

Mitchell, Nathan D. *The Mystery of the Rosary: Marian Devotion and the Reinvention of Catholicism.* New York: New York University Press, 2009.

Molina, Alonso de, and Miguel León Portilla, Miguel. *Vocabulario en lengua castellana y mexicana y mexicana y castellana.* Mexico City: Porrúa, 2004.

More, Alena. *Baroque Sovereignty: Carlos de Sigüenza y Góngora and the Creole Archive of Colonial Mexico.* Philadelphia: University of Pennsylvania Press, 2013.

Mosquera, Daniel. "Nahuatl Catechistic Drama: New Translations, Old Preoccupations." *Nahuatl Drama Series* 1. Edited by Louise Burkhart and Barry D. Sell. Norman: University of Oklahoma Press, 2004.

Motolinia, [Toribio de Benavente]. *Memoriales o Libro de las cosas de la Nueva España.* Edited by Edmundo O'Gorman. Mexico City: Universidad Nacional Autónoma de México, 1971.

Moyssen, Xavier. "Las pinturas murales en Epazoyucan." *Boletín del Instituto Nacional de Antropología e Historia* No. 22 (1965): 20–27.

Mullen, Robert J. *Architecture and Its Sculpture in Viceregal Mexico.* Austin: University of Texas Press, 1997.

Mundy, Barbara. "The Emergence of Alphabetic Writing: Tlahcuiloh and Escribano in Sixteenth-Century Mexico." *The Americas* 77 (July 2020): 361–407.

Olivier, Guilhem. *Mockeries and Metamorphoses of an Aztec God: Tezcatlipoca—"Lord of the Smoking Mirror."* Translated by Michel Besson. Boulder: University Press of Colorado, 2003.

Oroz, Pedro. *The Oroz Codex.* Translated and edited by Angelico Chavez. Washington, DC: Academy of American Franciscan History, 1972.

Osowski, Edward W. *Indigenous Miracles: Nahua Authority in Colonial Mexico.* Tucson: University of Arizona Press, 2010.

———. "Passion Miracles and Indigenous Historical Memory in New Spain. *Hispanic American Historical Review* 88, no. 4 (2008): 607–38.

Osuna, Joaquin de. *Peregrinacion Cristiana por el camino real de la celeste Jerusalén. que son unas estaciones devotas al modo de Via Crucis y Guirnaldas a la Sagrada Passion de Christo, y Dolores de la Santissima* Madre. Mexico City: Biblioteca Mexicana, 1760.

Palomera, Esteban J. *Fray Diego de Valadés, OFM. Evangelizador humanista de la Nueva España. El hombre, su época y su obra.* Mexico City: Universidad Iberoamericana, 1988.

———. Introduction to *Rhetorica Cristiana*, by Diego Valadés. Mexico City: Fondo de Cultura Económica, 1989.

Panofsky, Erwin. "Once More 'The Friedsam Annunciation and the Problem of the Ghent Altarpiece.'" *Art Bulletin* 20 (December 1938): 419–42.

Pascha, Jan. *Een devote maniere om gheestelyck pelgrimagie.* Louvain: Hieronymum Welle, 1563.

Paso y Troncoso, Francisco del, ed. *Papeles de la Nueva España.* 7 vols. Madrid: Sucesores de Ribadeneyra, 1905–1906.

Paz, Octavio. *Sor Juana*. Cambridge, MA: Harvard University Press, 1988.

Peterson, Jeanette Favrot. *The Paradise Garden Murals of Malinalco: Utopia and Empire in Sixteenth-Century Mexico*. Austin: University of Texas Press, 1993.

Poole, Stafford. "Opposition to the Third Mexican Council." *The Americas* 25 (1968): 111–59.

———. *Our Lady of Guadalupe: The Origins of a Mexican National Symbol, 1531–1797*. Tucson: University of Arizona Press, 1995.

———. *Pedro Moya de Contreras: Catholic Reform and Royal Power in New Spain, 1571–1591*. Berkeley: University of California Press, 1978.

Ragon, Pierre. "La colonización de lo sagrado: La historia del sacromonte de Amecameca," *Relaciones, Estudios de Historia y Sociedad 75* (Colegio de Michoacán) 19 (1998): 281–300.

Richel, Dionisio. *Este es un cōpēdio [compendio] breue que tracta de la manera de como se hā de hazer las p[ro]cessions*. Mexico City: Cromberger, 1544.

Robin, Alena. *Las capillas del Vía crucis de la ciudad de México: Arte, patrocinio, y sacralización*. Mexico City: Universidad Nacional Autónoma de México, 2014.

———. "Vía crucis y series pasionarias en los virreinatos latinoamericanos." *Goya* 339 (2012): 130–45.

Romero, Diego. *Meditaciones de la passion de Christo vida nuestra*. Puebla: Diego Fernandez de Leon, 1683.

Rudy, Kathryn M. *Virtual Pilgrimages in the Convent: Reimagining Jerusalem in the Late Middle Ages*. Turnhout, Belgium: Brepols, 2011.

Ruiz Martínez, Rafael, and Juan Manuel Armenta Olvera. *Las capillas del vía crucis en Puebla, su historia*. Puebla: Gobierno del Estado de Puebla, Secretaría de Cultura, 1992.

Sahagún, Bernardino de. *Florentine Codex*. 13 vols. Translated and edited by Arthur J. O. Anderson and Charles Dibble. Salt Lake City: University of Utah Press, 1950–82.

———. *Primeros memoriales*. Paleography and Translation by Thelma Sullivan. Norman: University of Oklahoma Press, 1997.

Salas Cuesta, Marcela. *La iglesia y el convento de Huejotzingo*. Mexico City: Universidad Nacional Autónoma de México, 1982.

Salutacion a las Sacratissimas cinco Llagas de Christo nuestro redentor, para alcanzar una feliz y santa Muerte. Mexico City: D. Felipe de Zuñiga y Ontiveros, 1777.

Sant'Elia A Piasini, Antoninius. *De pio Viae Crucis exercitio disquisitio histórica iuridica ritualis*. Rome: Centro Nazionale del TOF, 1950.

Schuessler, Michael K. *Foundational Arts: Mural Painting and Missionary Theatre in New Spain*. Tucson: University of Arizona Press, 2013.

Schwaller, John F. “The Brothers Fernando de Alva Ixtlilxochitl and Bartolomé de Alva: Two ‘Native’ Intellectuals of Seventeenth Century Mexico.” In *Indigenous Intellectuals: Knowledge, Power, and Colonial Culture in Mexico and the Andes*, edited by Gabriela Ramos and Yanna Yannakakis. Durham, NC: Duke University Press, 2014.

———. “Don Bartolomé de Alva, Nahuatl Scholar of the Seventeenth Century.” In *A Guide to Confession Large and Small in the Mexican Language, 1634* by Bartolomé de Alva, edited by Barry Sell and John F. Schwaller. Norman: University of Oklahoma Press, 1999.

———. *The Fifteenth Month: Aztec History in the Rituals of Panquetzaliztli.* Norman: University of Oklahoma Press, 2019.

———. “The *Ilhuica* of the Nahua: Is Heaven Just a Place?” *The Americas* 62 (January 2006): 391–412.

———. “The ‘Ordenanza del Patronazgo’ in New Spain, 1574–1600.” *The Americas* 42 (1986): 253–74.

Sell, Barry D. “The Classical Age of Nahuatl Publications and Don Bartolomé de Alva’s *Confessionario* of 1634.” In *A Guide to Confession Large and Small in the Mexican Language, 1634* by Bartolomé de Alva, edited by Barry Sell and John F. Schwaller. Norman: University of Oklahoma Press, 1999.

———. “Two Eminent and Classical Authors of the Discipline: Father Horacio Carochi, S. J., and Don Bartolomé de Alva, Nahuatl Scholars of New Spain.” In *Spanish Golden Age Drama in Mexican Translation*, edited by Barry D. Sell, Louise M. Burkhart, and Elizabeth R. Wright. Vol. 3 of *Nahuatl Theater.* Norman: University of Oklahoma Press, 2008.

Sell, Barry D., and Louise M. Burkhart, eds. *Nahuatl Theater.* 4 vols. Norman: University of Oklahoma Press, 2004–2009.

Short, William. *The Franciscans.* Collegeville, MN: Liturgical Press, 1989.

Snodin, Michael, and Nigel Llewellyn. *Baroque: Style in the Age of Magnificence, 1620–1800.* London: V&A Publishing, 2009.

Soria, Francisco. *Manual de exercicios para los desagravios de Christo nuestro señor.* Mexico City: Herederos del Lic. D. Joseph de Jauregui, 1778.

Sousa, Lisa, Stafford Poole, and James Lockhart, eds. *The Story of Guadalupe: Luis Lasso de la Vega’s Huei tlamahuiçoltica of 1649.* Stanford, CA: Stanford University Press, 1998.

Storme, Albert, *The Way of the Cross: A Historical Sketch.* Jerusalem: Franciscan Printing, 1984.

Sticca, Sandro. “The Via Crucis: Its Historical, Spiritual, and Devotional Context.” *Mediaevalia* 15 (1989): 93–126.

Taylor, William B. “An ‘Evolved’ Devotional Book from Late-Eighteenth-Century Mexico.” *Catholic Historical Review* 101 (2015): 65–79.

———. *Magistrates of the Sacred: Priests and Parishioners in Eighteenth-Century Mexico.* Stanford, CA: Stanford University Press, 1996.

———. *Theater of a Thousand Wonders: A History of Miraculous Images and Shrines of New Spain*. Cambridge: Cambridge University Press, 2016.

Tavarez, David. "Nahua Intellectuals, Franciscan Scholars, and the *Devotio Moderna* in Colonial Mexico." *The Americas* 70 (2013): 203–35.

Thurston, Herbert. *The Stations of the Cross*. London: Burns & Gates, 1914.

Torquemada, Juan de, and Miguel León-Portilla. *Monarquía indiana*. Mexico City: Porrúa, 1986.

Torre Villar, Ernesto de la. *Fray Pedro de Gante. Maestro y civilizador de América*. Mexico City: Seminario de Cultura Mexicana, 1973.

Toussaint, Manuel. *Colonial Art in Mexico*. Austin: University of Texas Press, 1967.

Townsend, Camilla. *Annals of Native America: How the Nahuas of Colonial Mexico Kept Their History Alive*. Oxford: Oxford University Press. 2017.

Truitt, Jonathan. *Sustaining the Divine in Mexico Tenochtitlan: Nahuas and Catholicism 1523–1700*. Norman: University of Oklahoma Press, 2018.

Valadés, Diego, *Rhetorica Cristiana*. Perugia: Apud Petrumiacobum Petrutium, 1579.

Valton, Emilio. *El primer libro de alfabetización en América*. Mexico City: Antigua Librería Robredo, 1947.

Van der Horst, Pieter W. "Silent Prayer in Antiquity." *Numen* 41 (1994): 1–25.

Vélez, Karin. *The Miraculous Flying House of Loreto: Spreading Catholicism in the Early Modern World*. Princeton, NJ: Princeton University Press, 2019.

Vetancurt, Augustín de. *Teatro Mexicano*. 4 vols. Madrid: Editorial Porrua Turanzas, 1960–61.

———. *Via crucis en mexicano*. Mexico City: Francisco Rodríguez Lupercio, 1680. Manuscript copied by Matheo de San Juan Chicahuastla, 1738. Academy of American Franciscan History Collection, Copley Library, University of San Diego.

Wake, Eleanor. *Framing the Sacred: The Indian Churches of Early Colonial Mexico*. Norman: University of Oklahoma Press, 2010.

Webster, Susan Verdi. *Art and Ritual in Golden-Age Spain: Sevillian Confraternities and the Processional Sculpture of Holy Week*. Princeton, NJ: Princeton University Press, 1998.

Webster, Susan Verdi. "Art, Ritual, and Confraternities in Sixteenth-Century New Spain: Penitential Imagery at the Monastery of San Miguel, Huejotzingo." *Anales del Instituto de Investigaciones Estéticas* no. 70 (1997): 5–43.

Winston-Allen, Anne. *Stories of the Rose: The Making of the Rosary in the Middle Ages*. University Park: Pennsylvania State University Press, 1997.

Wunder, Amanda. "Classical, Christian, and Muslim Remains in the Construction of Imperial Seville (1520–1635)." *Journal of the History of Ideas* 64 (2003): 195–212.

Zedelgem, Amédée de. "Aperçu historique sur le devotion au chemin de la croix." *Collectanea franciscana* 19 (1948–49): 45–142.

Index

CPSIA information can be obtained
at www.ICGtesting.com
Printed in the USA
LVHW110413080622
720722LV00003B/3/J

9 780806 176536